IMAGES
of America

WILMINGTON

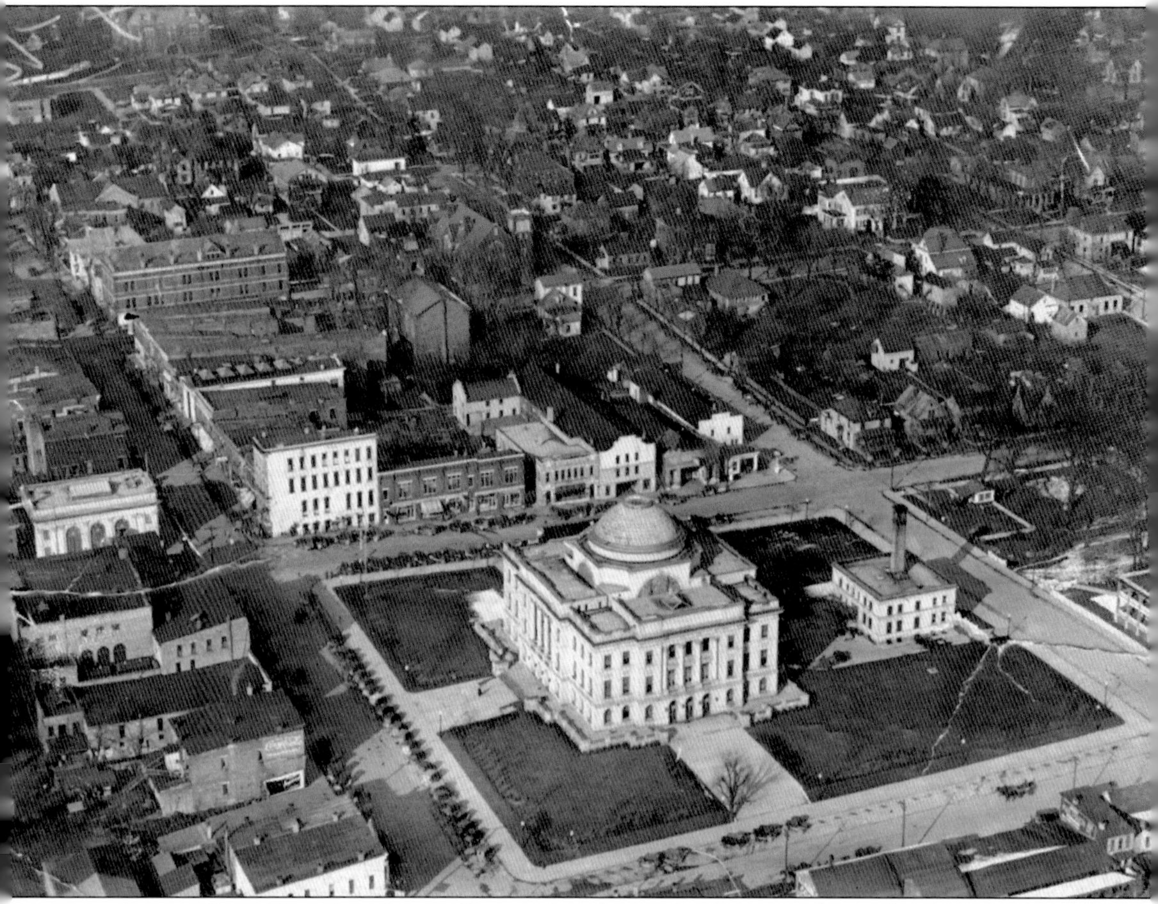

Aerial View. Near the Clinton County Courthouse, built in 1918, horse-drawn carriages were still being used while motorcars were becoming popular in downtown Wilmington. (Courtesy of Clinton County Historical Society.)

On the Cover: Open-house visitors lined up to view the experimental gliders at the Clinton County Army Air Field in 1944. The airfield has been reincarnated several times and awaits its newest tenant. (Courtesy of Clinton County Historical Society.)

IMAGES
of America

WILMINGTON

Laura Lanese and Eileen Brady in association with
the Clinton County Historical Society

ARCADIA
PUBLISHING

ISBN 978-0-7385-8444-7

Published by Arcadia Publishing
Charleston, South Carolina

Printed in the United States of America

Library of Congress Control Number: 2009942713

For all general information contact Arcadia Publishing at:
Telephone 843-853-2070
Fax 843-853-0044
E-mail sales@arcadiapublishing.com
For customer service and orders:
Toll-Free 1-888-313-2665

Visit us on the Internet at www.arcadiapublishing.com

For my parents and Mike, Michael, Camille, and Francesca

—Laura Lanese

For my parents and my husband, Brian, and our daughter, Pearl

—Eileen Brady

Contents

Acknowledgments

We are grateful for all the people through the years who have donated their photographs and memorabilia to the Clinton County Historical Society, which was the source of most of the photographs included in this book, unless otherwise noted. These contributions make a historian's life much easier and the task more enjoyable. We encourage anyone with history to share to do likewise.

The keeper of this wealth of information at the Clinton County Historical Society is Kay Fisher. Her impressive ability to recall and find exactly what we were looking for was a tremendous help. She also assisted with the less glamorous tasks, such as scanning and copying. Additionally, we would like to acknowledge Bernie Quigley, local historian extraordinaire, who has been researching Wilmington and Clinton County history for a long time and knew the minutia of most of the questions we asked of him. He was truly a pleasure to work with. And we would like to thank his wife, Cindy, for being supportive of his time with us. We would like to especially thank Patti Kinsinger, head reference services/Quaker research coordinator at Wilmington College, who was so good at her job that we almost never felt guilty asking her for help. She was meticulous in her research and quick to respond to any inquiries. Also thanks go out to Lee Bowman, librarian/college archives coordinator at Wilmington College, who always went above and beyond in his assistance—all we had to do was ask, and there was the photograph or piece of information we were looking for. We would also like to thank several others who provided us with photographs, stories, sketches, expert advice, and other support: Randy Sarvis, Karen Campbell, Ruth Dobyns, Gary Kersey, Paul Presta, Mike Sutton, Earl Nicholson, Mary Wall, Shari Murphy, Virgene Peterson, Beverly Barrett Browning, Jean Rachford Barrett, Amy Miller, Don Wells, Tom Ford, Mary Thomas Watts, Kathy Schwab, Sharon Newton, Rita Anderson, Rita Butcher, David Ellis, Neil Snarr, Jill Thompson, Richard and Pam Thompson, Alyssa Alden, Marilynn Wilson, Dee Tamplin, Toni Jenkins, Scott Wells, JoAnn Culberson, Marie Butts, June Fryman, Ellen Keim, Mary Anne Perry, Diane and Doug Borton, Debbie Stamper, Dennis and Barb Atley, Carole Moore, Dung Nguyen, Ingrid Sanden, Jan Chong, Roselee Papandrea, Roger and Connie Spurlock, and Camille Brady.

Any errors or omissions belong to us alone.

INTRODUCTION

Wilmington, Ohio, is situated on land that was once part of the Virginia Military District, land that was payment to Virginia's Revolutionary War soldiers for their military service. The passage of the Northwest Territory Act of 1787 and the defeat of the Native Americans at the Battle of Fallen Timbers in 1794 ushered in an era of expansion into Ohio. A handful of pioneers started arriving in the Wilmington region about the same time Ohio was becoming a state in 1803. These early settlers had to be resolute and resourceful to establish homesteads in the wilderness. If they arrived during the cold months when traveling was easier, they needed enough supplies to get them through the harsh Ohio winters. If natural hardships were not challenging enough, the settlers also had to contend with swindlers dealing in fraudulent land titles and the confusing metes and bounds system, which often led them to the wrong property and caused years of litigation.

Many of the original settlers came for the fertile farmland. The Wilmington region benefitted from the Wisconsin glaciers that helped create a landscape perfect for agriculture. For many pioneers, the Ohio terrain offered more opportunities than the rocky lands of the eastern seaboard. Other settlers were Quakers, who were either relocating to be near family and friends, coming for the farmland, or leaving the slave states of the South. Still other pioneers were led to Wilmington by their sense of adventure.

In 1810, Clinton County was carved out of surrounding counties and was named after George Clinton, then vice president and former governor of New York. Appointed by the state legislature, the first county commissioners were responsible for choosing the county seat. David Faulkner and Joseph Doan offered 50 and 10 acres respectively for this purpose, which was accepted by the commissioners. Doan kept two lots for himself, and two more were reserved for public use. Choosing a name was more difficult, and the new townsfolk went through several name changes before they settled on Wilmington.

When Wilmington was platted in August 1810, the villagers built log houses, churches, schools, and businesses. The Quakers set up their first house of worship around 1805 on Center Road. In 1811, Warren Sabin established the first permanent tavern and inn, and his descendants still operate a family business in downtown Wilmington. As commerce developed, the residents eventually found time for other activities in the new village, including publishing newspapers and participating in educational societies.

For a primarily agricultural town, Wilmington has produced a rich tapestry of talented individuals who have become, among other things, abolitionists, artists, and adventurers.

Among Wilmington's abolitionists was Dr. Abraham Brooke, one of the most active conductors on the Underground Railroad. Around 1839, Brooke was involved in a slave rescue that landed him in jail. Although different versions of the story have been told, it seems that Brooke and several others liberated the slaves of a Virginia family traveling along State Route 73 on the way to Missouri. The slave owner prosecuted the case in the Warren County Common Pleas Court, where the defendants' attorneys argued that the slaves became free once the owner voluntarily brought them to a free state. The local judge disagreed and sentenced Brooke and the other defendants to a fine and five days in the jail with only bread and water. The Ohio Supreme Court sided with the abolitionists and released them. The slaves were safely resettled in Ohio.

Among the nationally known artists from Wilmington was Carl Moon. Born in 1879, Moon graduated from Wilmington High School and moved to New Mexico to become a photographer, painter, and illustrator. His primary interest was depicting the lives of southwest Native Americans before their culture was completely lost. In 1907, Pres. Theodore Roosevelt requested Moon's work to be exhibited at the White House. Moon and his wife, Grace, collaborated on 22 children's books. Their first book was *Indian Legends in Rhymes*, published in 1917. Moon's goal was to replace the stereotypes of Native Americans with a more accurate portrayal.

Jeremiah Reynolds was an adventurer in the true sense of the word. He began his career as a newspaper man in Wilmington in the 1820s and later became interested in John Cleves Symmes's hollow Earth theory, which asserted that the Earth was hollow with openings at both poles. Reynolds earned his living traveling and lecturing about Symmes's hollow Earth theory. Reynolds agitated for government funding for an expedition to Antarctica, but incoming Pres. Andrew Jackson canceled the trip. Reynolds privately outfitted his own expedition to Antarctica, but on the return trip his crew mutinied and abandoned him in Chile. As part of his adventures, he wrote a true story of a bellicose, white sperm whale, nicknamed Mocha Dick, known for his tendency to fight with small fishing boats. Reynolds published his account in *The Knickerbocker* in 1839. He called it "Mocha Dick: Or the White Whale of the Pacific." His story is believed to have influenced Herman Melville's legendary *Moby-Dick*. Reynolds's theory of a hollow Earth is also thought to have shaped Edgar Allen Poe's work *The Narrative of Arthur Gordon Pym of Nantucket*, published in 1838.

Another adventurer was one of Wilmington's most recognizable names and colorful characters, Gen. James W. Denver. Denver would eventually become a California state senator, U.S. congressman, a territorial governor of Kansas, and the namesake for the capital city of Colorado. He is less known, however, for his role in a deadly duel. Although accounts differ as to when and how events transpired, it appears that after Denver led a group of travelers overland through the mountains to California in the wake of the gold rush, he became active in California politics. In 1852, as a result of travelers trapped in the mountains en route to California, the governor placed Denver in charge of providing relief supplies to the stranded migrants. Edward Gilbert, a newspaper editor, criticized the governor's decision and Denver's handling of the situation. Denver responded angrily, and Gilbert challenged Denver to a duel. Denver was recognized as one of the best shots in the state, and as Gilbert shot wide, Denver chivalrously grounded his own shot. Gilbert nonetheless felt his honor was at stake and challenged Denver again. Denver dropped Gilbert with a shot through the heart. And although dueling had been outlawed in California, no action was taken against Denver, as popular opinion was on his side.

These are just a few of the stories of Wilmington's citizens. This book tells the story of many more Wilmingtonians, from the time of the town's founding in 1810 until its sesquicentennial in 1960. We have included the geographic area of Wilmington according to its current zip code so as to tell as broad a story as possible. Wilmington, known as a town that "honors its champions," is a city that celebrates its past. It also looks forward to its future. While many cities have neglected their downtown districts, Wilmington has chosen a different route and invested in its historic infrastructure. Our goal is that this book contributes to the historic preservation of one of America's best small towns.

One

Early History

Wilmington's first settlers began arriving in the early 1800s, around the time Ohio was becoming a state. Many of these early settlers were Quakers fleeing the slaveholding states of North Carolina and Tennessee. By 1810, Clinton County was carved out of surrounding counties and needed a government seat. Wilmington was chosen several months later after 60 acres were donated for this purpose.

The citizens decided that one of the first orders of business as the county seat was to develop the court system. The first criminal trial was held in June 1810, before either a courthouse or jail had been built. This trial involved Cornelius Quick, a horse thief, and was prosecuted by Joshua Collett from Warren County, later an Ohio Supreme Court justice. The trial was held in a barn, and Quick was found guilty but escaped after Sheriff Jonathan Harlan unchained him from an apple tree. The county built the first jail around 1811 and the first courthouse in 1813. One of the jail's first occupants was Caleb Kirk, a Quaker, who was held for several days for refusing to muster with the militia during the War of 1812.

In addition to seating the county government, Wilmington served the needs of the surrounding farmers, villagers, and travelers. Not surprisingly, taverns were one of the most common forms of business, and licenses were granted as early as 1811. Taverns provided food and drink to travelers and newly arrived settlers. They were also a major source of news, especially information relating to business opportunities and travel conditions. The town quickly grew to support other businesses needed by pioneers. These businesses included dry-goods shops, tanneries, cabinet and furniture makers, grist and sawmills, blacksmiths, and even a hatmaker.

Churches and schools sprang up almost immediately. Then, after settling their spiritual and educational affairs, the residents turned to other activities. Newspapers and educational societies took off, and a variety of social groups appeared on the scene. By the time Wilmington celebrated its centennial in 1910, it was a thriving, well-established community.

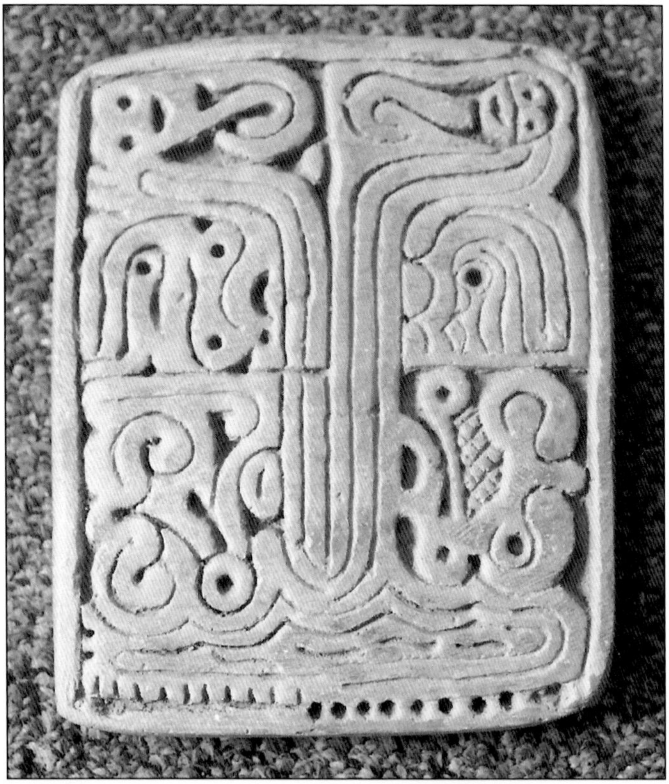

WILMINGTON OR RICHARDSON TABLET. Found by semi-amateur archaeologists Dr. L. B. Welch and J. M. Richardson in 1879 near the Sparks mound on the Seth Linton farm, the Wilmington tablet was a relic from the Adena culture. The original tablet now resides at the Ohio Historical Society.

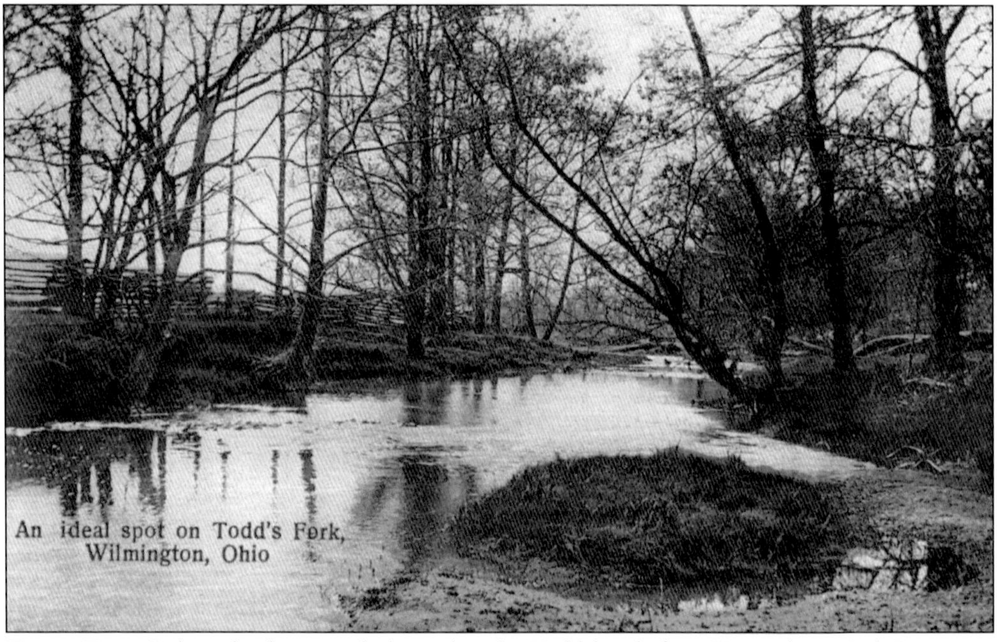

TODD'S FORK. Believed to be named after either the Todd family from Kentucky or Col. Benjamin Todd of the Kentucky militia, Todd's Fork became one of the earliest and largest settlements in the area. In 1803, George Haworth built a mill on the creek. It is the oldest creek in the county and at one time flowed north instead of south.

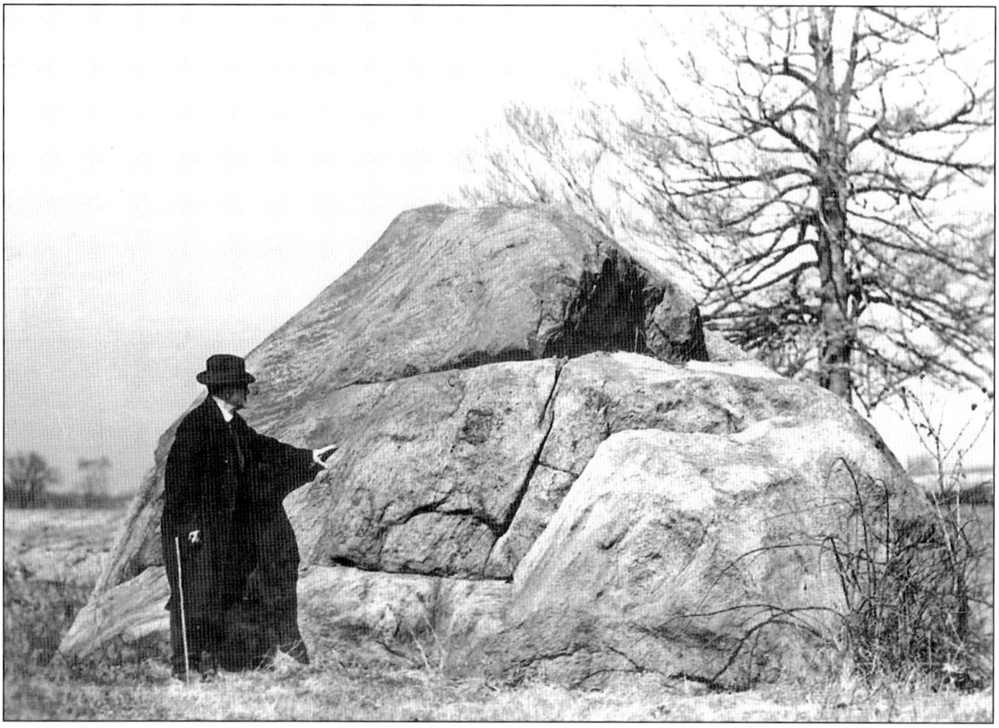

Dr. George Austin, 1930. Austin, a well-known amateur archaeologist and amateur geologist, is shown above standing by the glacial boulder near what was at the time the Clinton County Infirmary. The boulder originated from northern Canada and is the largest and oldest in the region, dating from the Early Wisconsin Glacial period, about 24,000 years ago. The estimated weight is 80 tons. Below, Austin is studying the valley between Wilson's Branch and Cowan's Creek. Lake Cowan was created in 1950–1951 by the damming of Cowan's Creek. Austin grew up in this area and was interested in the prehistoric mounds found on this land. He donated his scientific collection to Wilmington College, where Austin Hall is named in his honor.

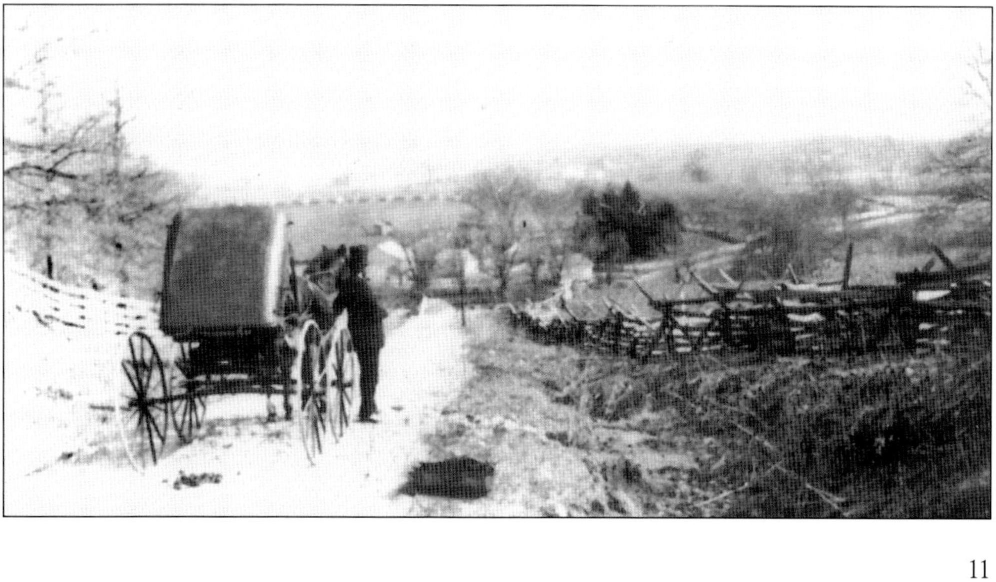

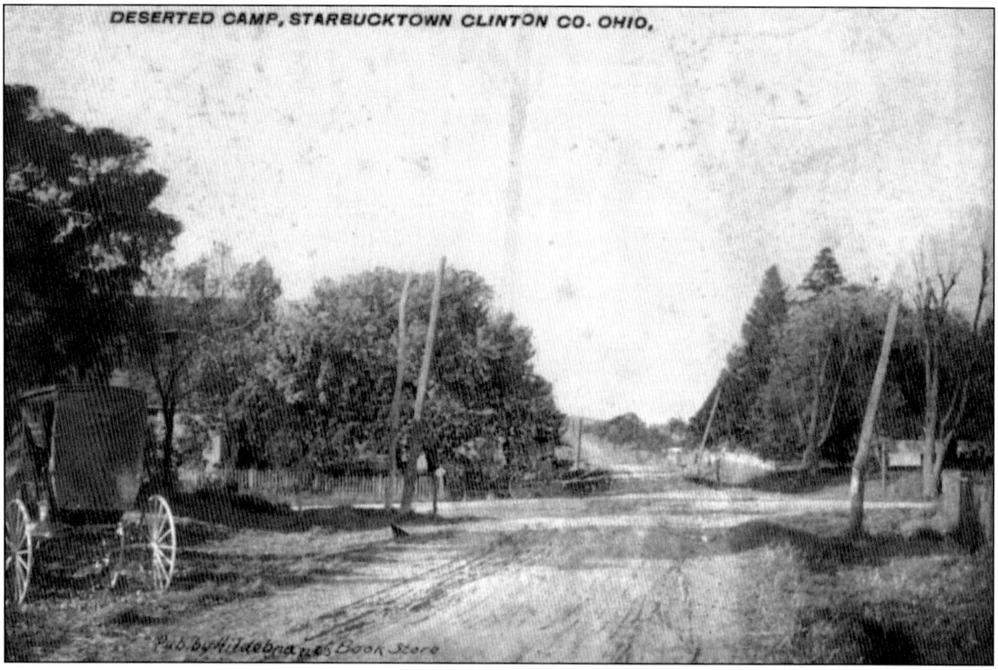

DESERTED CAMP. Located on Prairie Road, the camp was named after a trail guide who deserted the 700 Kentucky Volunteers serving under Gen. Benjamin Logan in 1786. The guide successfully alerted the Native Americans that the military was in pursuit of them. This infamous spot served as a marker in five early military surveys.

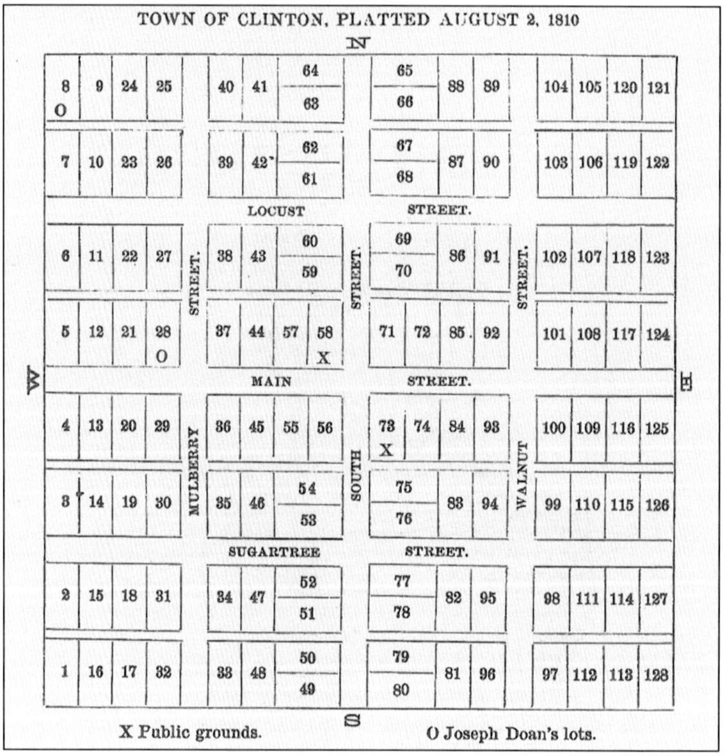

TOWN PLAT, 1810. When selecting a name for the village, the town first chose Clinton, then Armenia, next Mount Pleasant, and finally Wilmington. A court ordered no further name changes without legislative approval. Platted on August 2, 1810, the town originally consisted of 60 donated acres. The highest price paid for a lot was $100 for lot No. 71 by William Ferguson, and the lowest amount was paid for lot No. 82, which cost Isaiah Morris $4.12½.

DR. AQUILA JONES. Jones was born in 1807 and arrived in Wilmington in 1810. He served the community as a general practitioner and local mentor to doctors in training and as the president of the local medical society. Additionally he served as county auditor, co-owned a newspaper, kept a meteorological journal, wrote poetry, and recorded local history.

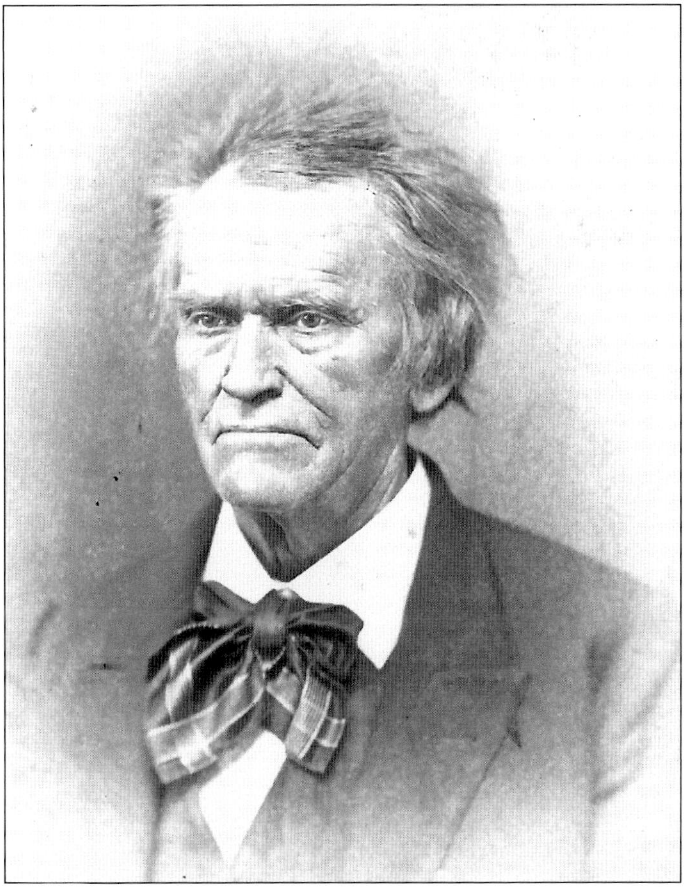

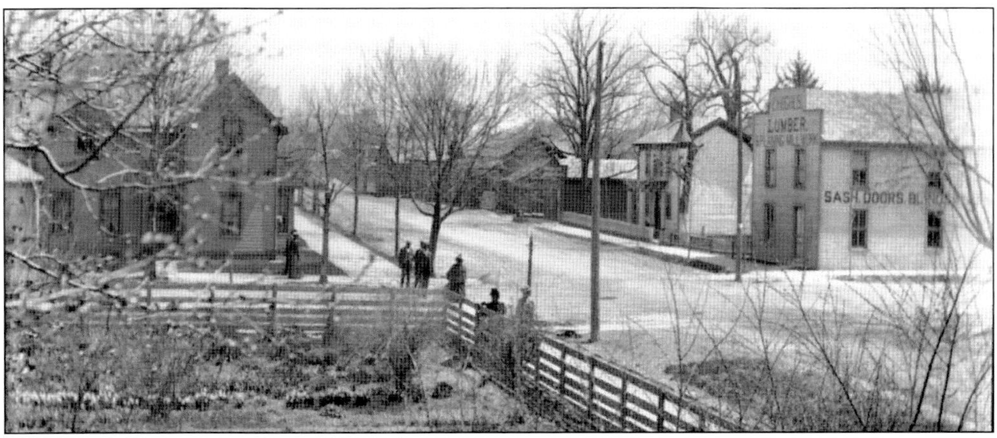

DOWNTOWN, 1900s. This is the intersection of Main and Lincoln Streets with Church's Lumber on the southeast corner. Notice the woman with the parasol out for a walk on a nice spring day. Located on this spot today is the parking lot for National Bank and Trust employees, next to KFC.

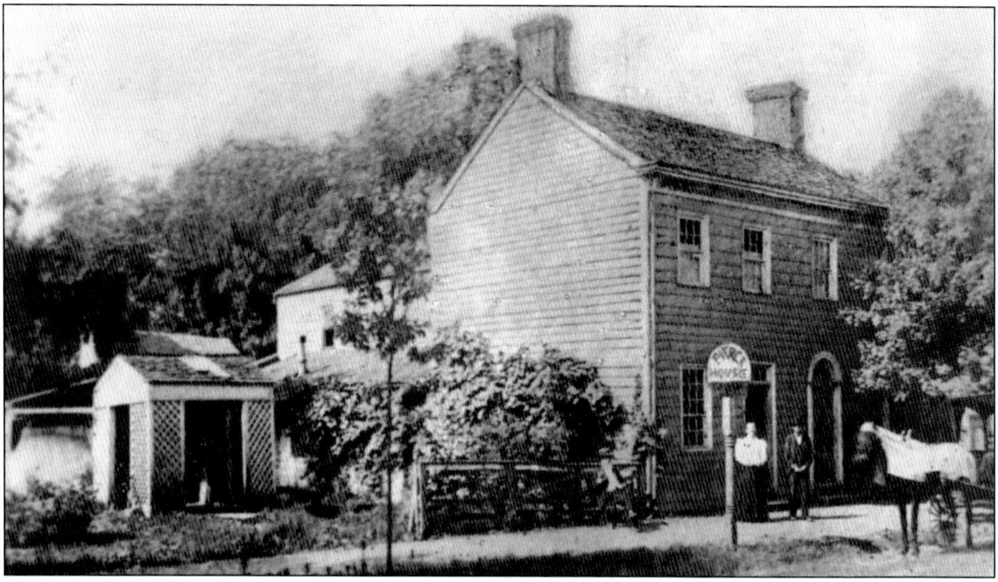

Pierce House. Richard Pierce (or Peirce) arrived in Wilmington in 1813. In 1833, he built this hotel, which was located on East Main Street. It was the site of a boisterous Fourth of July party in 1834.

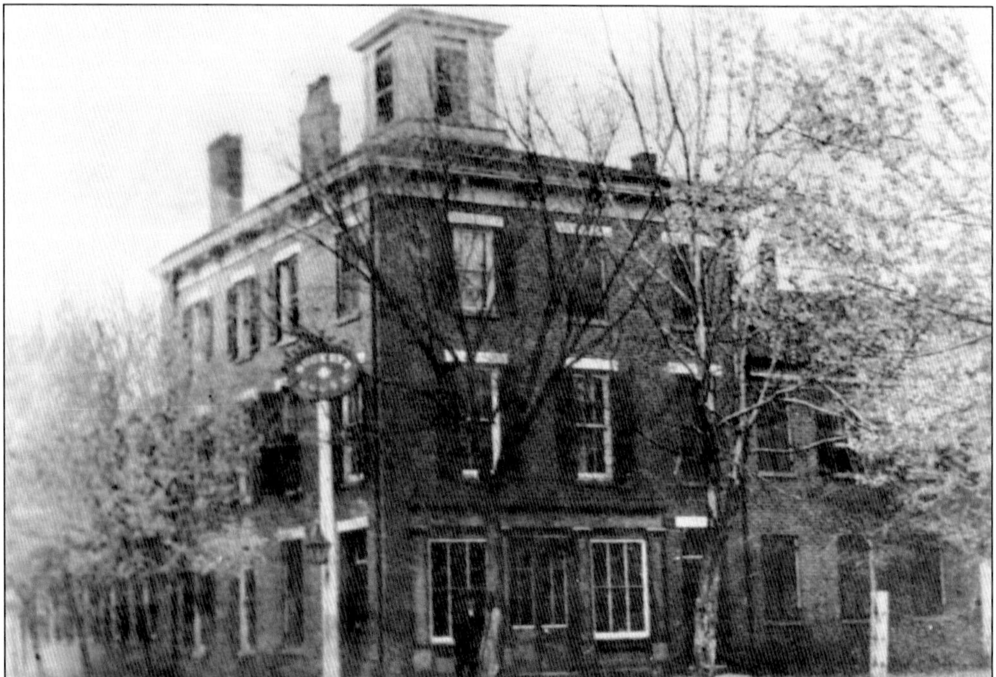

Buckeye House, 1840–1876. Located at Locust and North South Streets, where Rose and Dobyns law firm now stands, this building was set afire by a stable hand in 1876. During the 1840 presidential campaign, Gen. William Henry Harrison stayed here at George Haworth's home. Haworth built a brick addition to his home, converting it into the Buckeye House. Hotels then were often affiliated with political parties, and this was considered a Whig hotel.

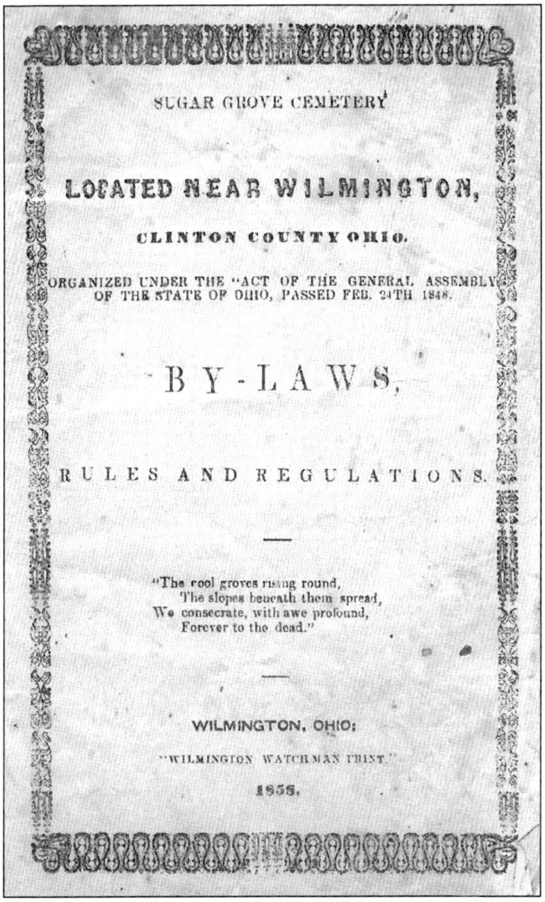
SUGAR GROVE CEMETERY

LOCATED NEAR WILMINGTON,

CLINTON COUNTY OHIO.

ORGANIZED UNDER THE "ACT OF THE GENERAL ASSEMBLY OF THE STATE OF OHIO, PASSED FEB. 24TH 1848.

BY-LAWS,

RULES AND REGULATIONS.

"The cool groves rising round,
The slopes beneath them spread,
We consecrate, with awe profound,
Forever to the dead."

WILMINGTON, OHIO:

"WILMINGTON WATCHMAN PRINT."

1858.

SUGAR GROVE CEMETERY, 1857. In 1857, Leo Weltz designed the grounds of this early Wilmington cemetery. Weltz was born in Prussia in 1825 and was the head gardener to Russian czar Alexander III. Sugar Grove Cemetery's beautifully landscaped hills include the Children's Cemetery, the Irish section, the Pet Cemetery, and Soldier's Point. In the Soldier's Point section are graves of unknown Civil War veterans, a number of African American war veterans, and Mary Taylor Adams, the first Ohio nurse to volunteer in the Civil War.

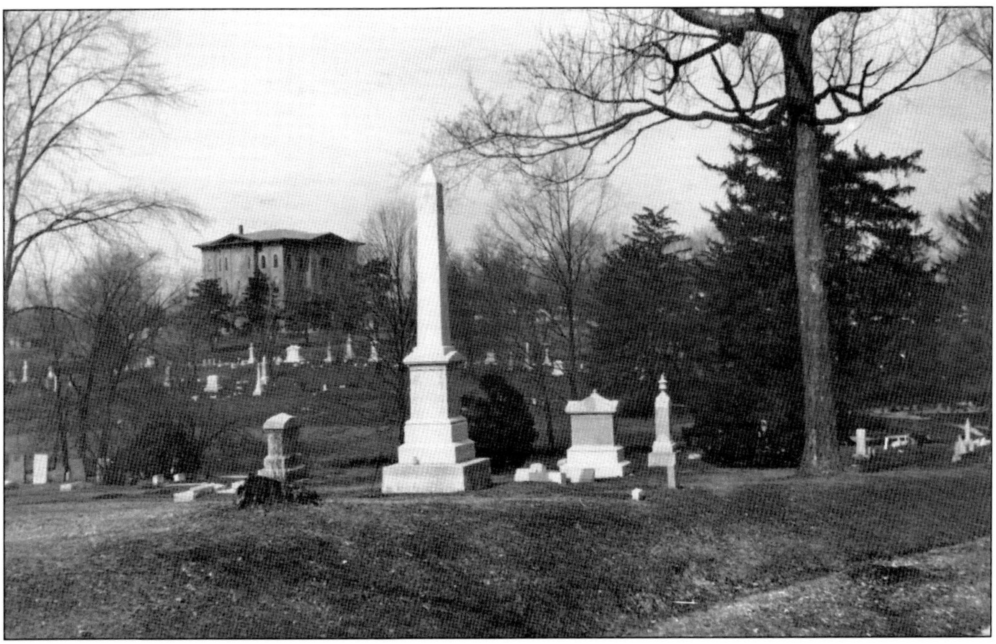

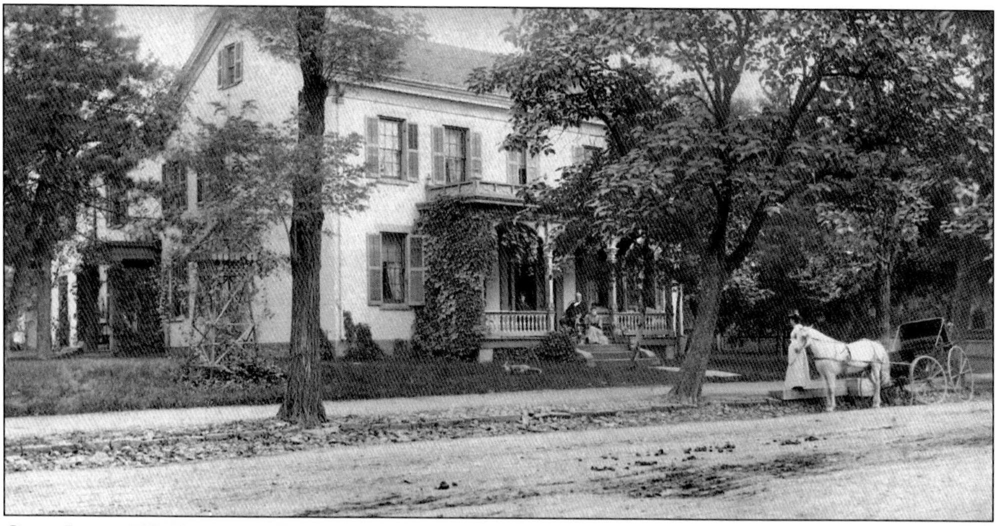

GEN. JAMES W. DENVER HOME, 1880s. Denver is seen with his family, wife, Louise Rombach Denver, on their porch; daughter Kate St. Clair Denver Williams on the steps; and daughter Mary Louise Denver Lindley at the curb. The Clinton County Historical Society purchased the home in 1955 from David Williams, Denver's great-grandson, and the building was placed on the National Register of Historical Places in 1979.

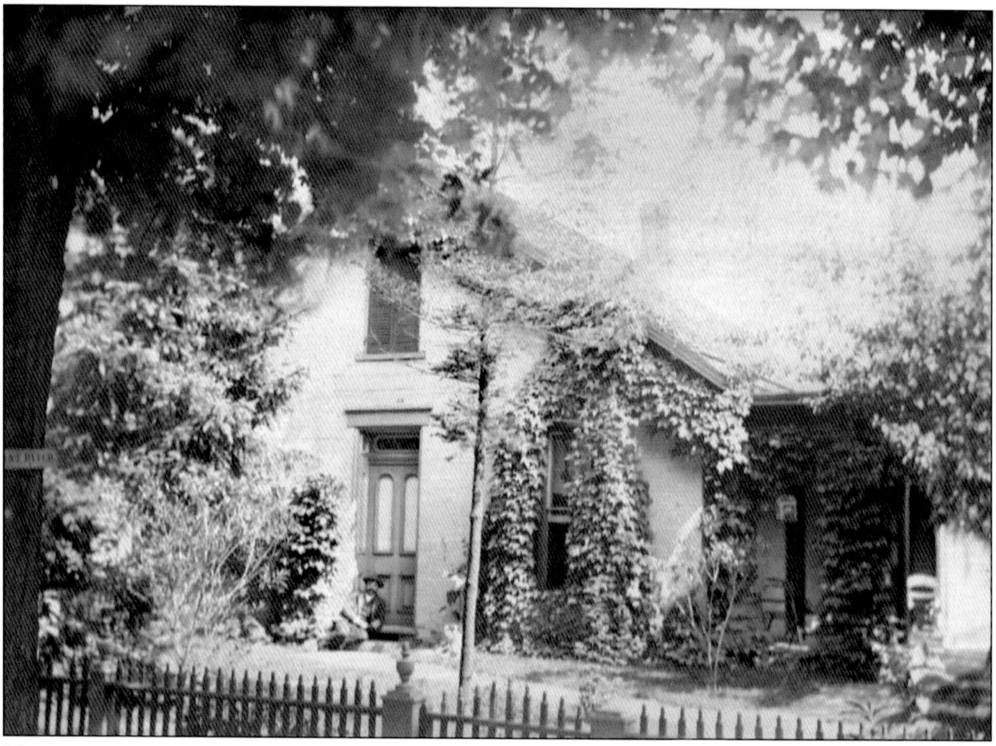

UNDERTAKER'S HOME. In this photograph is the home of Columbus and Martha Ann (Quinn) Marble. Columbus Marble had both a furniture business and an undertaking business. In 1875, Marble employed Carey Holladay, a 10-year-old orphan. Holladay eventually took over the business in 1893.

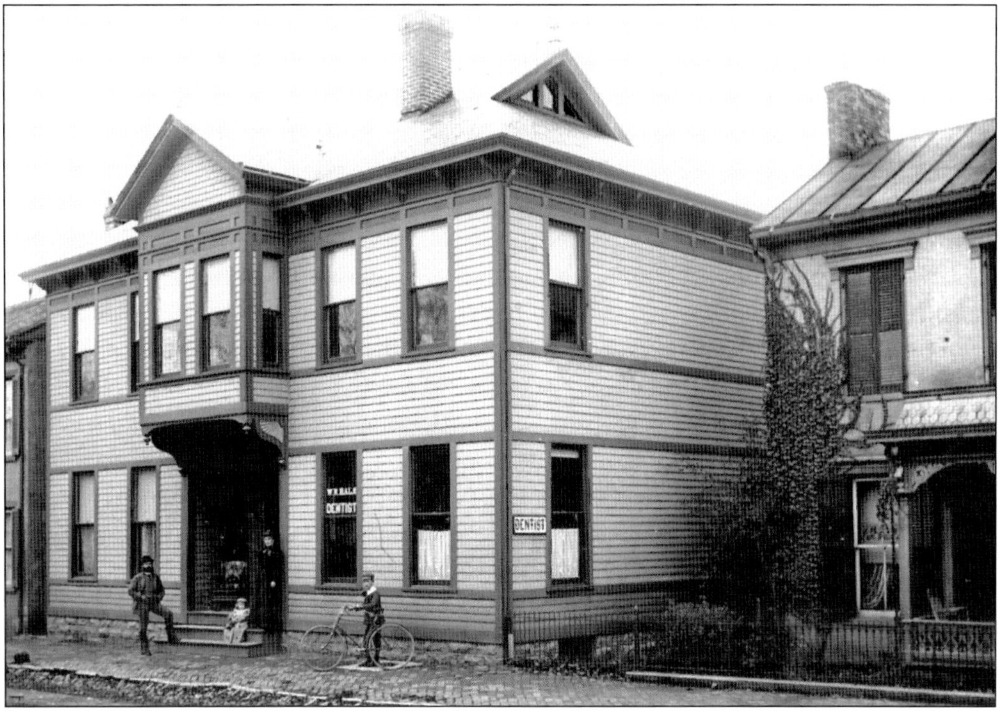

Hale Dentist c. 1882. Pictured from left to right are Will Hale, his wife, Amy, and children Mary Louise and Russell in front of Hale's practice on Main Street. Born in 1854, Hale graduated from Wilmington College and received his dental training from the Ohio Dental College in Cincinnati.

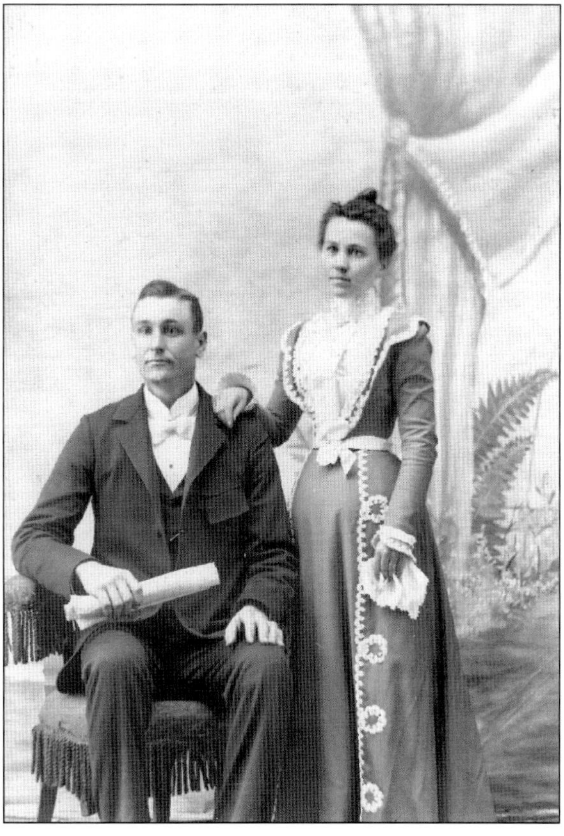

Brown Wedding, 1899. Andrew Jackson Brown married Martha Jane Conover, and they had nine children: Ernest, Frank, Grace, Alice, Catherine, Clifford, Andrew, Stella, and Ruth. Andrew Brown worked as a farmer and horse trainer and in the kitchen at the General Denver Hotel in the 1940s and 1950s. They lived on South Walnut Street for many years. (Courtesy of Marilynn Wilson.)

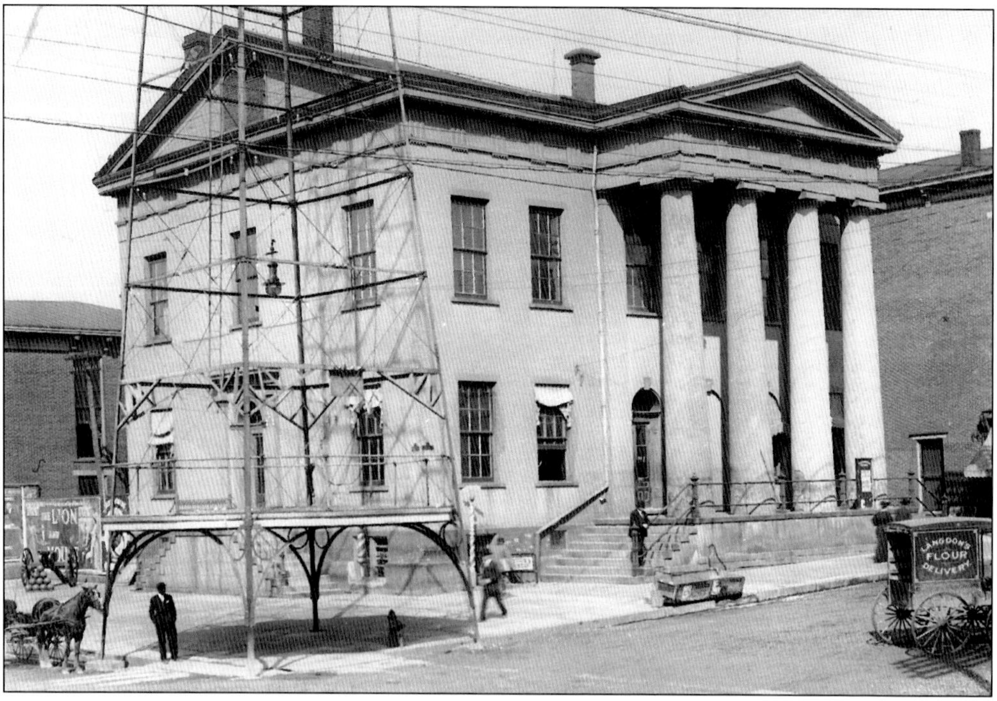

SECOND COURTHOUSE. In 1812, the citizens of Clinton County passed a tax levy for the first courthouse, which lasted until 1838, when it was sold for $240. The second courthouse served from 1839 until 1918. Wilson's flag tower (see page 92) stands next to the courthouse and was dedicated on Peace Day in August 1898. The columns from the bell tower from the second courthouse can be found on the Fisher-Edgington Funeral Home on West Locust Street.

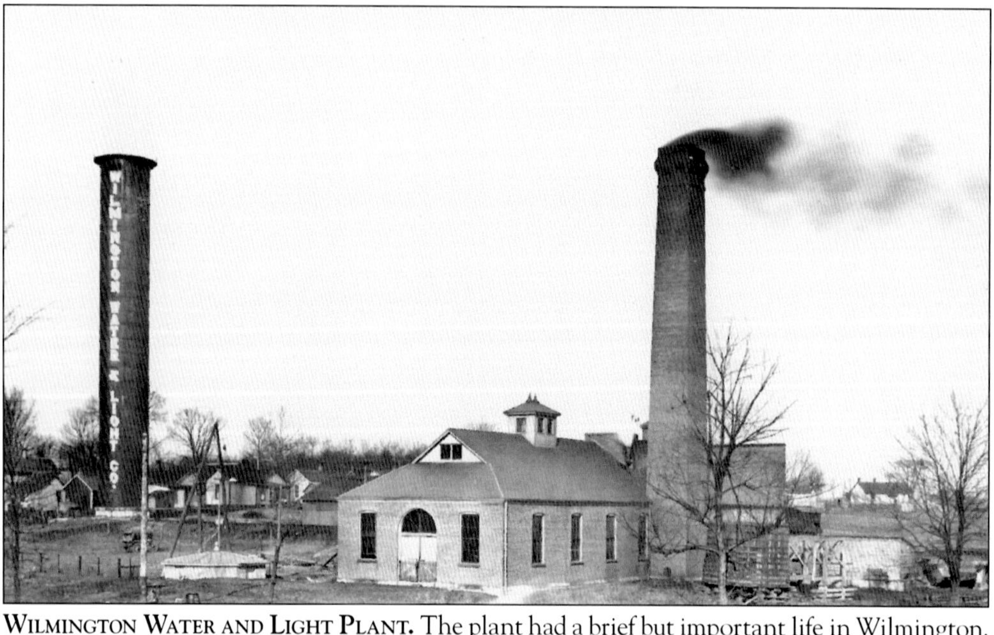

WILMINGTON WATER AND LIGHT PLANT. The plant had a brief but important life in Wilmington. After several false starts, it began operating in 1906 and stopped in 1914 when its franchise was taken over by Dayton Power and Light.

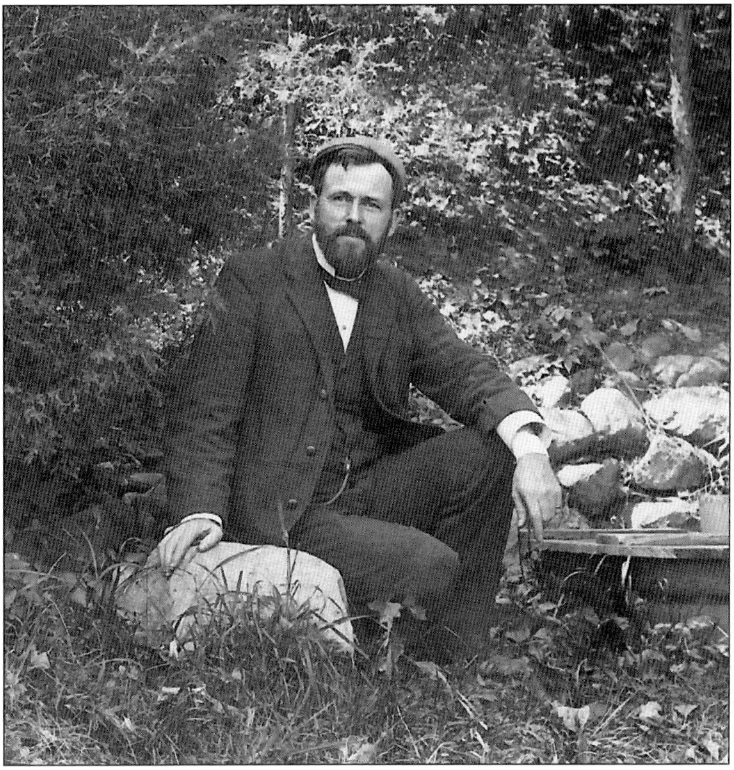

Orange Frazer. Frazer was a well-known, well-liked Wilmington resident who owned Frazer Brothers Grocery with his brother, John. He also worked for the local post office and the Ohio Supreme Court. However, it was probably Frazer's travel adventures that made him a favorite of his friends. His often humorous writings captured some of his escapades, including his trips to the Middle East and his purloining of a mummy's head.

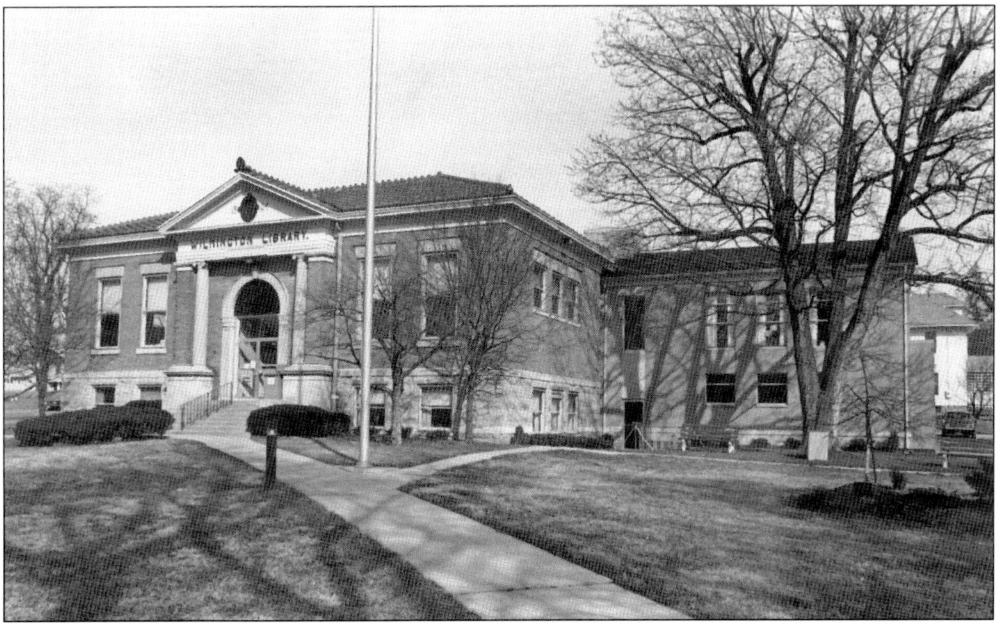

Library. In 1816, Wilmington launched its first private library association. In 1899, a subscription library was located in the Fife and Bosworth building. For $1, a subscriber could use the library for one year. In 1903, Andrew Carnegie donated $10,000 for a public library, pictured above on North South Street. Previously Samuel Walker had donated a building and funds for the same purpose.

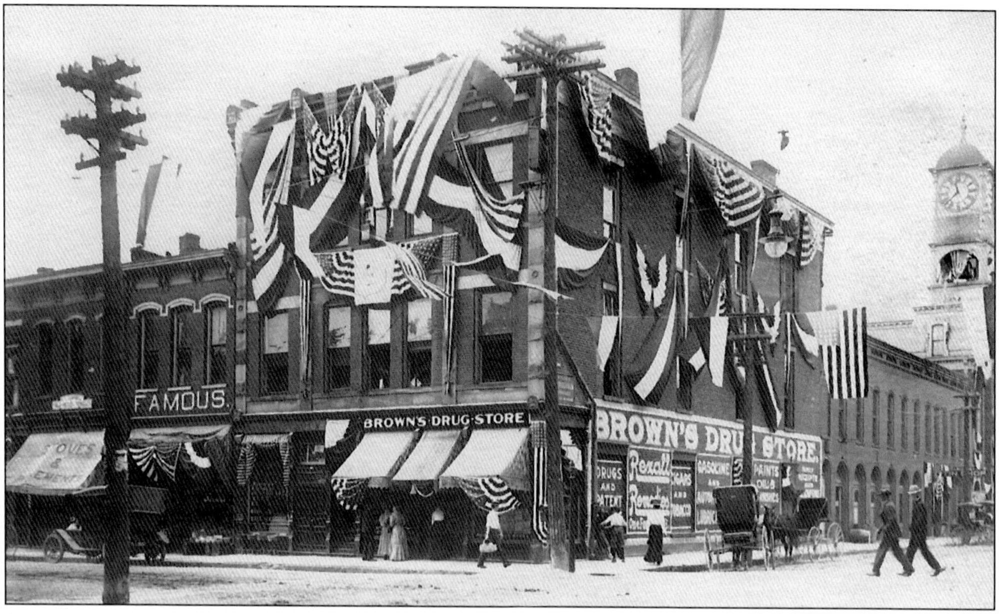

CENTENNIAL CELEBRATION, AUGUST 25–28, 1910. Town officials rolled out the red carpet for the homecoming celebration. Professional decorators worked day and night to dazzle the village. More than 20,000 revelers poured into the streets to enjoy the concerts, parties, public speeches, and fireworks. This photograph above was taken at the corner of North South and Main Streets.

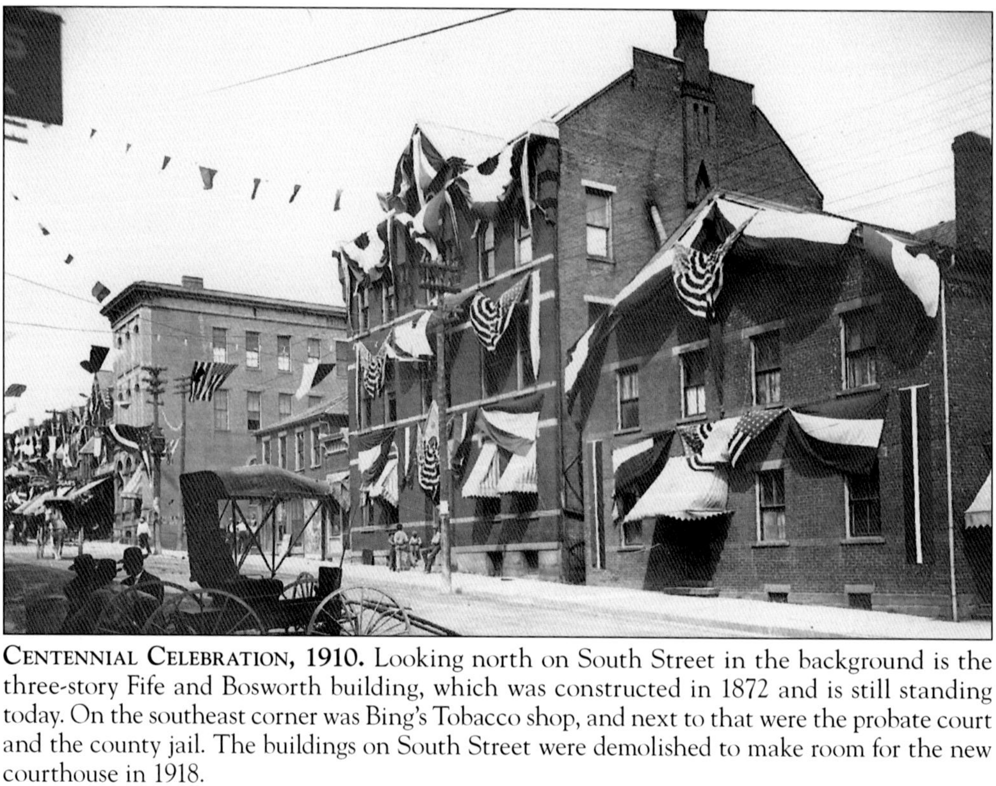

CENTENNIAL CELEBRATION, 1910. Looking north on South Street in the background is the three-story Fife and Bosworth building, which was constructed in 1872 and is still standing today. On the southeast corner was Bing's Tobacco shop, and next to that were the probate court and the county jail. The buildings on South Street were demolished to make room for the new courthouse in 1918.

Two

TRANSPORTATION

Wilmington was relatively isolated during its early years. Located miles away from a major waterway or large city, it was situated near a network of Native American trails. The first settlers would have arrived by horseback, oxen cart, or horse-drawn wagons. The pioneers had to travel light while transporting the necessities of everyday living to a primitive land. Stagecoach stops and stables sprang up to support the travelers.

The early roads were just traces or blazes marked on trees. Next, the underbrush would have been cleared and trees felled. Eventually some sort of material would have been placed on the ground, such as wood planks or stone chips. Travelers would have been lucky if all the stumps had been removed. Many early settlers limited their travel to the winter months when they were assured their carriages could pass freely over the frozen ground.

In 1853, one of the greatest technological innovations in transportation arrived in Wilmington: the Cincinnati, Wilmington, and Zanesville Railroad. Railroads enabled farmers to sell excess goods, manufacturers to import raw materials and export finished products, and passengers to visit one another—all on a large scale and in an expeditious manner.

After the railroad arrived, the bicycle was the next technological advancement, and while cycling was popular, it was mostly limited to leisure travel. Cycling, however, led to the demand for better roads, which helped the next emerging technologies: the automobile and paved roads. Today Wilmington, no longer isolated, is positioned along one of the largest interstate highways.

As automobiles became more popular during the 1920s, a new craze hit rural America: barnstorming. In Wilmington, local residents developed an airfield near the infirmary. This airfield eventually became an influential part of the fabric of Wilmington, as it was first converted to a military base during World War II and served as such until 1971. The airfield then became one of the largest air cargo terminals in the world. While the airfield sits nearly empty today, Wilmington residents hope that it will once again return to productivity.

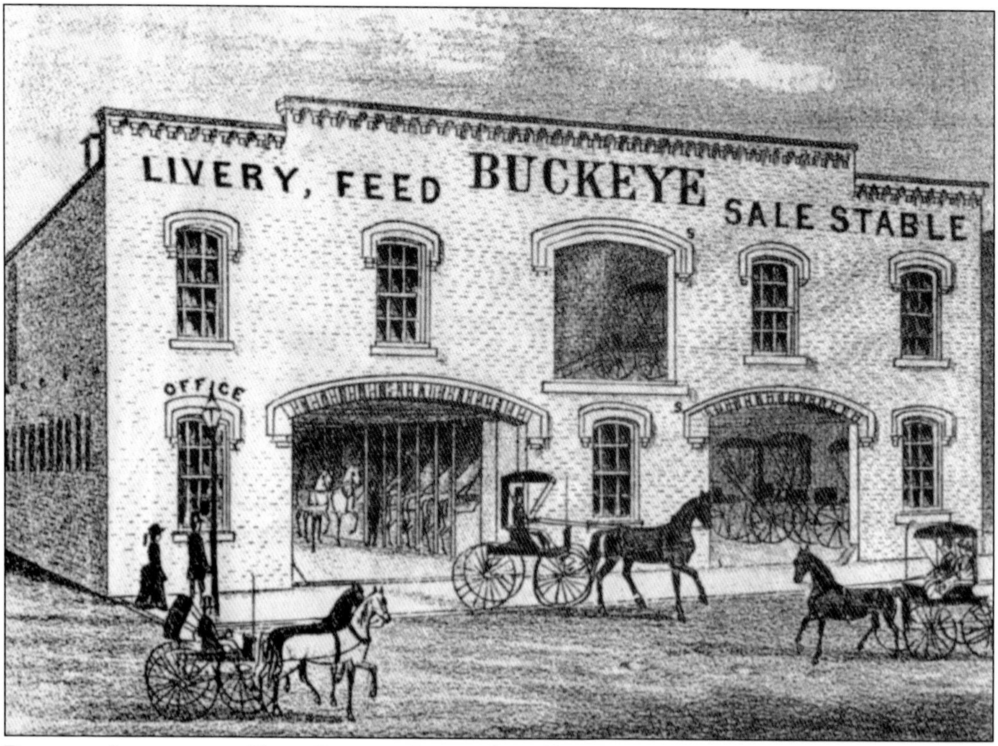

Buckeye Livery and Feed Stable. Located on East Locust Street, the livery served the Buckeye Hotel. In 1876, the hotel was destroyed by fire, but the livery survived. The building now houses the Buckeye Livery Café's Cassano's Pizzeria. (*An Illustrated Historical Atlas of Clinton County*, 1876).

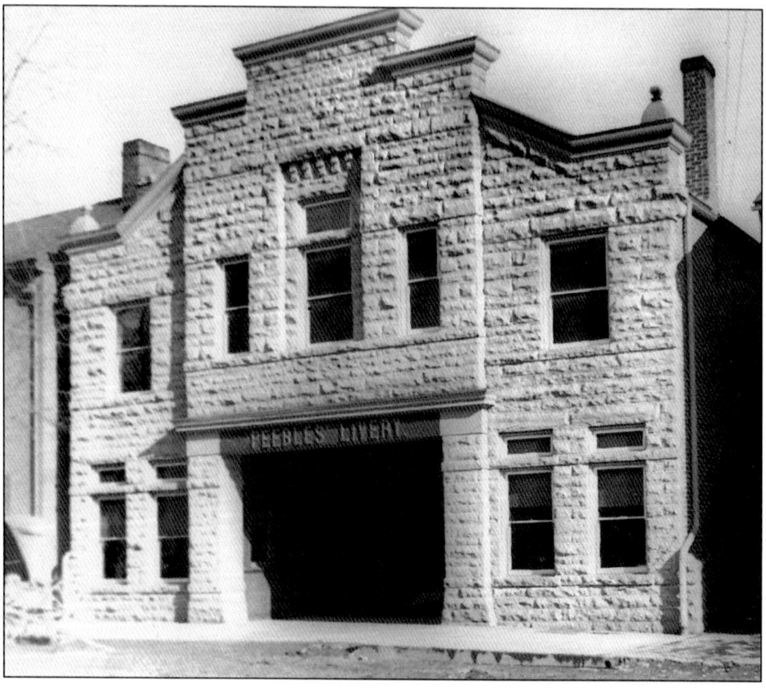

Peebles Livery. Situated on West Main Street next to the General Denver Hotel in what is now a parking lot, the livery served Wilmington customers in both the horse business and eventually the automobile business when it was converted to the Motor Inn. In the 1960s, the J. W. Bowling Alley and Clinton Sports were located in the building.

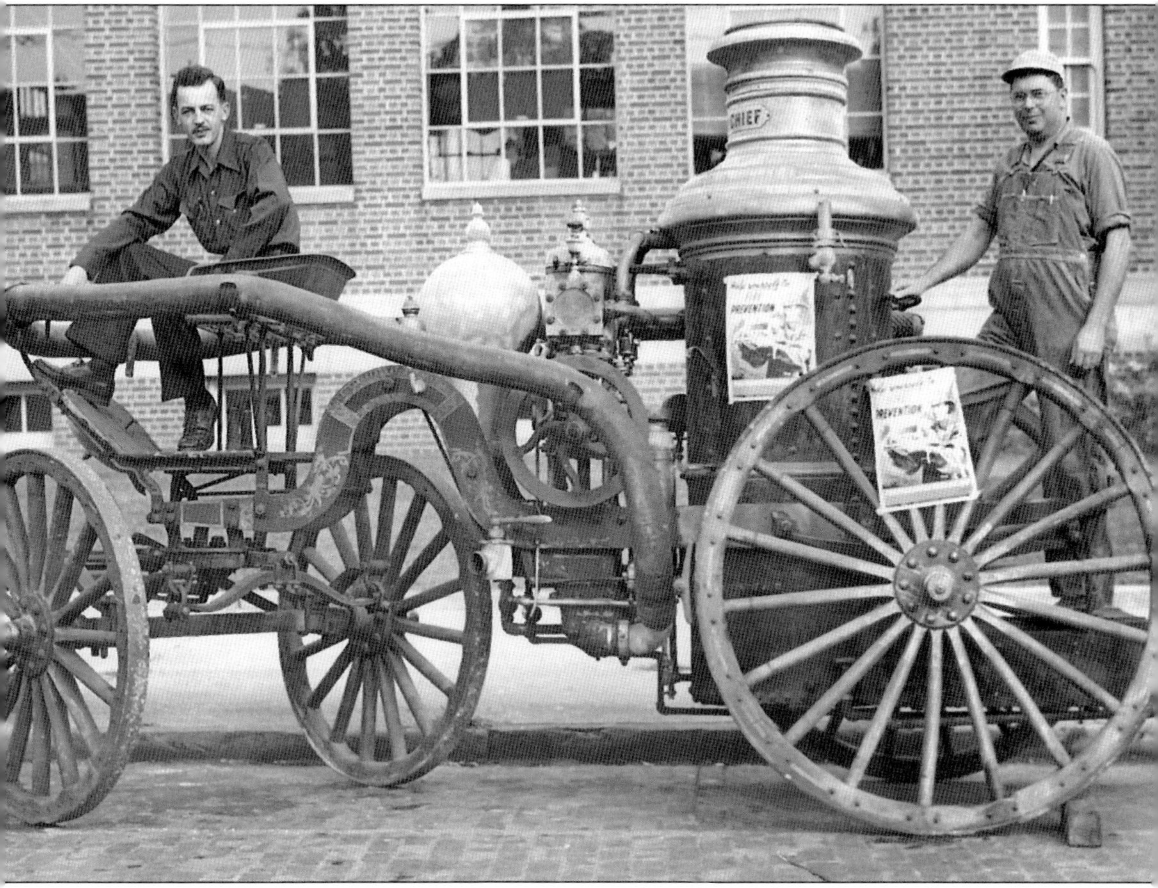

CLINTON STEAM FIRE ENGINE, 1948. The town council purchased the "Clinton Chief" steam fire engine in 1875 for $6,000 after a string of fires devastated the downtown infrastructure. In 1890, the fire department became a paid force. The Chief was used until 1910 and was pulled by a team of horses. Pictured are fire chief Harry Hague III (left) and firefighter Dr. Neil Myers.

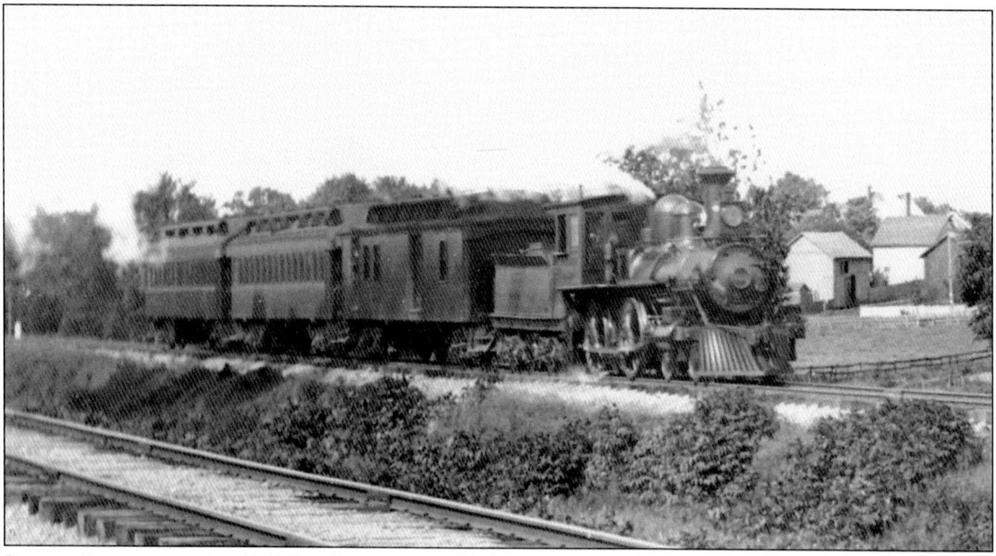

STEAM ENGINE, C. 1885. The Cincinnati, Wilmington, and Zanesville Railroad was the first line to serve Wilmington. This photograph shows both the Cincinnati line and the Baltimore and Ohio line. The Cincinnati, Wilmington, and Zanesville line transferred ownership several times due to financial difficulties. Segments of the line are now part of the bicycle path of the Rails-to-Trails Conservancy.

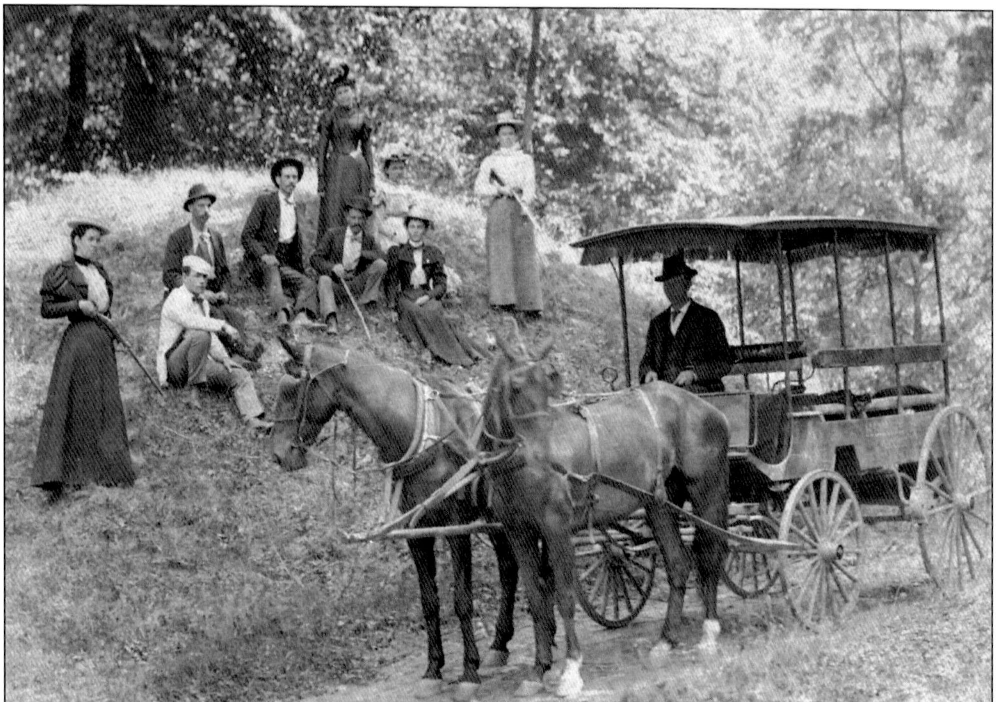

SOCIAL OUTING, 1898. For a leisurely trip to Fort Ancient, this group hired a carriage and driver and brought along their hunting gear. Pictured from left to right are Sadie Johnston, Frank Woolary, Albert Johnston, Allie Johnston, Clyde Hazard, Belle Hazard, ? Thomas, Eulalia Jefferis, Lucy Johnston, and the driver, ? Coakley. (Courtesy of Rita Butcher).

Bicycling Brindle Brothers, 1896. Twin brothers William "Will" Brindle (left) and Frank L. Brindle are pictured with their bicycles. When they married twin sisters Ada McKee (who wed Will) and Alma McKee (who wed Frank) on the same day in 1898, the wedding announcement was published by the *New York Times* and by a local paper in New Zealand.

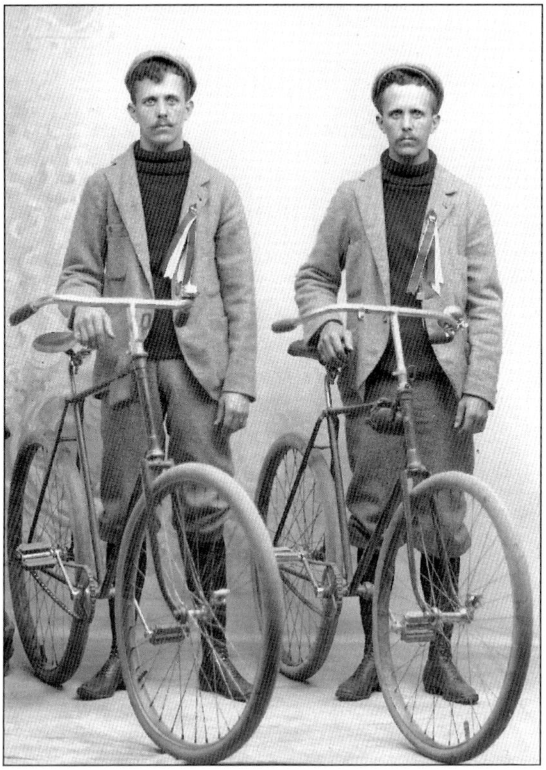

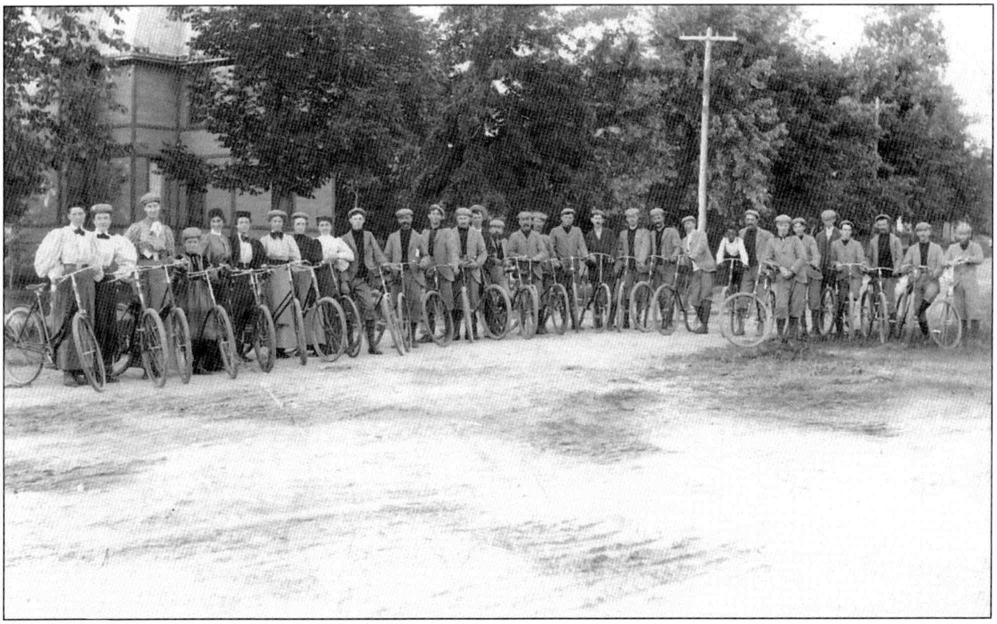

Wilmington Bicycle Club, c. 1890s. Cycling became popular in the 1880s and 1890s, and cyclists formed the League of American Wheelman, now the League of American Bicyclists. Pictured here is Wilmington's local cycling club, which included a number of female cyclists. In 1896, Susan B. Anthony said that bicycling had "done more to emancipate women than anything else in the world." Cycling also ushered in an era of commonsense clothing for women.

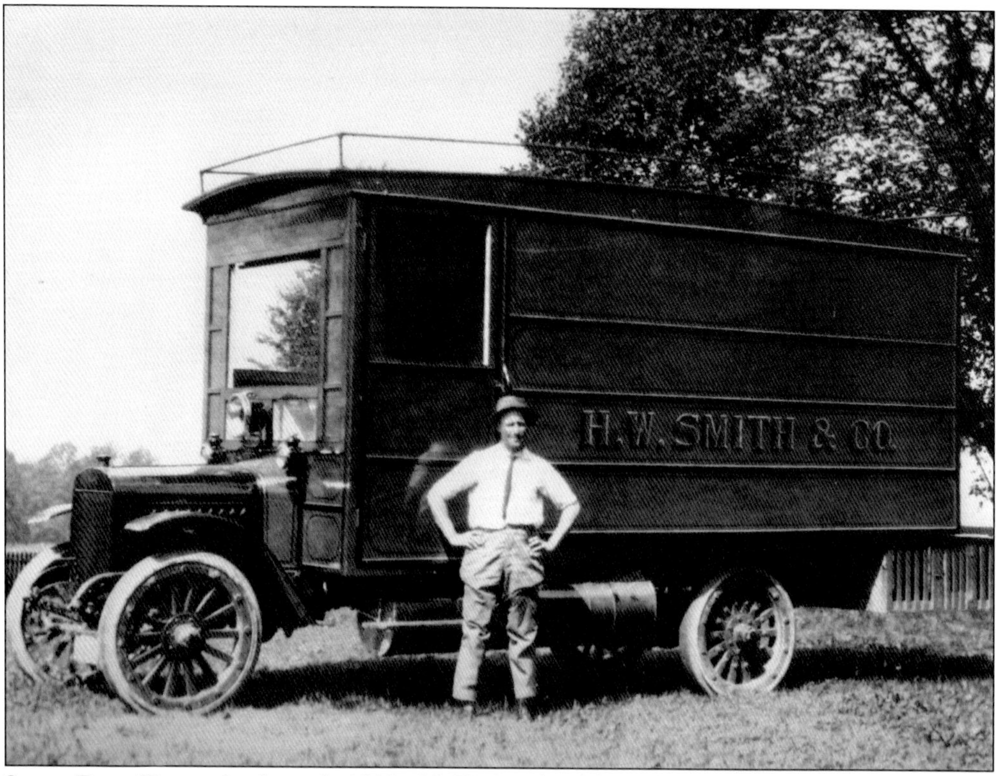

SMITH FARM TRUCK. In the early 1900s, H. W. Smith sold supplies from his truck to the farmers in the Kingman area of Wilmington. He also owned a country store in South Kingman. Smith is the great-grandfather of Wilmington farmer Richard Thompson. (Courtesy of Richard and Pam Thompson.)

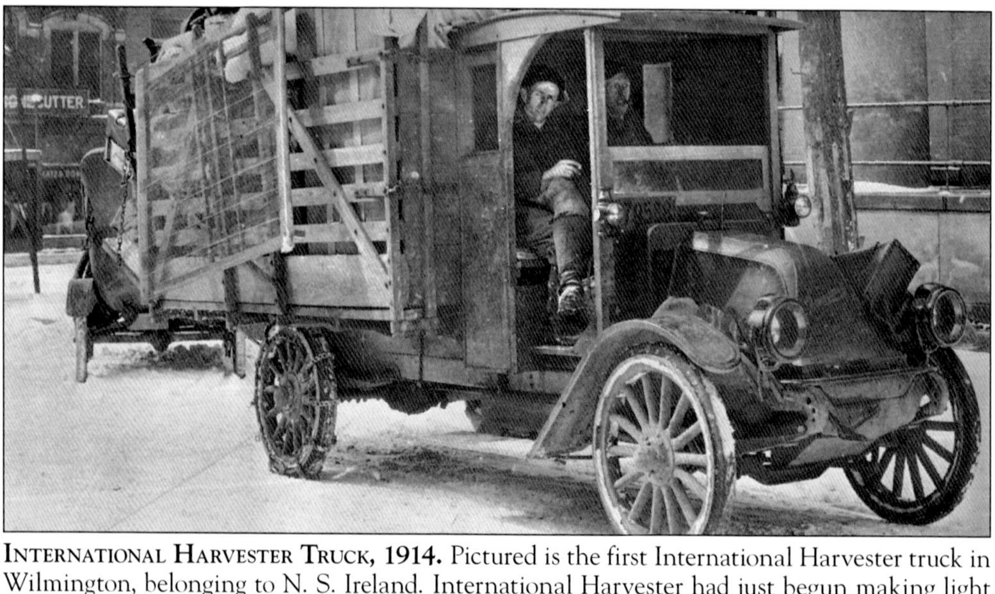

INTERNATIONAL HARVESTER TRUCK, 1914. Pictured is the first International Harvester truck in Wilmington, belonging to N. S. Ireland. International Harvester had just begun making light trucks in 1907. Trucks would become immensely useful to farmers over the years as horse-drawn vehicles and railroad usage diminished.

FIRST FEMALE PILOT IN WILMINGTON, 1935. Kathryn Hale, wife of Corwin "Kersey" Hale, was the first female pilot in Wilmington. Female pilots were still rare at the time, but the exploits of Amelia Earhart in the 1920s inspired women to become pilots. The first airfield, located across from the county infirmary, would later become home to Airborne Express and then DHL.

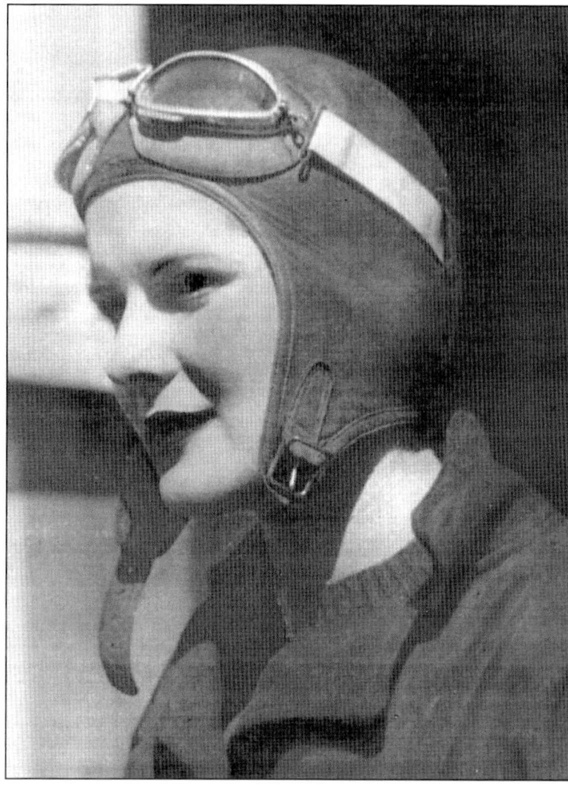

AIR MAIL RUN, 1938. Corwin "Kersey" Hale flew the first, last, and only mail run to Cincinnati from Wilmington. Hale took off from Wilmington at 3:15 p.m. and arrived in Cincinnati 35 minutes later with 293 letters. Pictured from left to right are Mr. and Mrs. Orville Hale, Mrs. W. F. Haines, W. F. Haines, Mrs. M. D. Barns, M. D. Barns, I. J. Jefferis, Grover Smith, and pilot Corwin Hale. (Courtesy of Rita Butcher.)

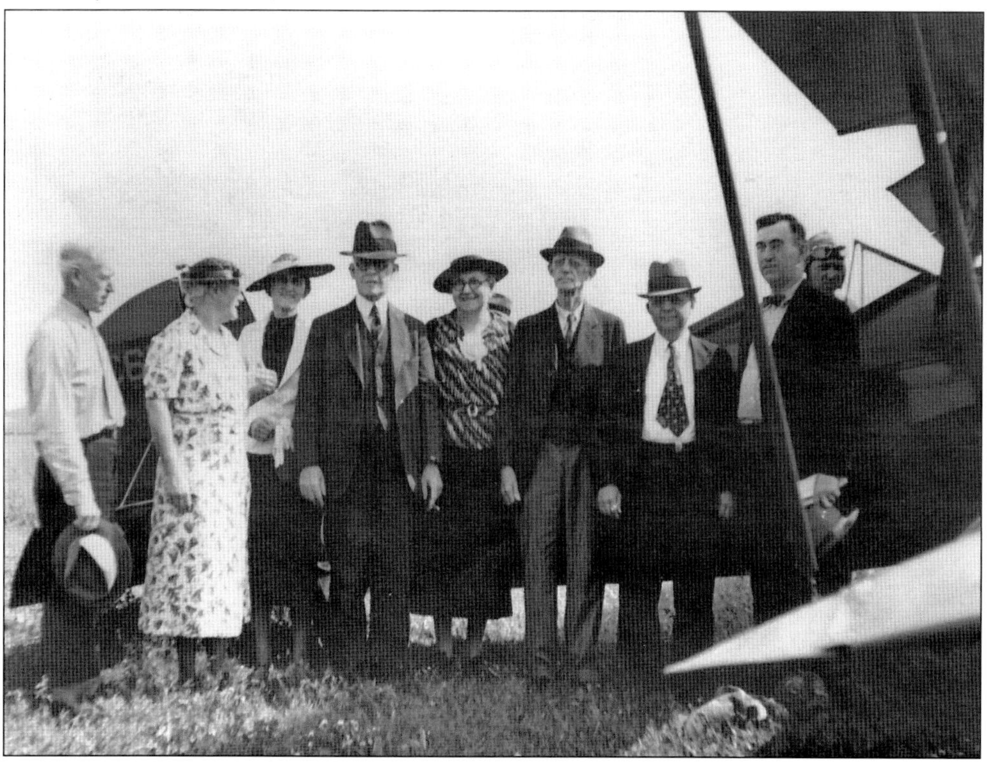

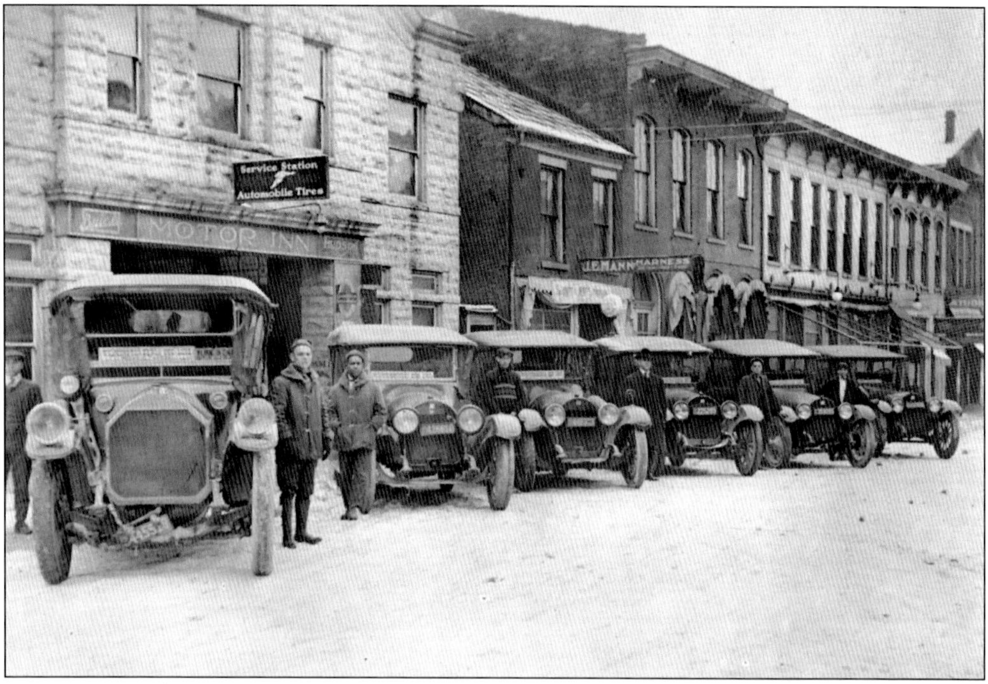

MOTOR INN. The Motor Inn dealership and service station was located on Main Street where the mural parking lot is today. It was formerly the Peebles Livery, but instead of stabling horses, it housed and sold automobiles.

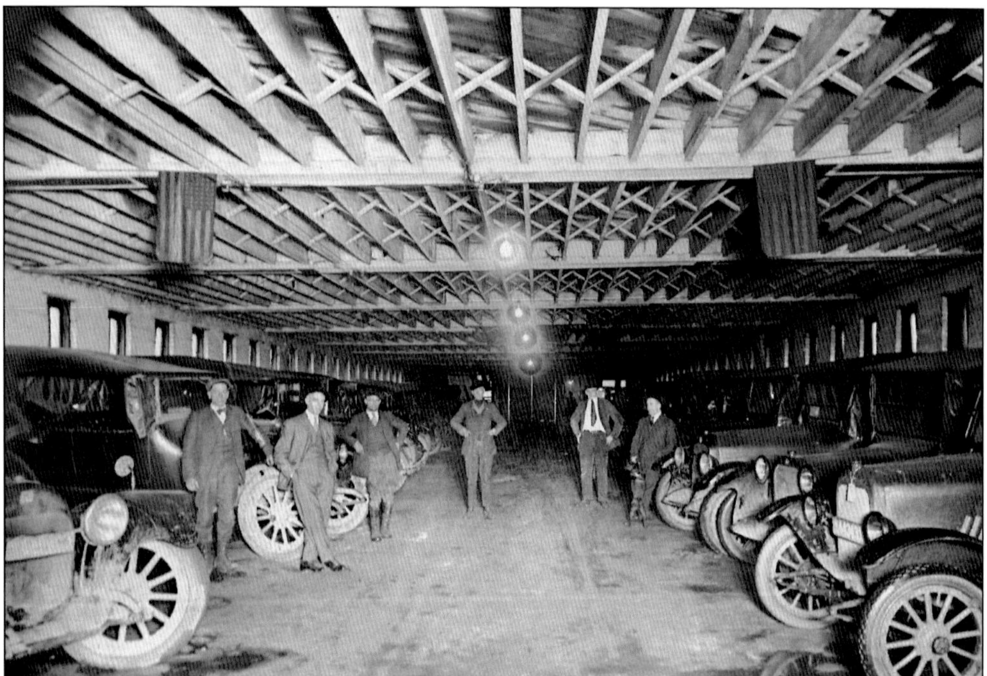

CLINTON GARAGE. Located on Sugartree and Mulberry Streets, Clinton Garage served as an indoor parking garage and service station.

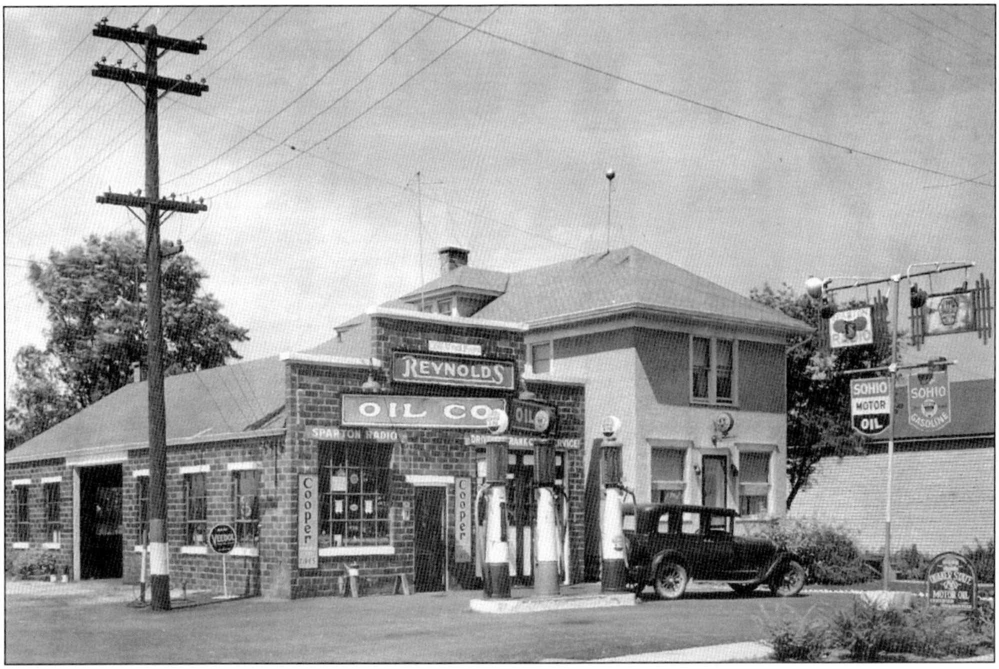

CRAIG REYNOLDS GARAGE, 1940s. The Craig Reynolds Garage was located on the corner of Josephine and West Main Streets. During the 1940s, service stations had a considerable drop in business due to gasoline rationing during World War II.

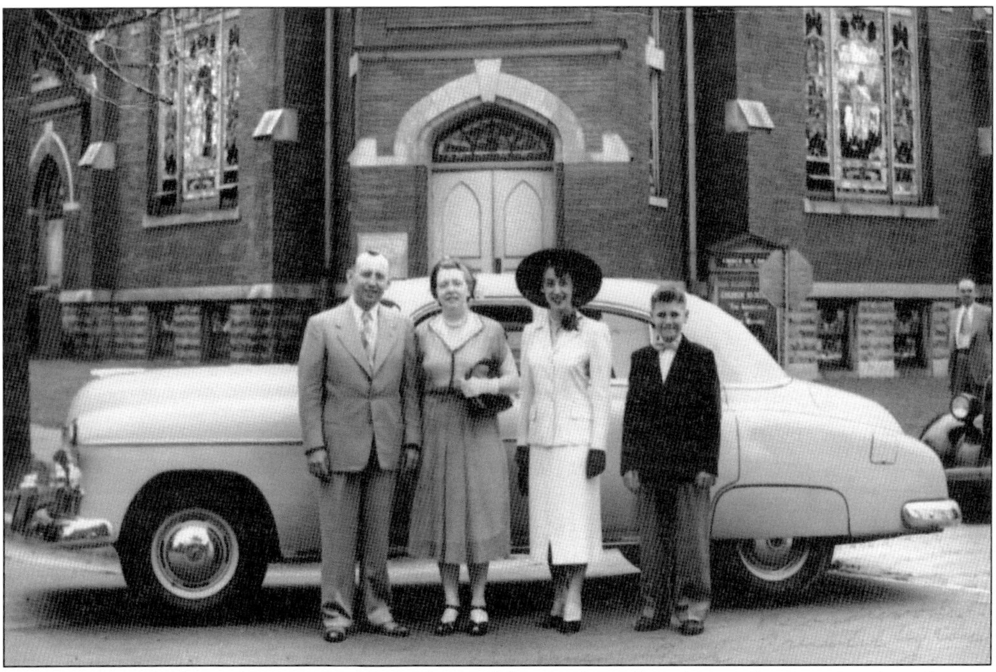

CHEVROLET. This brand-new 1950 Chevrolet Styleline Deluxe four-door sedan was purchased using a special fund raised by church members and given to Rev. Otha Clary (far left) and his family (from left to right, Mrs. Clary, June, and Paul). It cost $1,571.25 with delivery and taxes, plus $91.50 for the optional heater, defroster, and undercoating. (Courtesy of First Christian Church.)

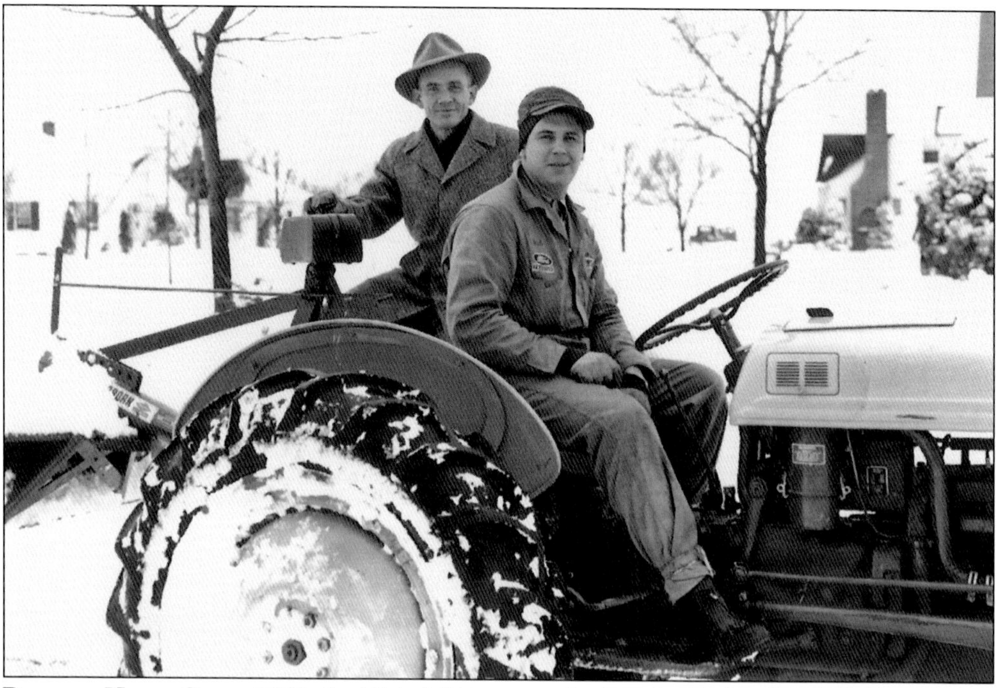

BLIZZARD HOUSE CALLS, 1950. Fred Fairchild is pictured taking Dr. Richard Bath (left) to a house call on his tractor during a big snow storm. A total of 17 inches of snow fell within three days, making travel by automobile treacherous. In the 1950s, house calls accounted for 40 percent of all physician-patient encounters.

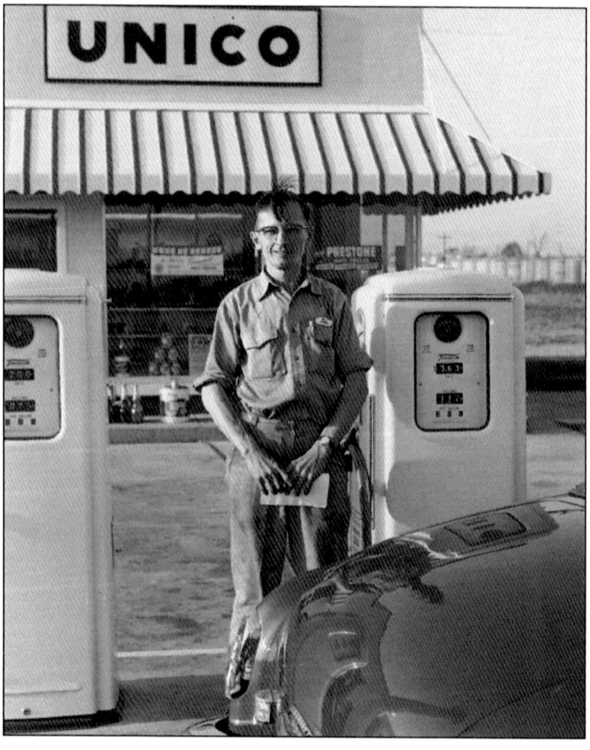

LANDMARK FILLING STATION, 1954. Located on Routes 22 and 3, Landmark was a farmers' cooperative that sold a variety of agricultural products, including petroleum, and is still in business today. Don Grove, a well-known member of the community, is pictured here during a time when station attendants pumped gasoline for customers. Notice the price of gasoline was about 30¢ per gallon.

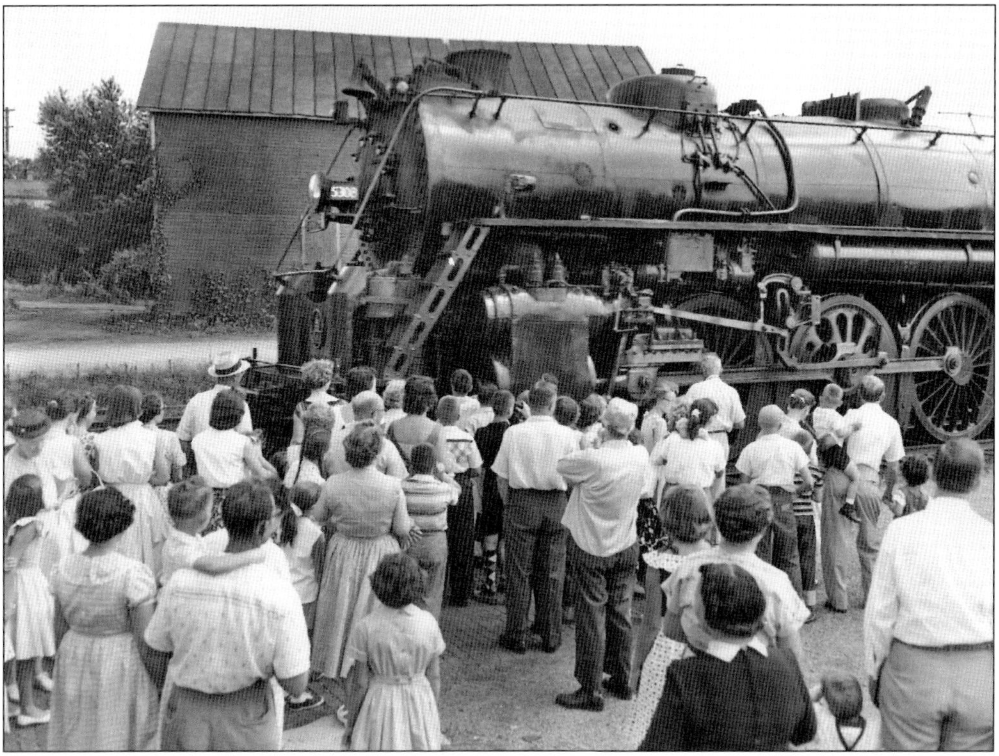

LAST PASSENGER TRAIN, 1956. The last passenger train serving Wilmington was part of the Baltimore and Ohio Railroad line. Wilmington residents turned out in force to say farewell. The growth of trucks, buses, automobiles, high-speed interstates, and airline travel proved to be the death knell for passenger rail service. Freight service continues through Wilmington today.

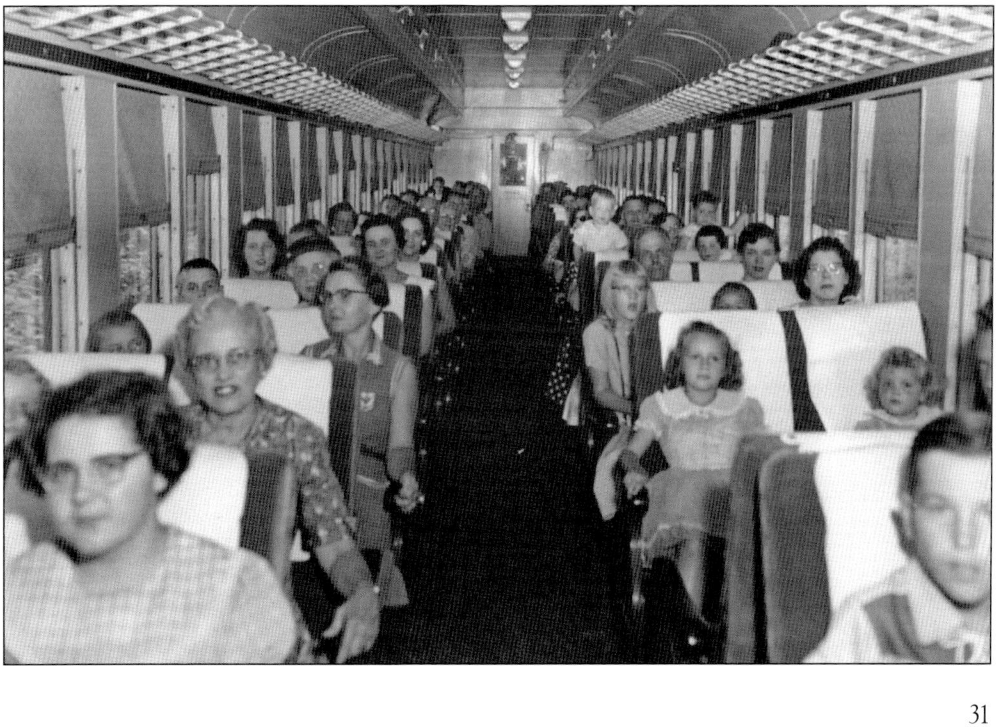

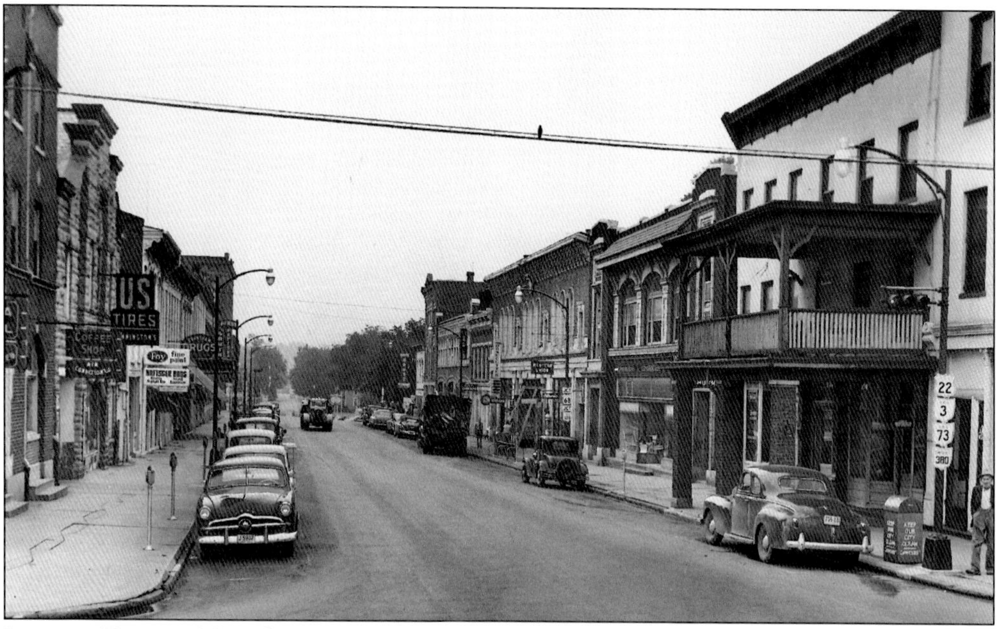

Looking East on Main Street, 1940s–1950s. At the time, Main Street was a two-way street. The first building on the left is the General Denver Hotel. At one time, this road and many others were laid with brick before they were paved. Notice the highway signs for Routes 22, 3, 73, and 380. In 1916, the state took control of Route 3 (the "3C" Highway) because of its importance in connecting Ohio's three largest cities: Cincinnati, Columbus, and Cleveland.

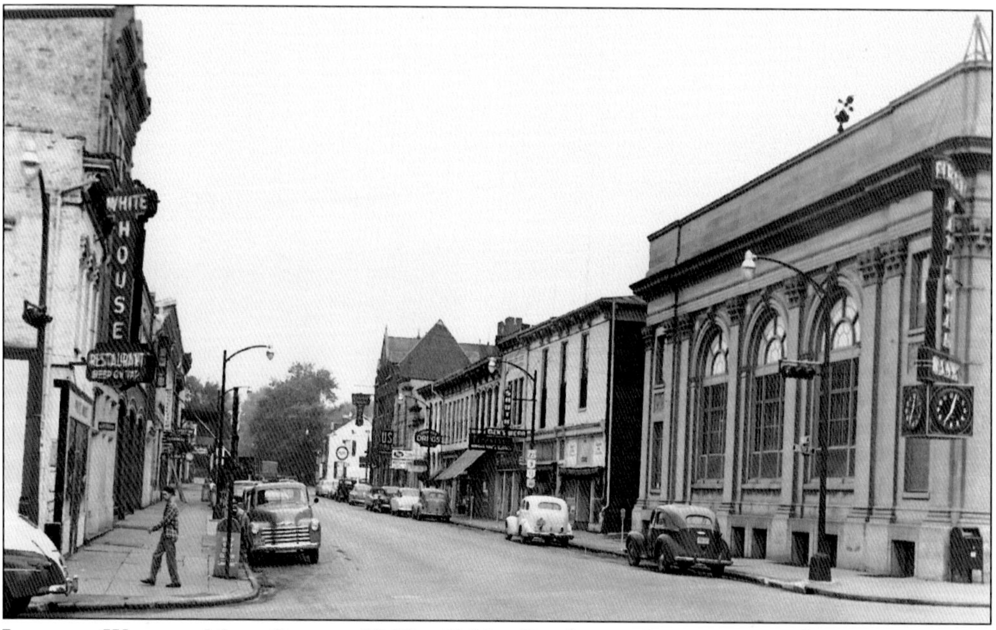

Looking West on Main Street, 1940s–1950s. On the southwest corner of Main Street near South Street sits the White House Restaurant, which was a popular hangout for service members during the World War II years. On the northwest corner is First National Bank. There were several apparel stores lining the streets, including Bonecutter's and Fort Pitt Shoe on the south side, and Jack and Jill's Clothing, Paris Clothing, and South Clothing on the north side.

Three

Quakers

The Quakers, or Society of Friends, were among the earliest arrivals to the Wilmington region. They established their first house of worship around 1805 at the Center Meeting with the monthly meeting starting around 1807. Springfield Monthly Meeting began in 1818, and Dover Monthly Meeting started in 1824. The Friends also built some of the earliest schools. Their teachings on social justice, humanitarian service, nonviolence, and simple living have placed them at the forefront of many social issues.

Perhaps ironically, the Friends' stances on social justice put them not only at personal risk, but also at risk within their religious community. While many Quakers were antislavery during the antebellum era, they had different ideas on the emancipation movement. Two of the best-known Quaker abolitionists were Abram (Abraham) Allen, a native of Ireland, and Dr. Abraham Brooke, both residents of the Oakland area (now Wilmington). Among Allen's unique abolitionist contributions was his "Mud Castle," modeled on Irish-style homes, where he housed the runaways, and his "Liberator," a carriage specially built to slip slaves away in secrecy. Brooke was known for Liberty Hall, an abolitionist convention hall built on his property, which played host to Frederick Douglass, among others.

Both Allen and Brooke were forced out of their Hicksite communities because of their radical views and joined the Congregational/Progressive Friends, continuing their antislavery mission. Others—both anonymous and well-known, Quaker and non-Quaker—served the abolitionist cause, including Eli Gaskill, Thomas Hibbens, David Sewell, W. H. Rogers, Parker Osborne, Elihu Oren, and Thomas Whinery. Some Friends served the antislavery cause in other ways, including creating a free trade store or meeting with Pres. Abraham Lincoln to discuss the plight of slaves.

The circumstances of the Civil War tested many of the local Quakers, given their views on slavery and nonviolence. Some chose to serve because of their antislavery position or their patriotic bent, and a few paid the commutation fee, while others risked imprisonment to stay true to their beliefs. After the war, the groups tried to reconcile their differences. Wilmington Monthly Meeting was started in 1868, with Wilmington Yearly Meeting formed in 1892.

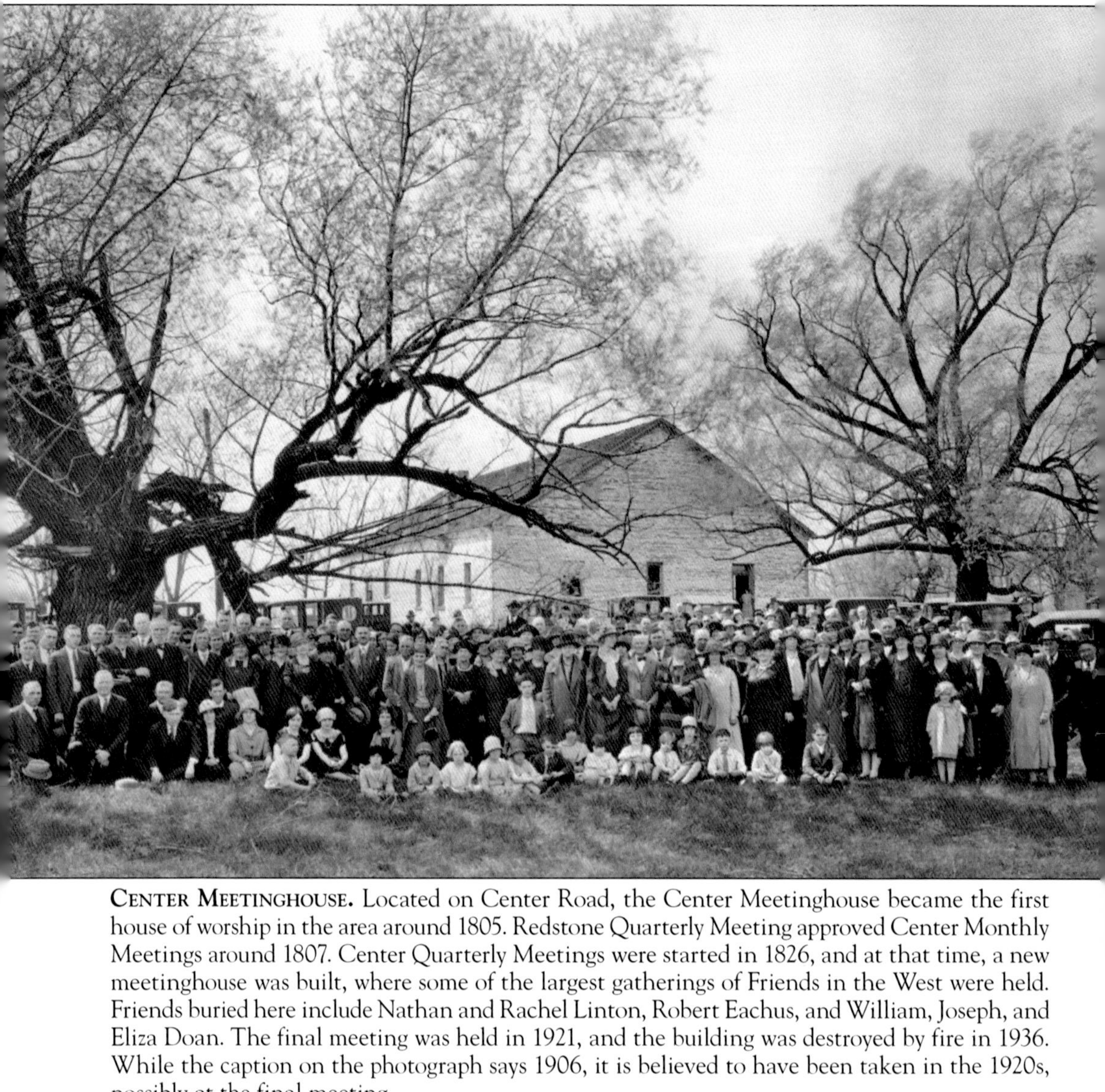

Center Meetinghouse. Located on Center Road, the Center Meetinghouse became the first house of worship in the area around 1805. Redstone Quarterly Meeting approved Center Monthly Meetings around 1807. Center Quarterly Meetings were started in 1826, and at that time, a new meetinghouse was built, where some of the largest gatherings of Friends in the West were held. Friends buried here include Nathan and Rachel Linton, Robert Eachus, and William, Joseph, and Eliza Doan. The final meeting was held in 1921, and the building was destroyed by fire in 1936. While the caption on the photograph says 1906, it is believed to have been taken in the 1920s, possibly at the final meeting.

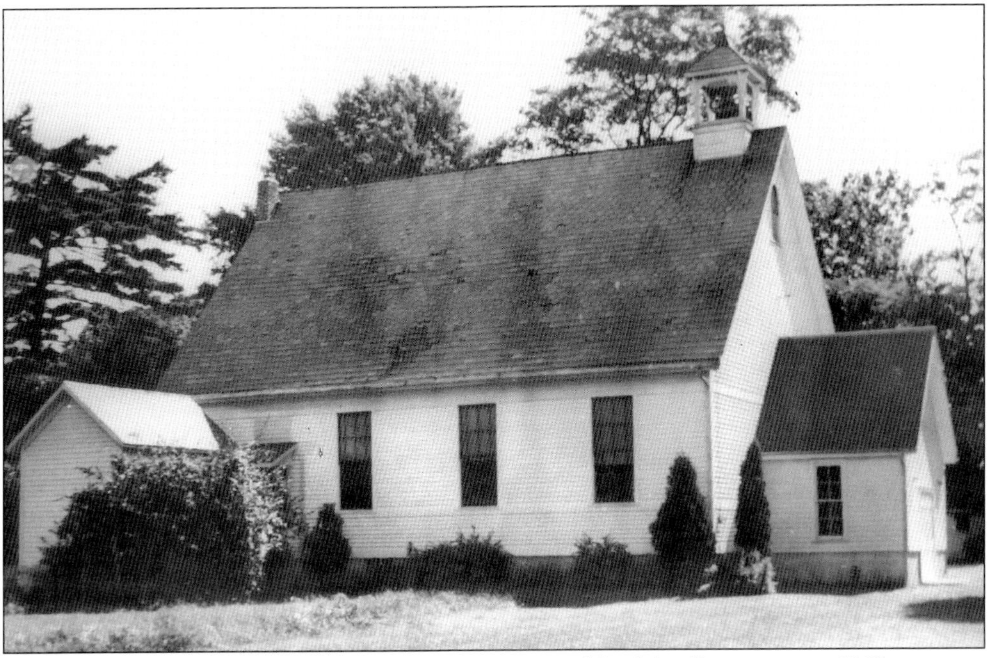

Springfield Meetinghouse. Springfield Meeting started "indulged" meetings in 1809 on a spot believed to have been a Native American altar near Todd's Fork. Monthly meetings began in 1818. The Quakers built the present meetinghouse in 1892. Some of the early families include the Harveys, the Hadleys, the Hales, and the Harlans. Members of the Harvey and Hadley families and others were active in Shawnee mission work for decades. The Springfield Friends celebrated their bicentennial in 2009.

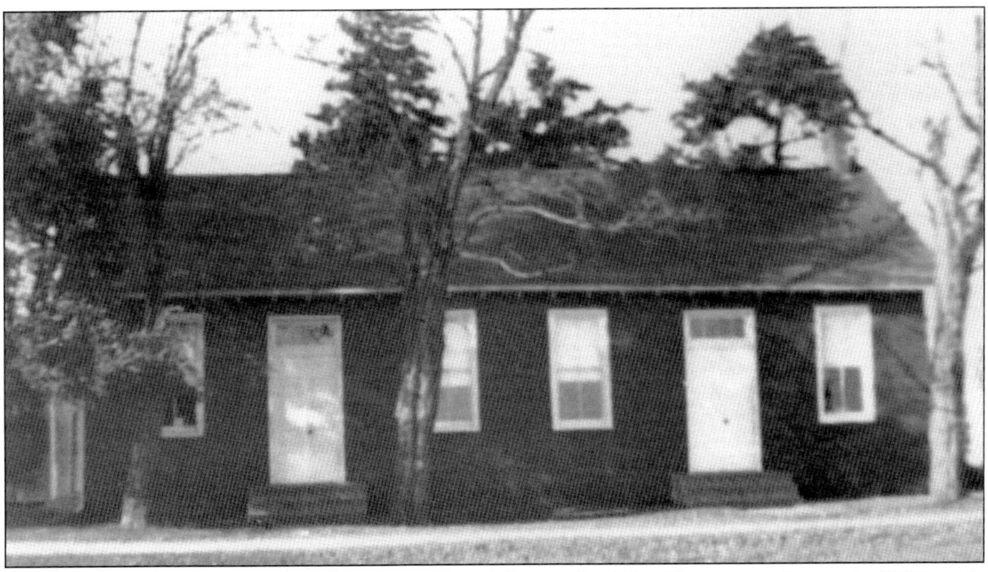

Dover Meetinghouse. Situated on Dover Road, Dover "indulged" meetings began in 1805, with monthly meetings in 1824. The original Dover log meetinghouse was replaced in 1844 with a brick structure that is still standing and used today. Some of the early names of Dover Meeting were the Haworths, the Wrights, the Dillons, and the Baileys. The Jones Meetinghouse, located on Wilmington College's campus, was designed to look like the Dover Meetinghouse.

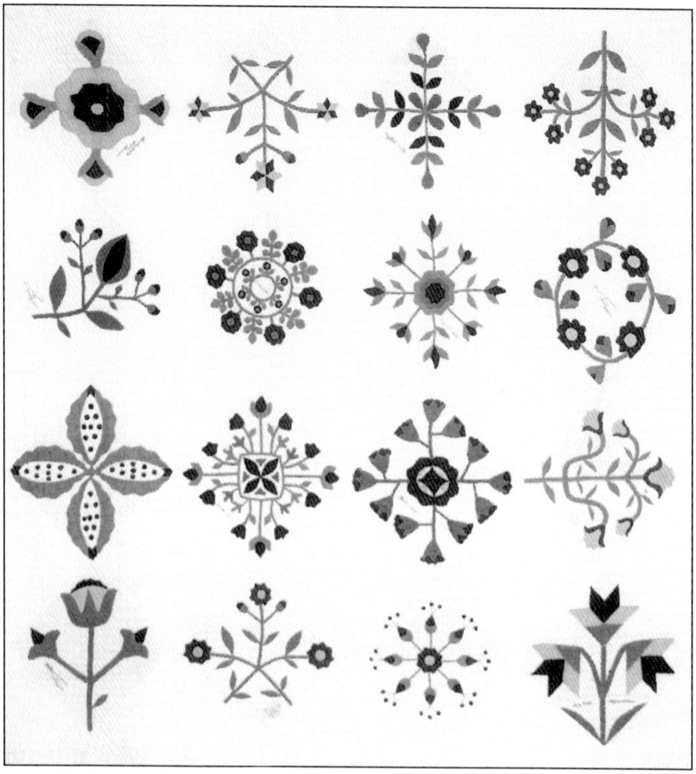

Friendship Abolitionist Quilt. The abolitionist women of Indiana Yearly Meeting from Clinton County, Ohio, and Wayne County, Indiana, created this friendship quilt in the 1840s. Rebecca Harvey Hadley and her daughters were signers of the quilt. In 1842, the women who had signed the quilt were "read out" of their meeting. This division lasted 13 years.

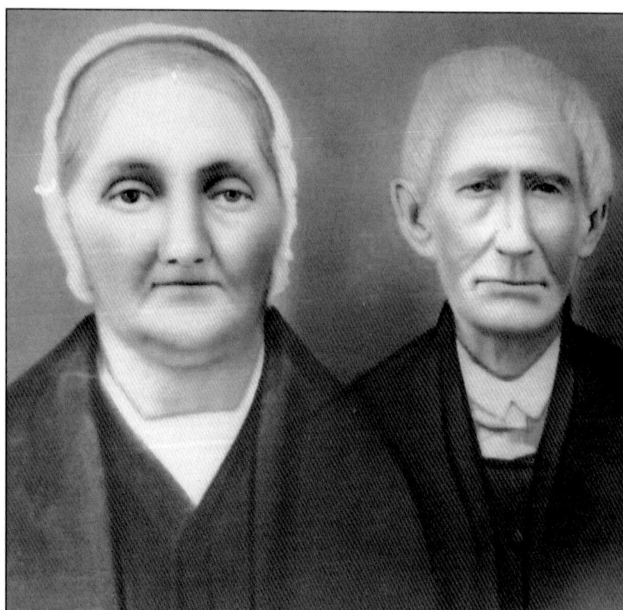

Sarah and Isaac Harvey. In 1862, Isaac Harvey convinced his wife that God wanted them to travel to Washington, D.C., to talk to Pres. Abraham Lincoln to discuss the conditions of slaves in the South. After an arduous journey, they arrived bewildered in the bustling capital city. They asked a well-dressed gentleman where they could find Lincoln. Somewhat surprised, this gentleman—Salmon P. Chase, President Lincoln's secretary of the treasury from Ohio—made arrangements for the Harveys to meet Lincoln the next day. Several literary versions of this event have been published.

Col. A. W. Doan, 1860s. In 1861, Doan was one of the first to respond to Lincoln's call for volunteers, serving first with the 12th Ohio Volunteer Infantry and later with the 79th Ohio Volunteer Infantry. After the march to Atlanta with Gen. William Tecumseh Sherman, Doan was promoted to colonel. Like other Quakers who fought in the war, he earned the moniker "Fighting Quaker."

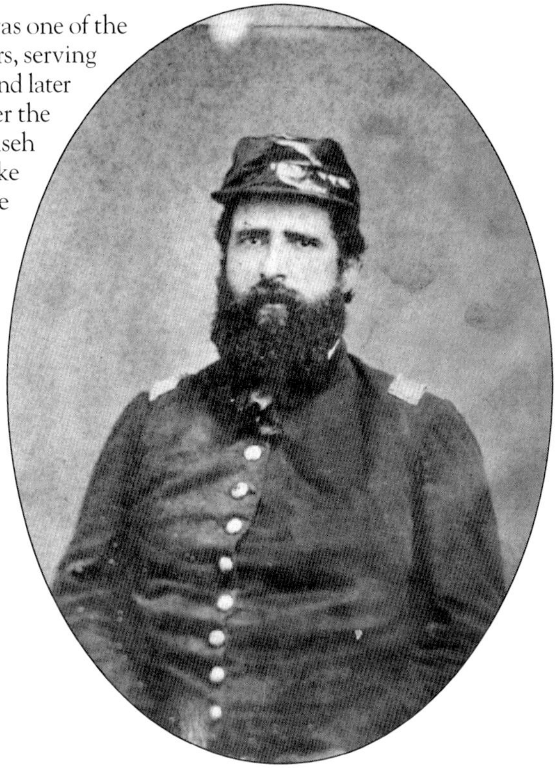

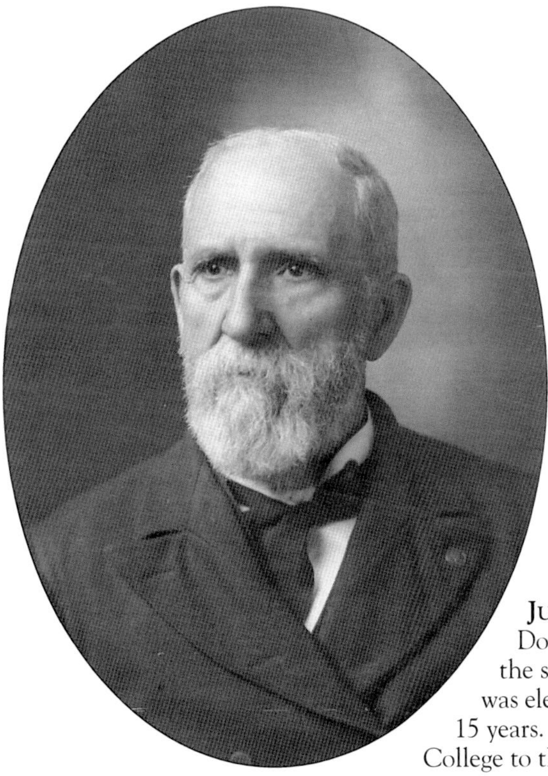

Judge Doan. After the Civil War, A. W. Doan served as a state senator and delegate to the state constitutional convention. In 1875, he was elected judge of the local court and served for 15 years. He also negotiated the sale of Wilmington College to the Friends.

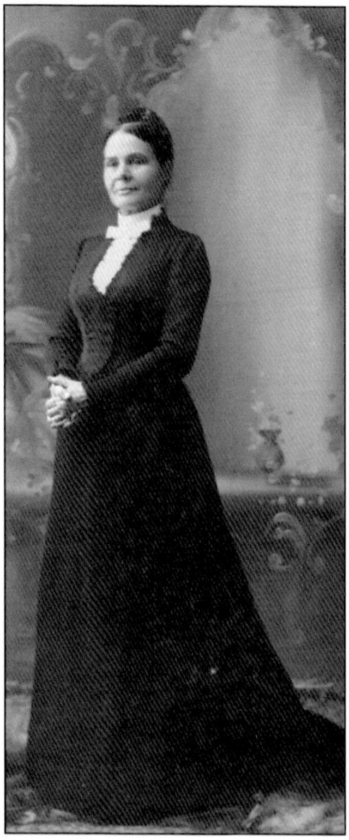

Esther Frame, 1840–1920. Born to a Methodist father and a Quaker mother, Frame is said to have turned to her Quaker heritage because Methodists did not offer women the opportunity for ministry. She and her husband, Nathan, traveled extensively to speak to Quaker groups throughout the country. She is credited with helping start both Wilmington Monthly and Yearly Meetings.

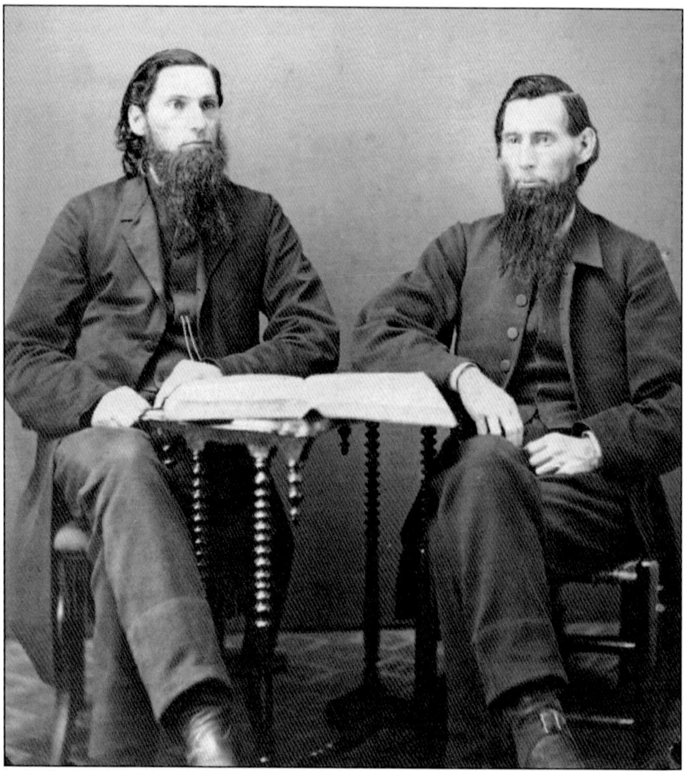

Douglas Brothers. John Henry (left) and Robert Douglas were well-known Quaker ministers and evangelists who helped form Wilmington Monthly Meeting. John Henry was instrumental in the purchase of Wilmington College, where he served as president of the board of trustees for 12 years.

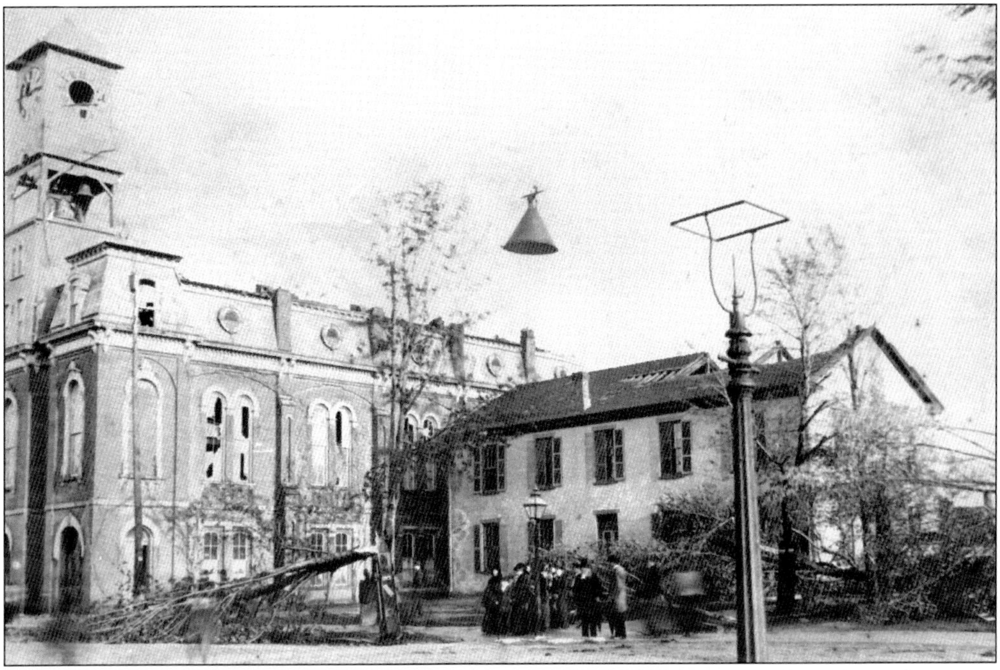

Tornado of 1893. A tornado struck Wilmington and caused destruction throughout the town. Pictured above are the damaged city hall and the former Wilmington Seminary (Academy), which served as a boardinghouse at the time. In 1896, the current Friends Meeting was constructed on this site at a cost of $25,000, making it one of the most expensive Quaker buildings at the time.

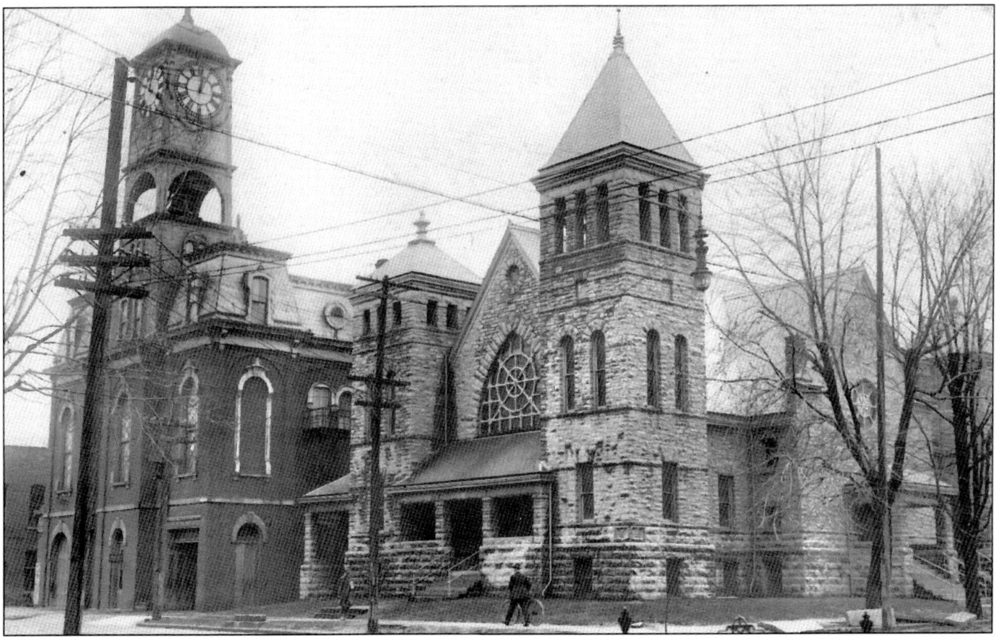

Wilmington Friends Meeting and City Hall, 1890s. While the presence of the Friends began in 1825 as an "indulged" meeting, Wilmington Monthly Meeting did not start until 1868 after a local Hicksite Friends Meeting had dissolved. The Friends first met in a former schoolhouse and later constructed this building.

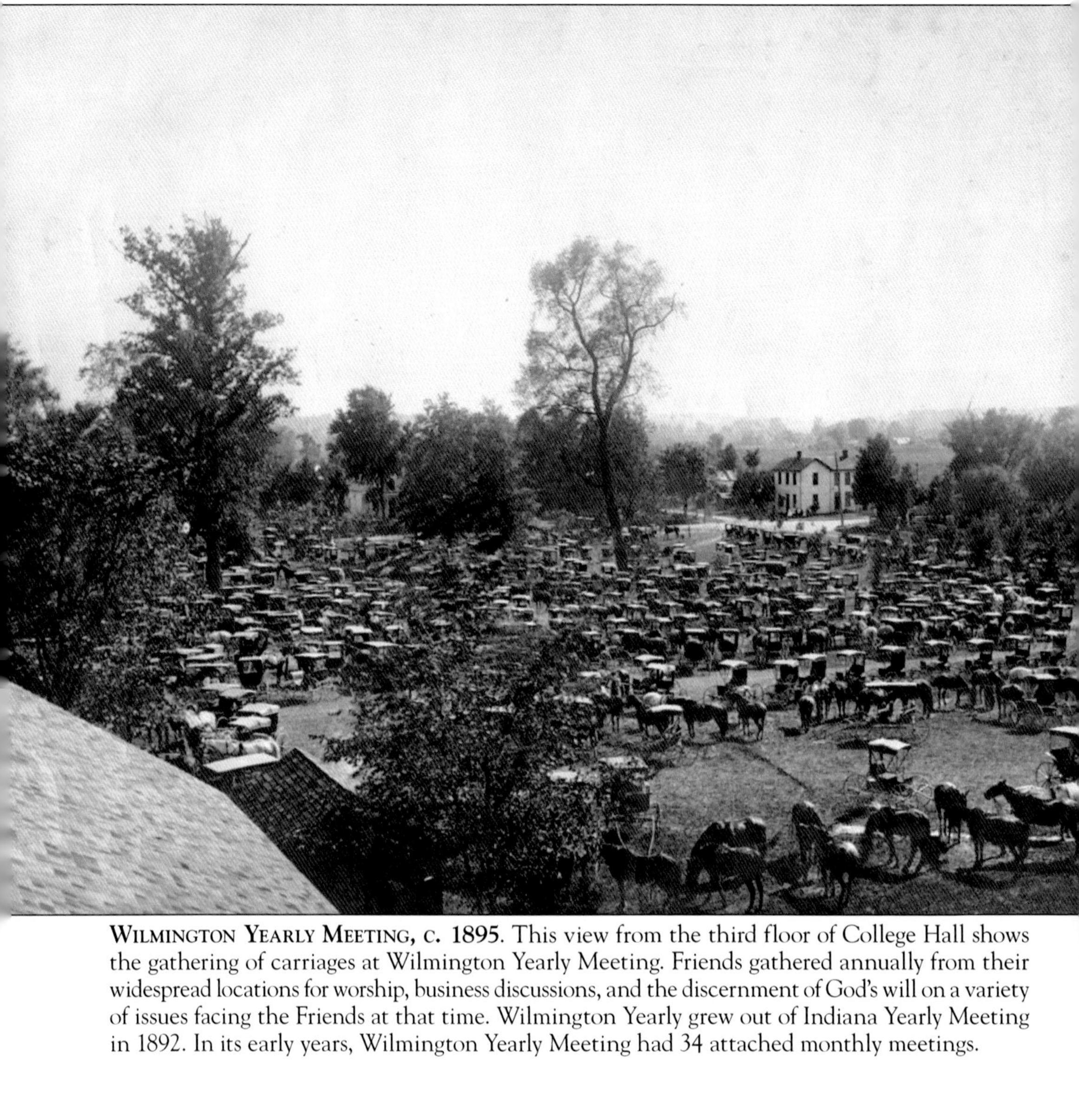

WILMINGTON YEARLY MEETING, c. 1895. This view from the third floor of College Hall shows the gathering of carriages at Wilmington Yearly Meeting. Friends gathered annually from their widespread locations for worship, business discussions, and the discernment of God's will on a variety of issues facing the Friends at that time. Wilmington Yearly grew out of Indiana Yearly Meeting in 1892. In its early years, Wilmington Yearly Meeting had 34 attached monthly meetings.

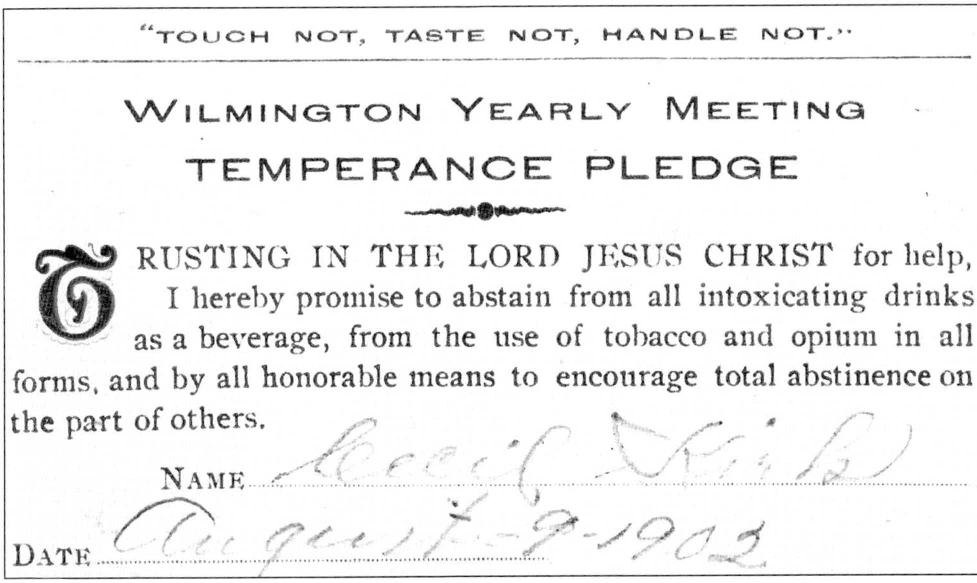

"TOUCH NOT, TASTE NOT, HANDLE NOT."

WILMINGTON YEARLY MEETING

TEMPERANCE PLEDGE

TRUSTING IN THE LORD JESUS CHRIST for help, I hereby promise to abstain from all intoxicating drinks as a beverage, from the use of tobacco and opium in all forms, and by all honorable means to encourage total abstinence on the part of others.

NAME Cecil Kirk

DATE August-9-1902

TEMPERANCE PLEDGE. Cecil Kirk signed this promise to refrain from all intoxicating drinks, tobacco, and opium, as well as to encourage abstinence on the part of others. Temperance pledges were popular among many religious groups.

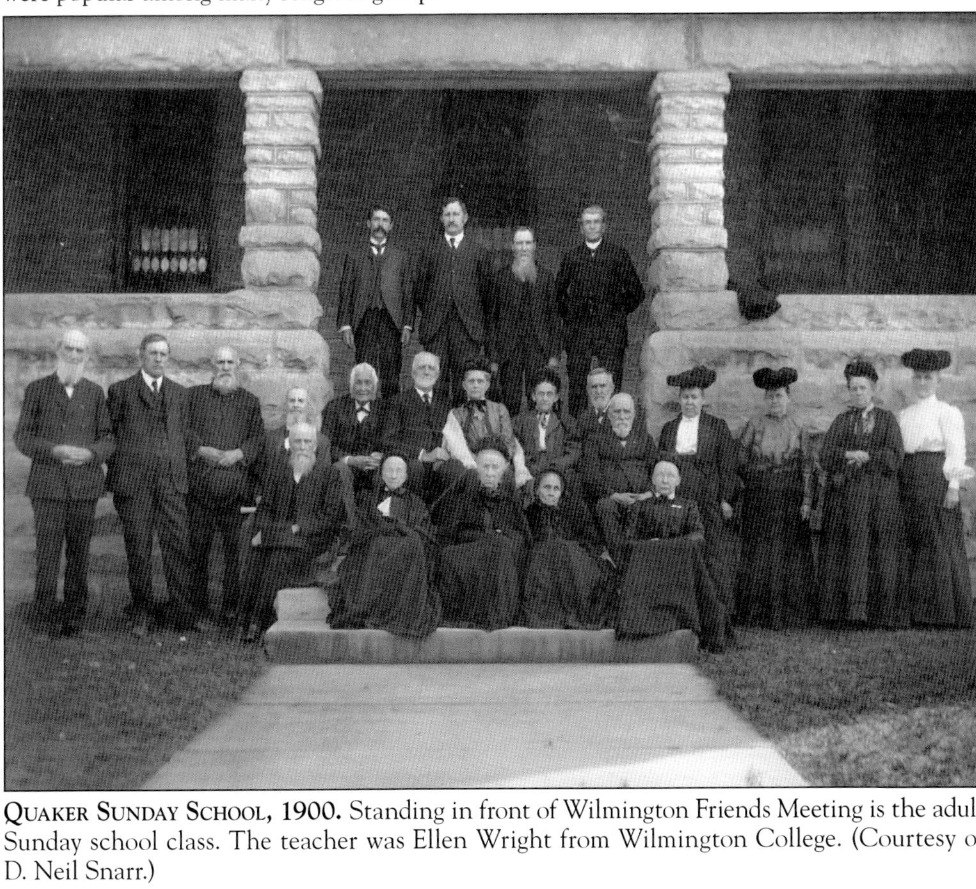

QUAKER SUNDAY SCHOOL, 1900. Standing in front of Wilmington Friends Meeting is the adult Sunday school class. The teacher was Ellen Wright from Wilmington College. (Courtesy of D. Neil Snarr.)

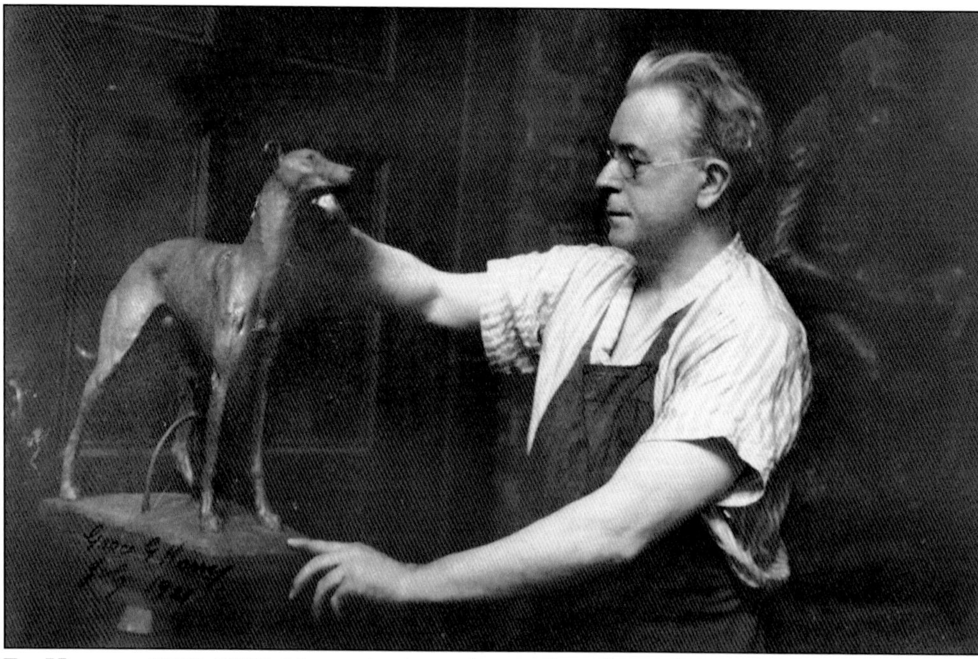

Eli Harvey, 1860–1957. Harvey is pictured at work sculpting his greyhound, Adonis, in his studio. Born near the Springfield Meetinghouse in 1860, Harvey trained in Paris and was a good friend of Norman Rockwell. Harvey was considered one of the best American sculptors of his time. He died in 1957, and his ashes were buried at the Springfield Meetinghouse.

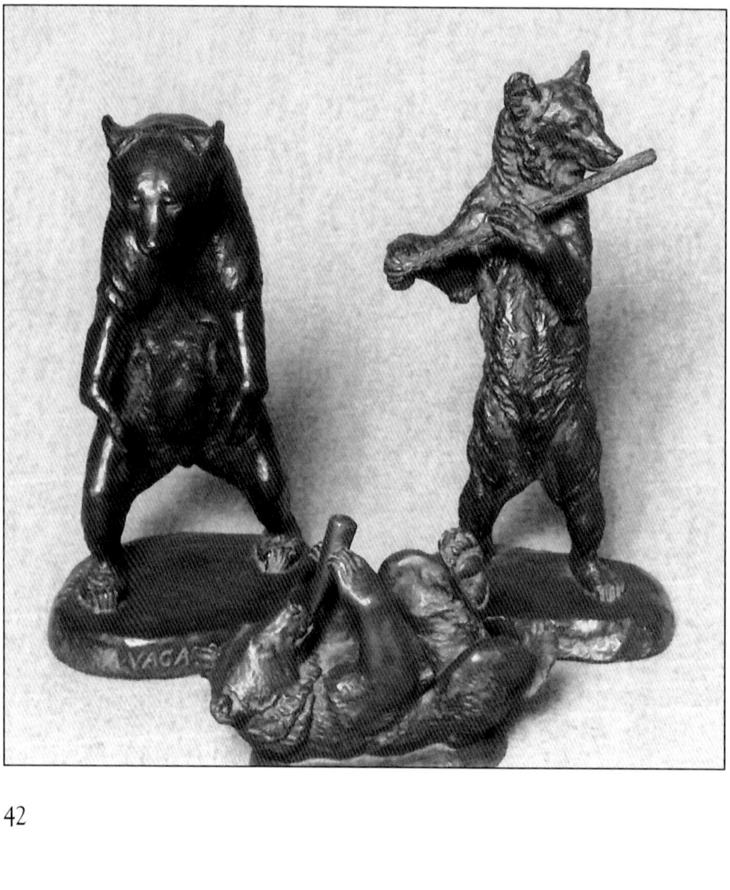

Vagabond Bear, Bear with Fife, and Bear with Bottle. Harvey was known for his animal sculptures, including Brown University's mascot, "Brown Bear," the J.C. Penney bull, and exhibits for the Bronx Zoo's Lion House. The Clinton County Historical Society showcases a collection of his works.

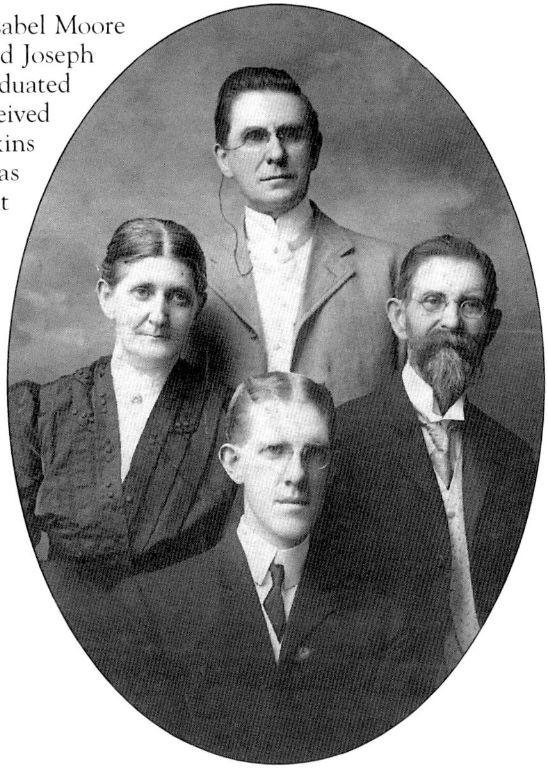

Moore Family. Pictured clockwise are Isabel Moore Hadley, Linley Moore, Oliver Moore, and Joseph Haines Moore. Joseph Haines Moore graduated from Wilmington College in 1897 and received his doctorate of philosophy from Johns Hopkins University in 1906 in astronomy. He was director of the Lick Observatory and taught at Berkeley College until his retirement in 1948. A lunar crater, the Moore, is named after him.

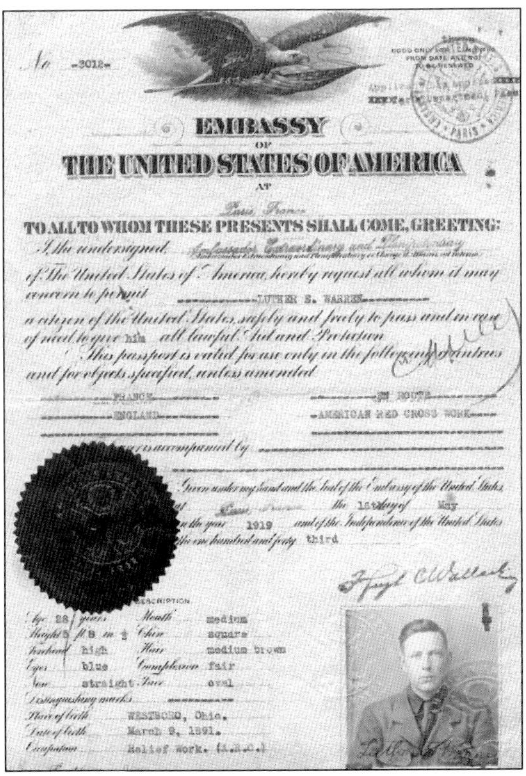

No -3012-

EMBASSY
OF
THE UNITED STATES OF AMERICA
AT
Paris, France

TO ALL TO WHOM THESE PRESENTS SHALL COME, GREETING:

I, the undersigned, ... of The United States of America, hereby request all whom it may concern to permit ——LUTHER S. WARREN—— a citizen of the United States, safely and freely to pass and in case of need to give him all lawful Aid and Protection.

This passport is valid for use only in the following countries and for objects specified, unless amended

FRANCE — EN ROUTE
ENGLAND — AMERICAN RED CROSS WORK

... is accompanied by

Given under my hand and the Seal of the Embassy of the United States at Paris, France the 1st day of May in the year 1919 and of the Independence of the United States the one hundred and forty third

DESCRIPTION

Age 28 years
Height 5 ft. 8 in. ½
Forehead high
Eyes blue
Nose straight
Mouth medium
Chin square
Hair medium brown
Complexion fair
Face oval
Distinguishing marks ———
Place of birth WESTBORO, Ohio.
Date of birth March 9, 1891.
Occupation Relief Work. (A.R.C.)

Luther Warren Passport. In 1917, Warren enrolled in a new program allowing conscientious objectors to serve with the Red Cross overseas in lieu of military service. Warren was a longtime peace activist in Wilmington, and the Luther Warren Peace Path has been named after him. Warren died in 1997 at the age of 106. (Courtesy of Wilmington College.)

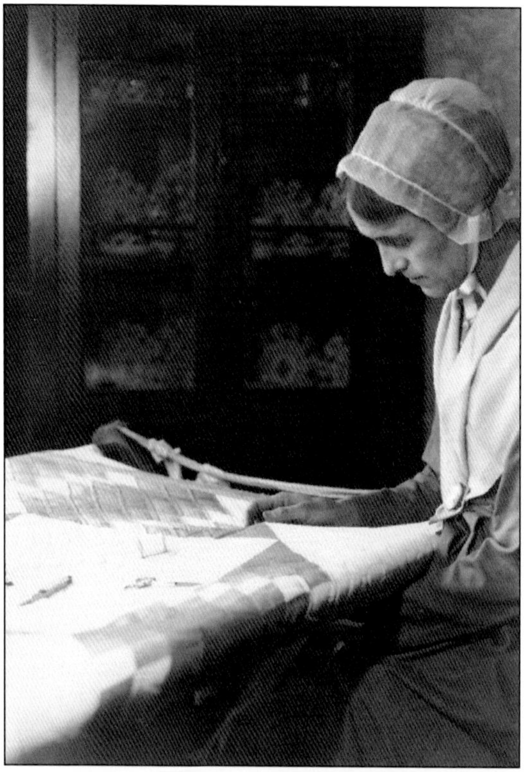

Hayes Quilt Portrait. Ethel Hale Hayes quilted while wearing a dress and bonnet belonging to her Hale grandmother. This photograph was taken in 1931 by Dr. Kelley Hale, who painted the same pose in life size in 1932. It hangs in the Wilmington College library. Quakers were known for their simplicity and chose to dress as plainly as possible for their meetings and to be a witness to the world.

Jacob and Esther Hale Home, 1917. Pictured below are, from left to right, (first row, on steps) Jacob Hale and Corwin Hale; (second row) Erskine Hayes, Ethel Hale Hayes, Fanny Babb Hale, Meredith Hayes, Edwin Hale, Fred Hale, and Orville Hale; (third row) Alta McFarland, Esther Hale, Ann Harlan, Sallie Hale, John Hale, William Harland, Ed McFarland, and Wilbur West; (fourth row) Mary Harris and Bess Hale West.

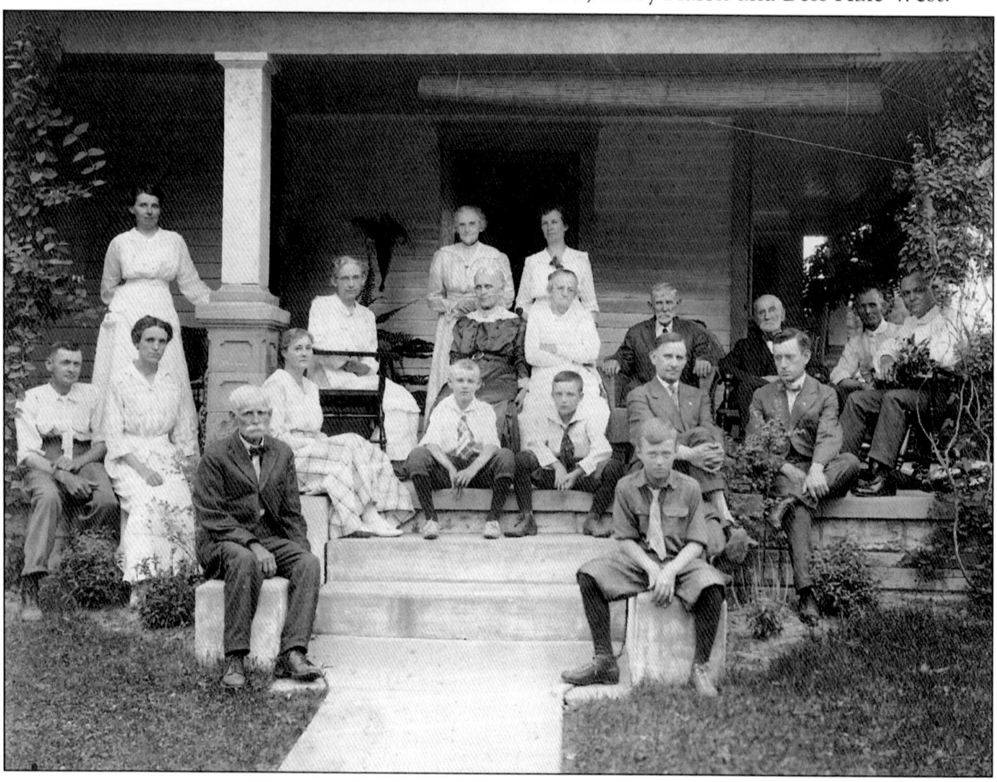

Four

Agriculture

The grain elevators, feed mills, farm-implement stores, and hardware stores that still populate Wilmington today reveal a strong agricultural presence that dates back to the area's beginnings.

Early Wilmington farms were often no more than a couple hundred acres, and they were self-sustaining operations where vegetables, livestock, and livestock feed were raised. Extra meat, grain, vegetables, or eggs were sold for profit.

In 1835, the Baltimore and Ohio Railroad was built to Charleston, West Virginia, at the same time a livestock auction house opened in Chillicothe. Both eliminated the long livestock drives to the East Coast, and the railroad also improved the market level of livestock. One of Wilmington's first livestock auctions was held in Morris Alley behind the Wilmington United Methodist Church parking lot on West Main Street.

Wool production was a booming business at Clinton County farms until about 1840, when the cotton baler was invented, making it faster and easier to ship cotton to northern mills from the South, which reduced the need for wool until the Civil War.

During the Civil War, the Spanish-American War, and World War I, the demand for horses increased, creating a strong equine market in Wilmington.

Longtime Wilmington teacher Virgene Webb Peterson, born in 1924 on a farm in Adams Township in Wilmington, watched firsthand how small, family farms evolved into large, mechanized agricultural operations. In 1900, the average U.S. farm size was 146 acres; in 2002, it was 441 acres. Peterson's parents, Ralph and Mary Webb, raised corn, wheat, beef cattle, and hogs, and she remembers when all the farm equipment was powered by horses.

Farming families often lived near each other, dividing plots among family members. Although their homes remained isolated as the population within Wilmington city limits increased, they networked with each other through schools, churches, or one of many farming organizations such as Farm Bureau or the National Grange of the Order of Patrons of Husbandry, known simply as the Grange.

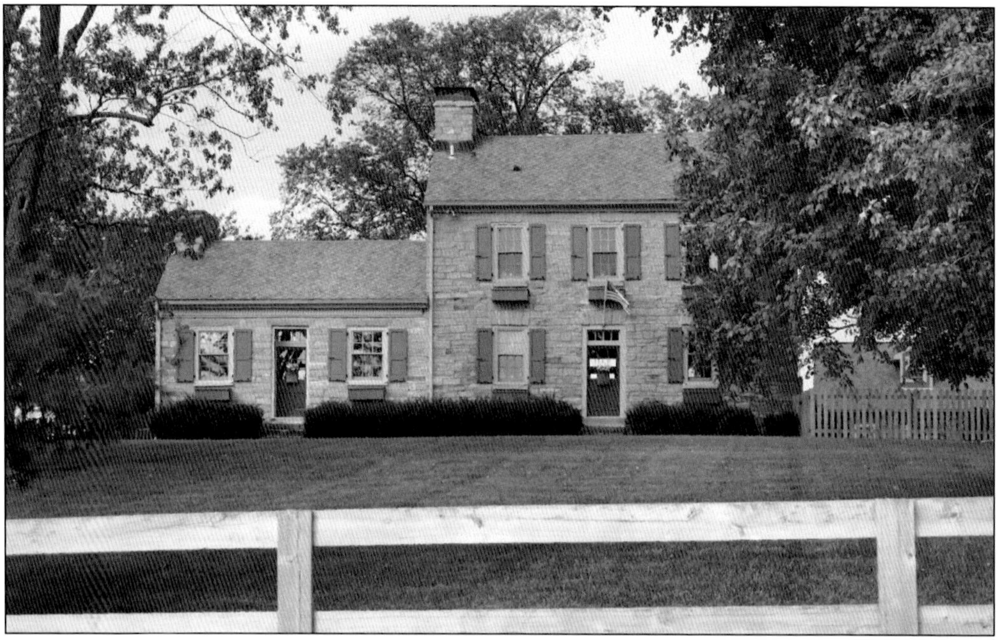

Center Road Farm. David Miars built this Federal-style stone house in 1811, making it one of the oldest homes in the area. When it was constructed, builders used a track-and-scaffolding system to haul the stone up to the second story by way of a wooden wheelbarrow. The 2-feet-deep stone walls and window casements are original.

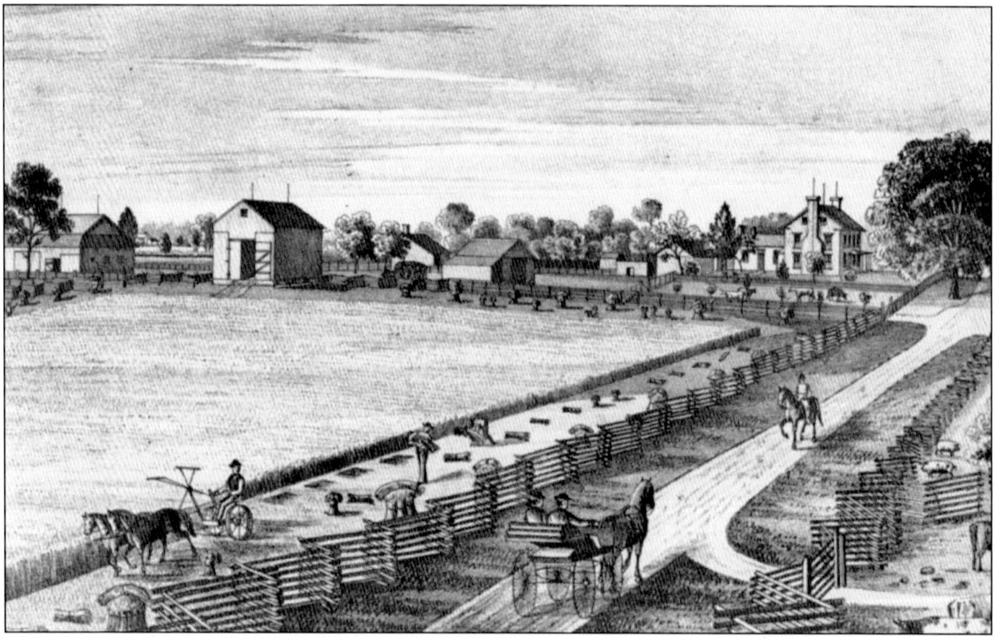

Starbuck Farm. This residence of Jesse Starbuck in Wilmington is depicted in the 1876 *Illustrated Historical Atlas of Clinton County*. Sawmills arrived around 1820, changing the zigzag of rail fencing into sawmill-cut fences built in a straight line, which freed at least 8 feet around fields for additional crop production. One of the first sawmills was located on Silver Creek and Cowan's Creek just off Cuba Road.

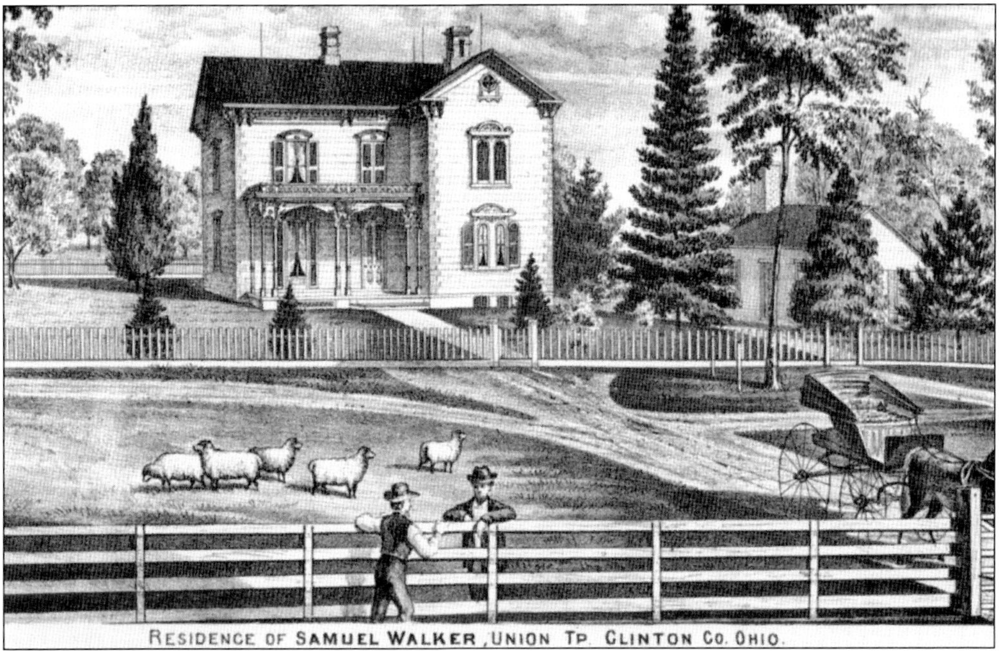

SAMUEL WALKER FARM. The residence of Samuel Walker in Wilmington is portrayed in the 1876 *Illustrated Historical Atlas of Clinton County*. A lover of reading, Walker donated money to the city to house a library, but before it could be built, funds were donated from steel magnate Andrew Carnegie. The town used Walker's money to construct the downtown Samuel Walker Building. Rice Furniture was the primary tenant for most of the building's existence.

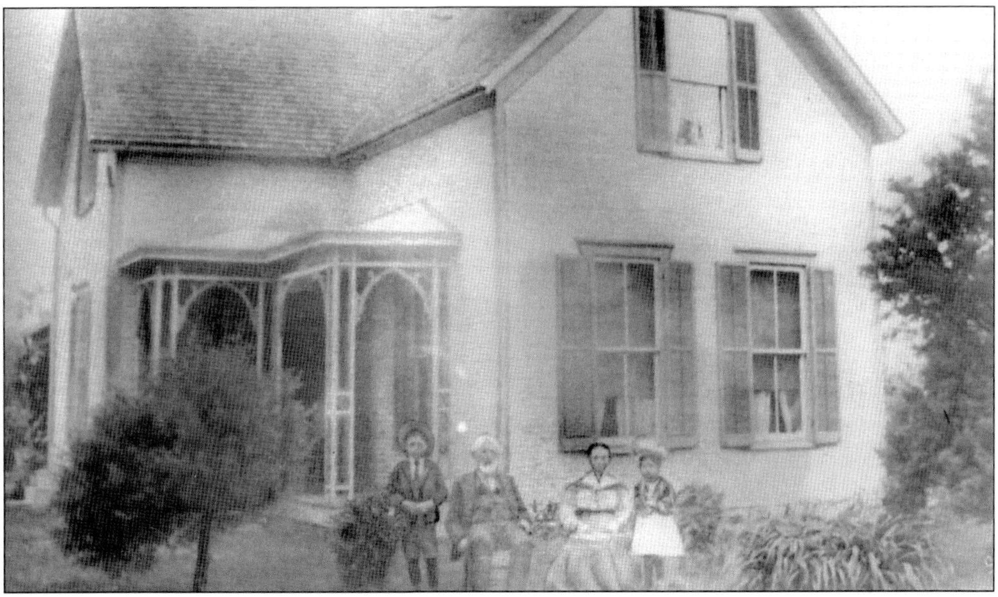

ATLEY FARM, C. 1886. In 1884, John and Eveline Atley, who had six children, purchased a 124-acre farm on Starbuck Road and built this house in 1885. Pictured from left to right are their son Christopher (who later was a reporter for the *Democrat* newspaper); John's parents, Henry and Sara; and their daughter, Nella. The farm remains in the family 126 years later; Bessie Atley and her late husband, James, moved there in 1943. (Courtesy of Dennis and Barb Atley.)

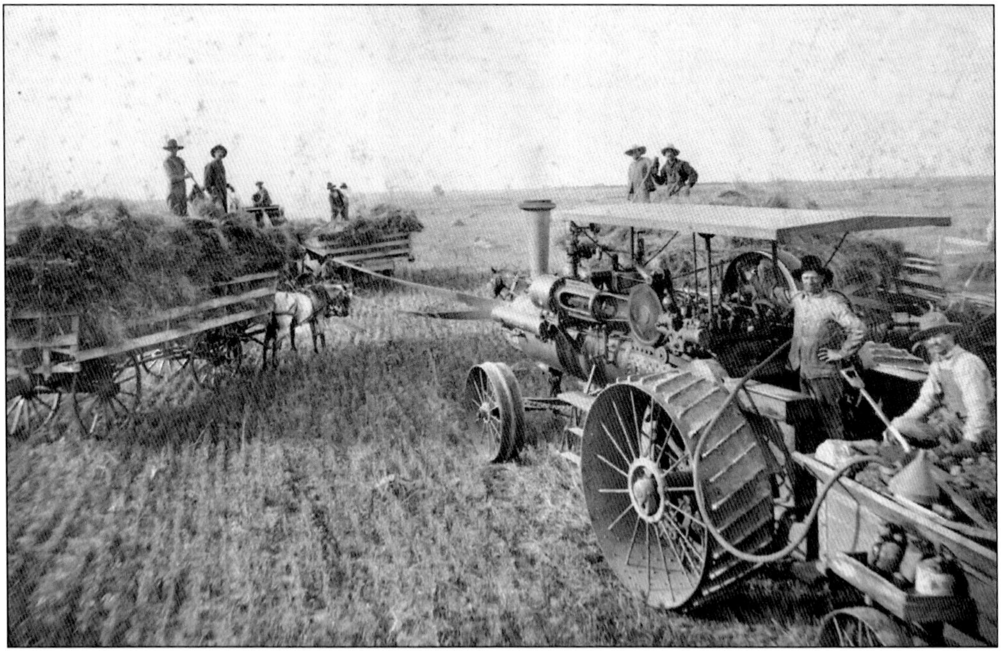

In the Fields. Early tractors, such as the steam-powered Case tractor on the right, had wide rear metal tires to disperse their weight. The ridges in the front wheels helped steer in dirt. The first steam-powered threshing machine was noted in Clinton County in 1867. At the same time, one of the world's largest distilleries, Workum and Friedberg, was located in Lynchburg and purchased large amounts of local grain.

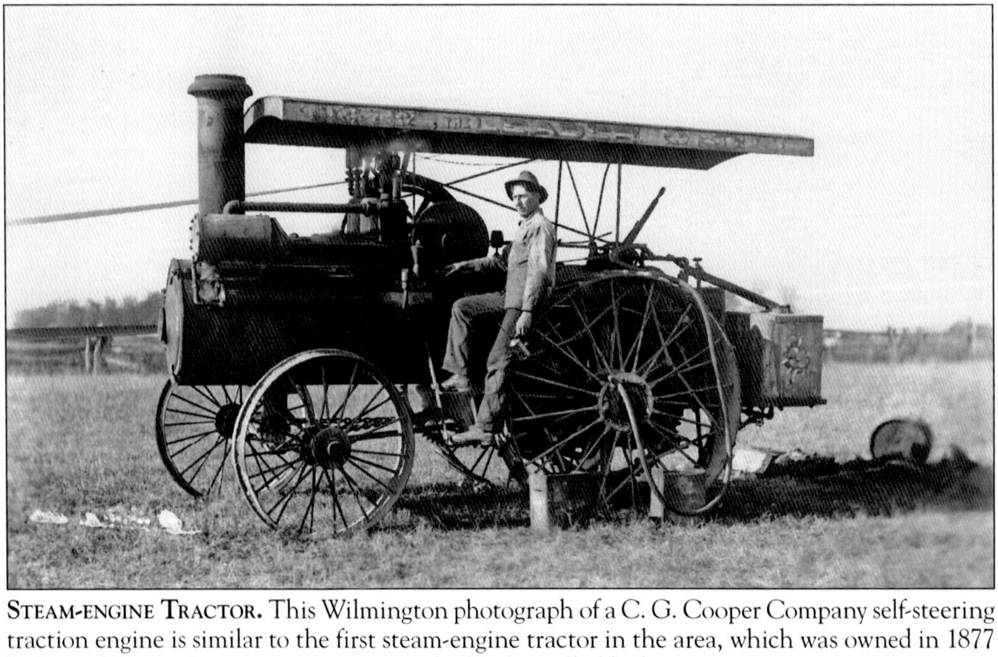

Steam-engine Tractor. This Wilmington photograph of a C. G. Cooper Company self-steering traction engine is similar to the first steam-engine tractor in the area, which was owned in 1877 by Daniel Kester. Previous steam engines had to be pulled by horses.

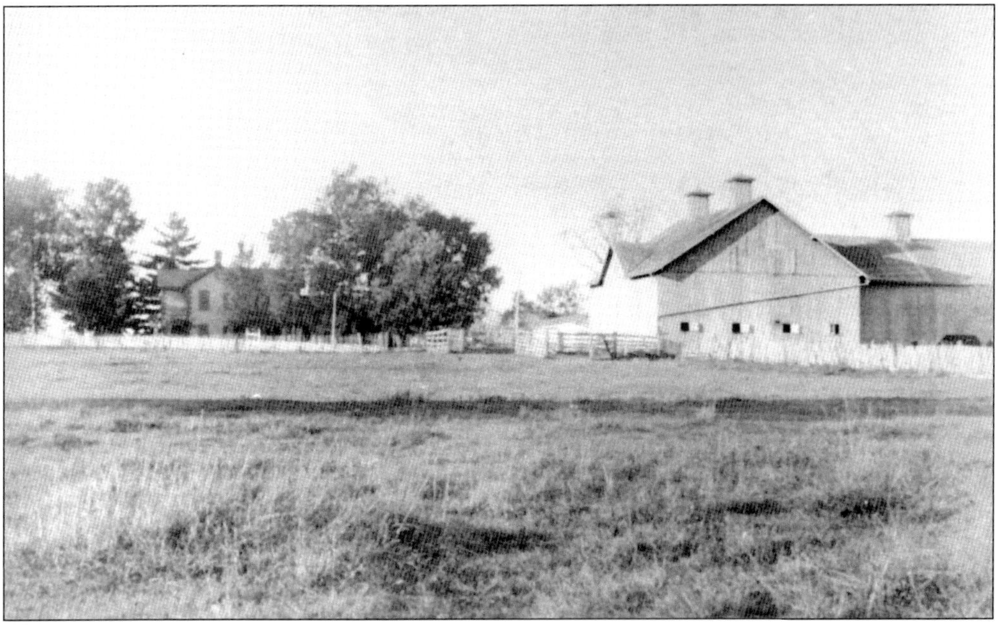

SMITH HOMESTEAD. The Sycamores Farm on Smith Road was the 1800s homestead of John Quincy Smith and later his son H. W. Smith. The second floor was lost to fire, and now the home has just one story. Richard and Pam Thompson have owned the farm since 1964. The barn was removed in 1979. Richard Thompson's mother was Ellen Smith Thompson, granddaughter of H. W. Smith. (Courtesy of Richard and Pam Thompson.)

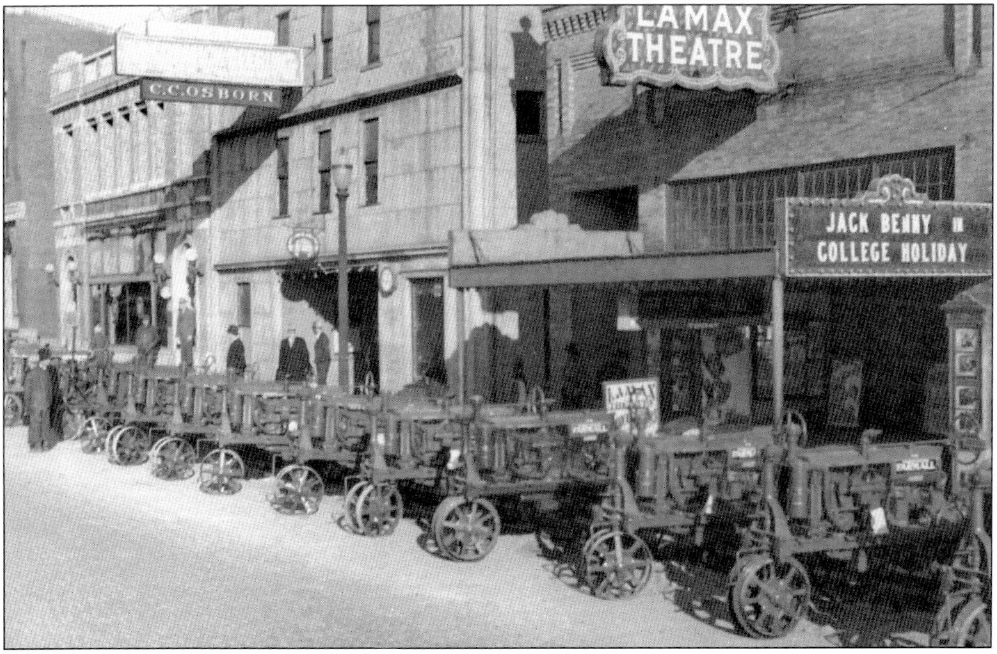

FARM STORE. The C. C. Osborn Farm Equipment store, shown here around 1936, was located at 53 East Main Street. The F-20 Farmalls were introduced by International Harvester. Other local farm equipment companies were Gumley Implement, Haines and Hill, Atley Tractor, Farm Bureau, and Schantz.

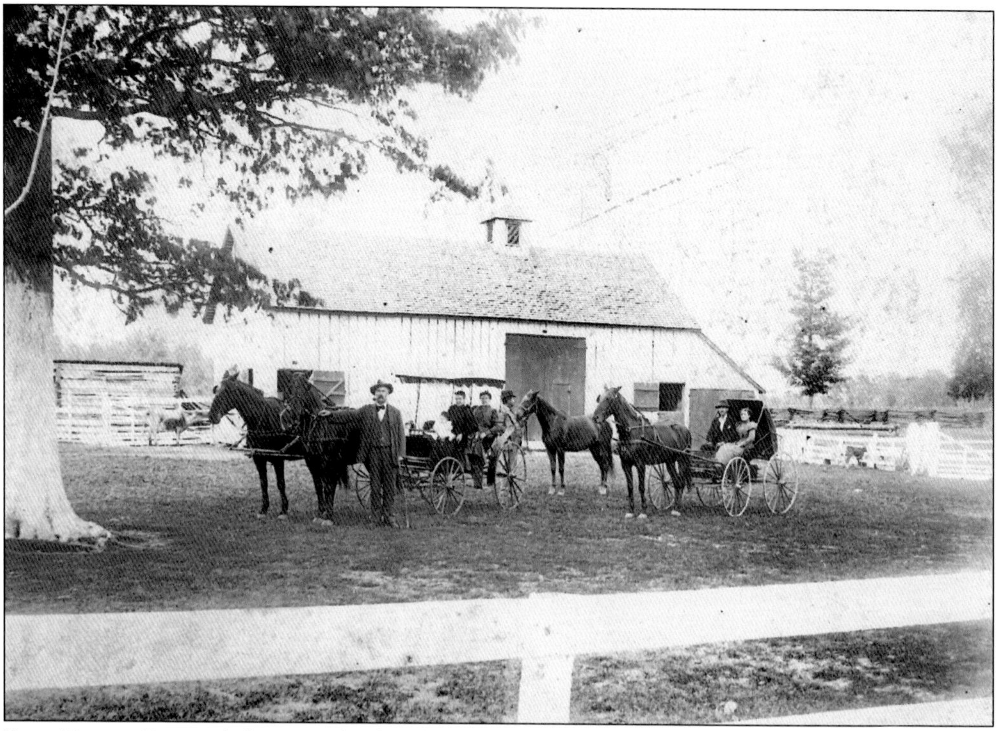

Ellis Farms. Pictured above on the family's Bailey Road farm around 1890 is Joshua Ellis, at left. At age 14, Joshua Ellis joined the 31st Regiment of the Ohio Volunteer Infantry (OVI), but the army released him to his parents when they discovered what he had done. At 16, he rejoined the OVI as a drummer in the 6th Regiment and was injured at Gettysburg. He returned to Wilmington and had one son, Harley Ellis, in 1871. Harley Ellis purchased the farm on State Route 134 (shown below) at an auction around 1929. Harley Ellis had one son, Orville, and one grandson, Dick, who had three sons: Richard "Dale," Dana, and David. David Ellis currently lives on the farm. (Both, courtesy of Dr. David Ellis.)

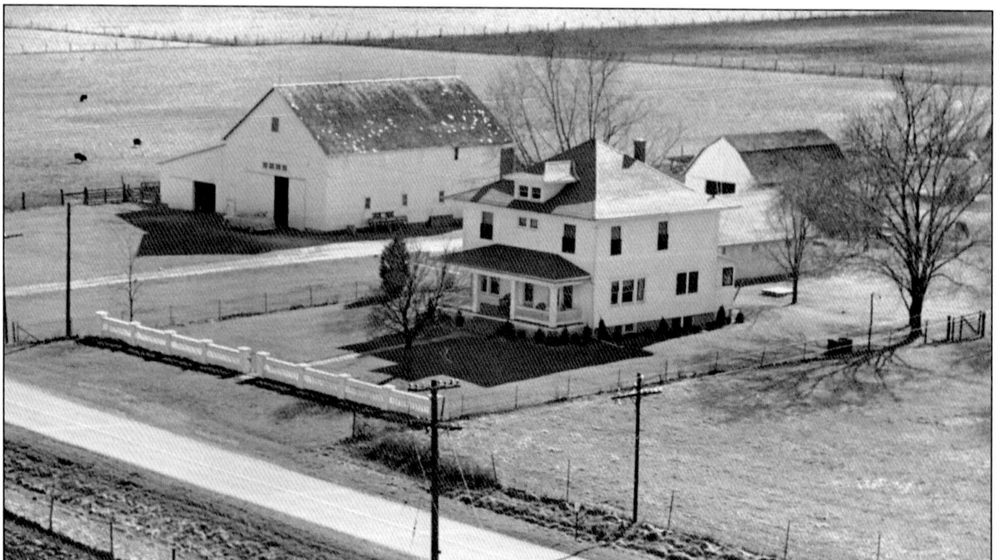

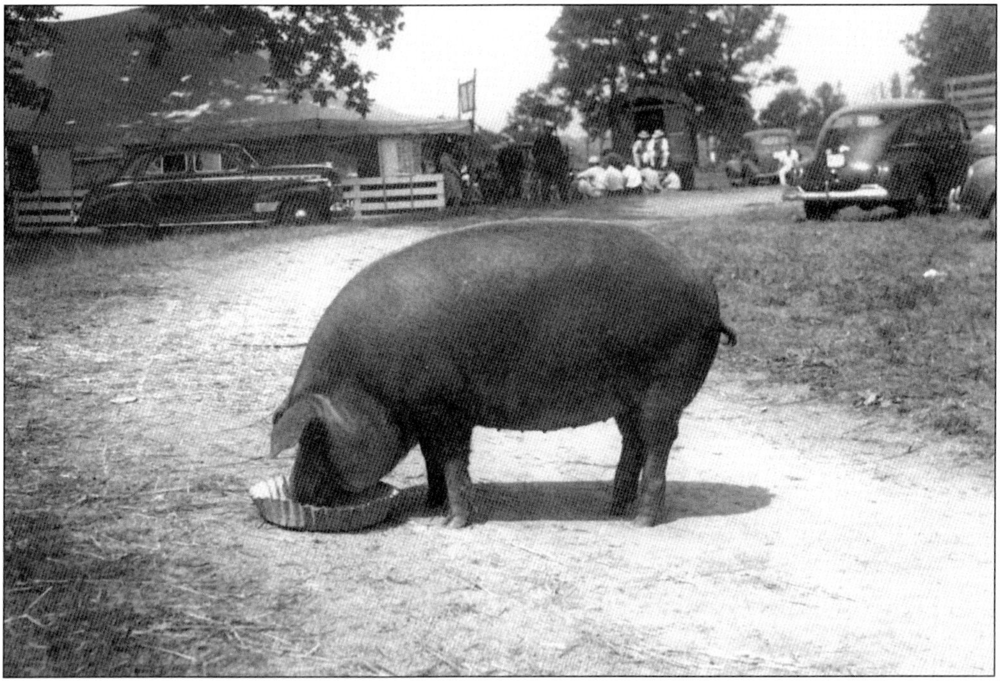

CHAMPION HOG. Howard Hackney owned the champion Duroc sow (pictured above) shown at the 1942 Clinton County Fair. Hog production has always been a major business in Clinton County. In 1940 and 1966, the county was the hog-raising capital of the State of Ohio. In 1964, around 57 percent of the personal income in the county was related to hog production.

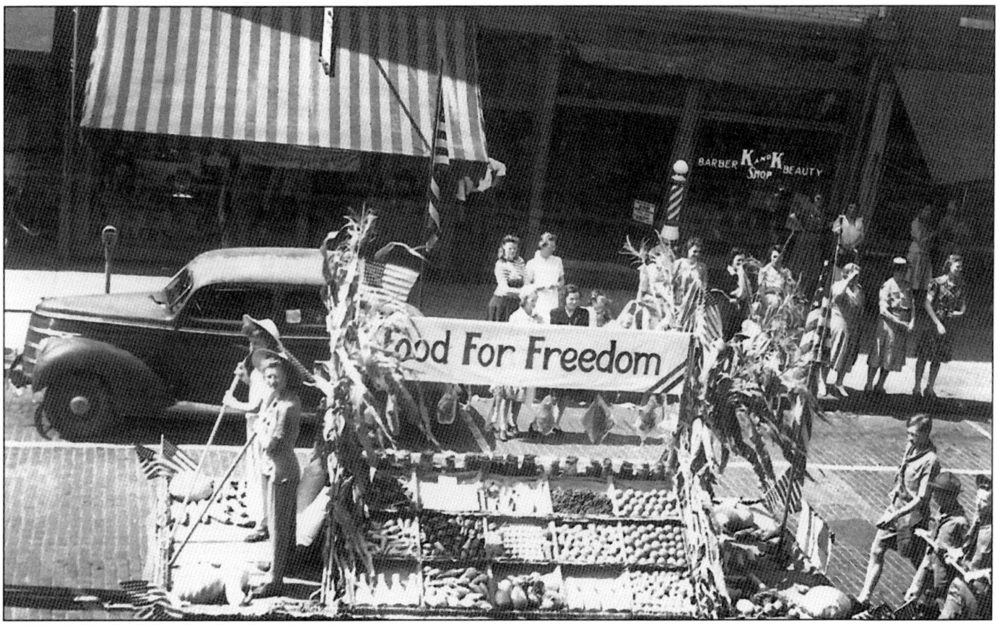

FOOD FOR FREEDOM. After the United States entered World War II, the U.S. Department of Agriculture asked farmers to increase food production, what the secretary of agriculture called "munitions of war." A Food for Freedom patriotic rally was held in Wilmington on September 14, 1942.

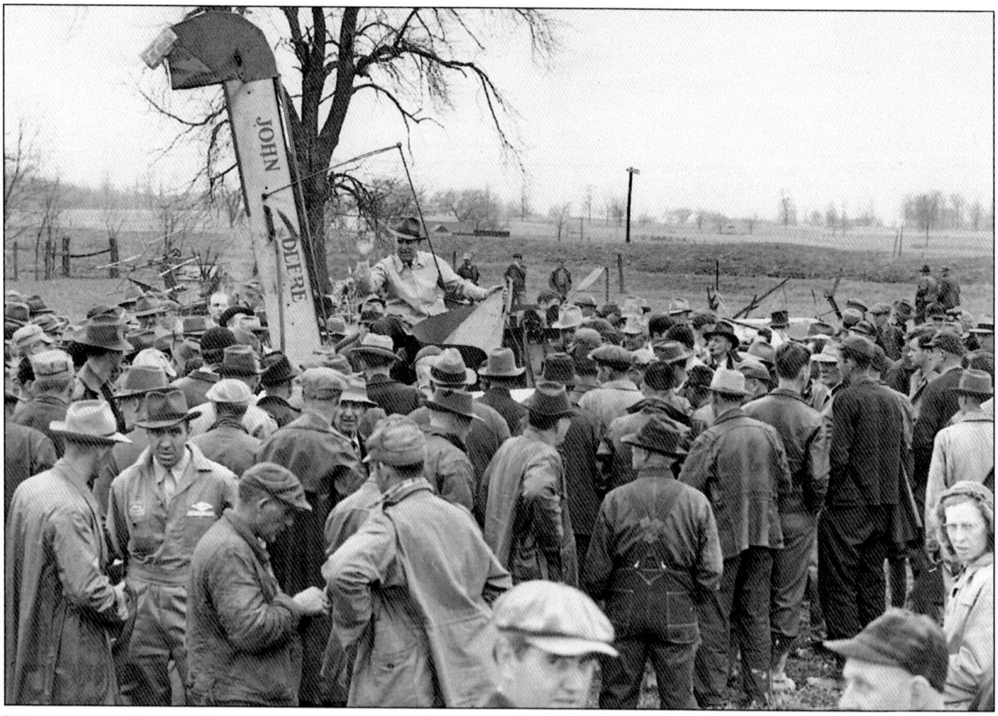

MACHINERY SALE. The sixth annual used farm machinery sale at Producers Livestock Cooperative Association, about 1 mile east of Wilmington on 3C Highway, was held on April 6, 1948. The machinery at left is a corn picker.

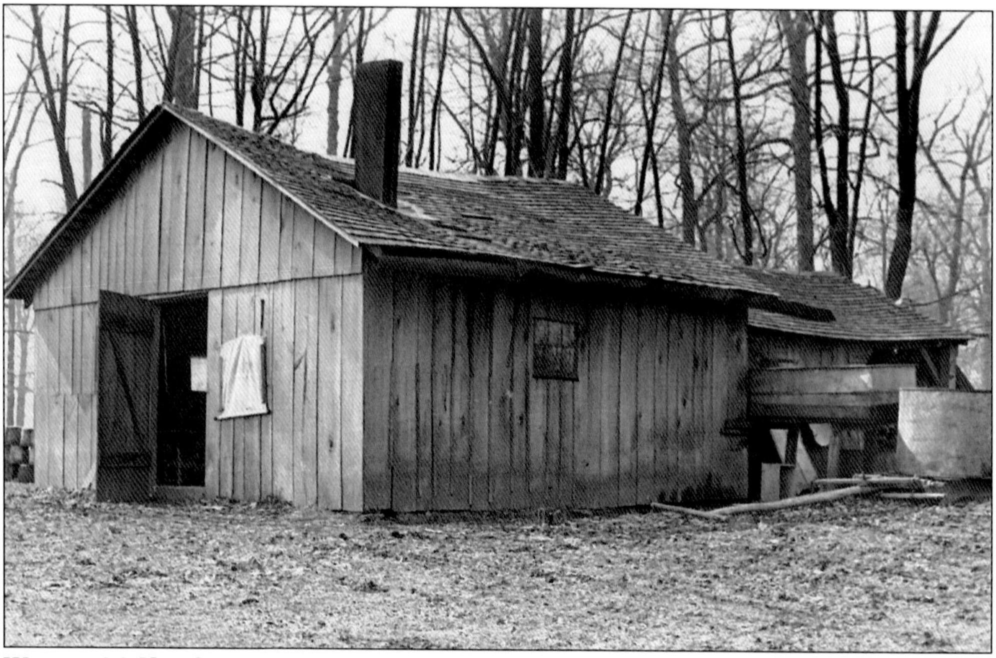

WILLIAM MCKAY SUGAR CAMP. From the early beginnings of the county, sugar was necessary because it was the only form of sweetener available. Sugar-making increased income for farmers. In the 1960s, sugar camps and fruit farms made up 5 percent of the county income.

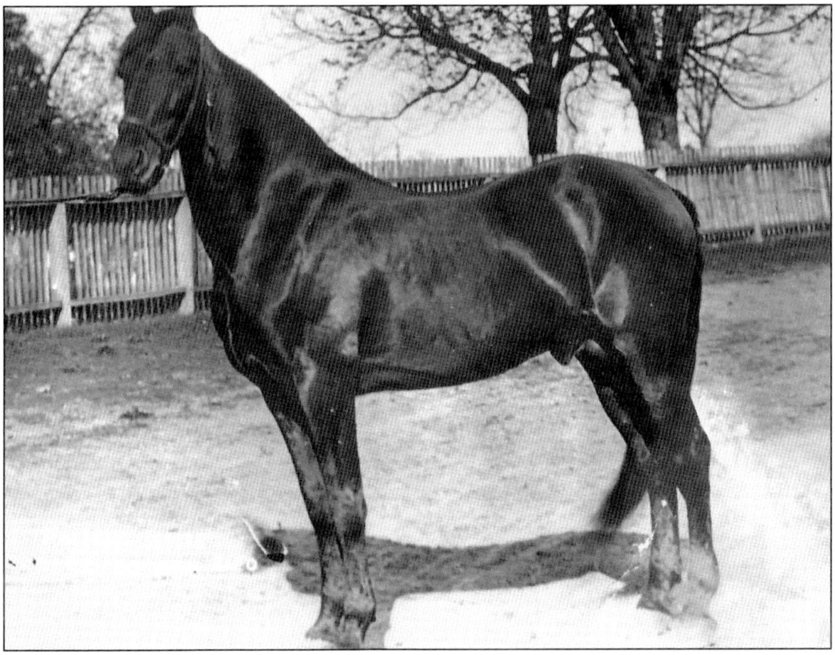

HORSE RACING. Police 16132, the fastest trotting stallion in Clinton County, set a record time and was a local 1909 sweepstakes winner. The horse also sired successive winners. In the 1950s and 1960s, racehorse farms were abundant in Wilmington, including Cloverdale, Green Acre, Fairmeade, and Reagan's. Wilmington native Colby Turner lost both forearms at age nine in a horse-drawn mower accident. He grew up to become a harness horse trainer and driver, and he is pictured below with Miss Jet Propulsion at the August 1946 Clinton County Fair. Turner used his teeth to wrap the reins around what remained of his arm, then hooked his whip between those lines. In the mid-1940s, Harness Racing Hall of Fame member McKinley Kirk and Turner earned a reputation for developing outstanding horses, including world champion Amortizor.

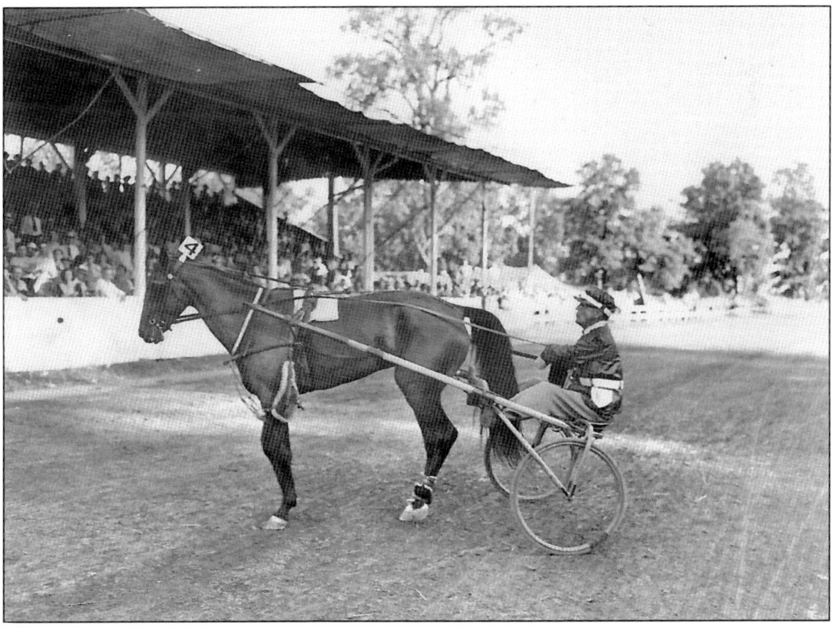

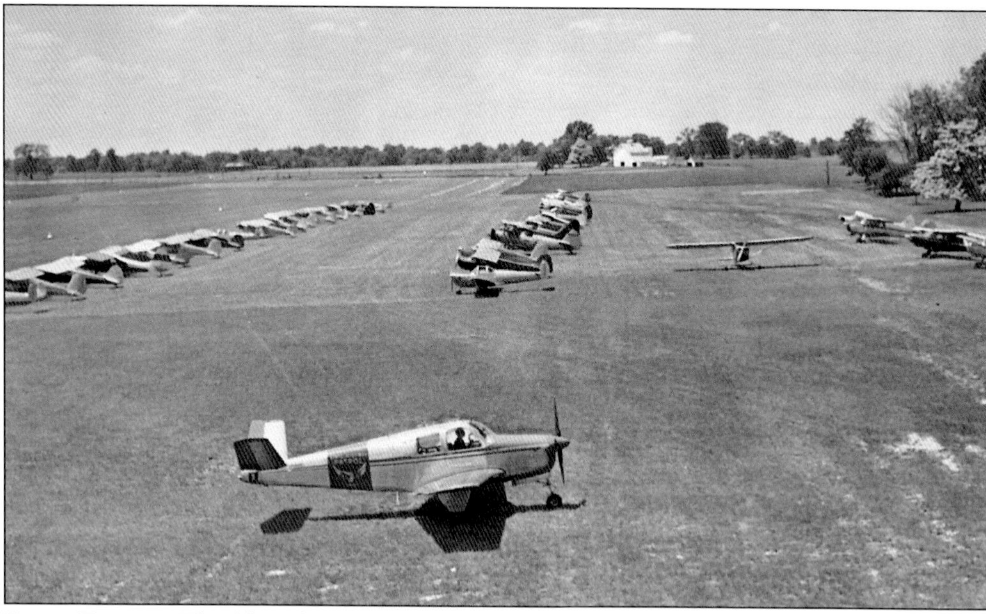

Flying Farmers. The Ohio Flying Farmers Association met in Wilmington on June 5, 1946. Flying Farmers is an international organization established in 1945. At the time, owning airplanes was not as complicated and expensive as it is today; farmers fixed their own tractors and airplanes. Among other uses, airplanes delivered groceries and livestock feed.

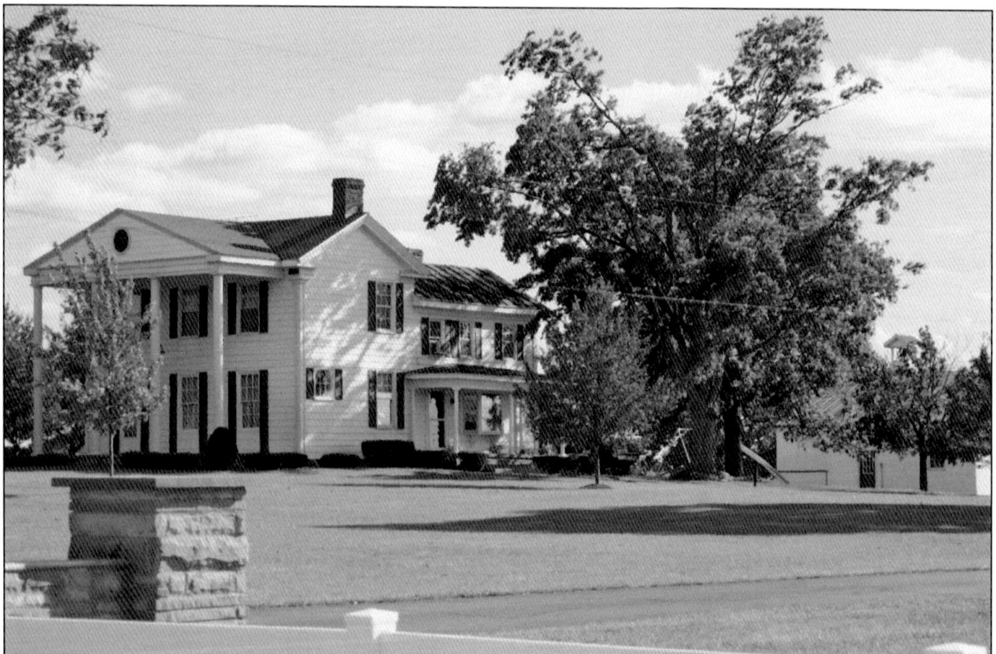

Former Dairy Farm. John Orebaugh of Champion Bridge owned this farm on Gurneyville Road but resided at a house he owned in town. Orebaugh's wife's family, the Owenses, had owned the dairy farm since the 1900s. The Orebaughs sold the farm to Marvin and Virgene Peterson in 1960 and donated the profits to Children's Hospital in Cincinnati. The farm remains in the Peterson family.

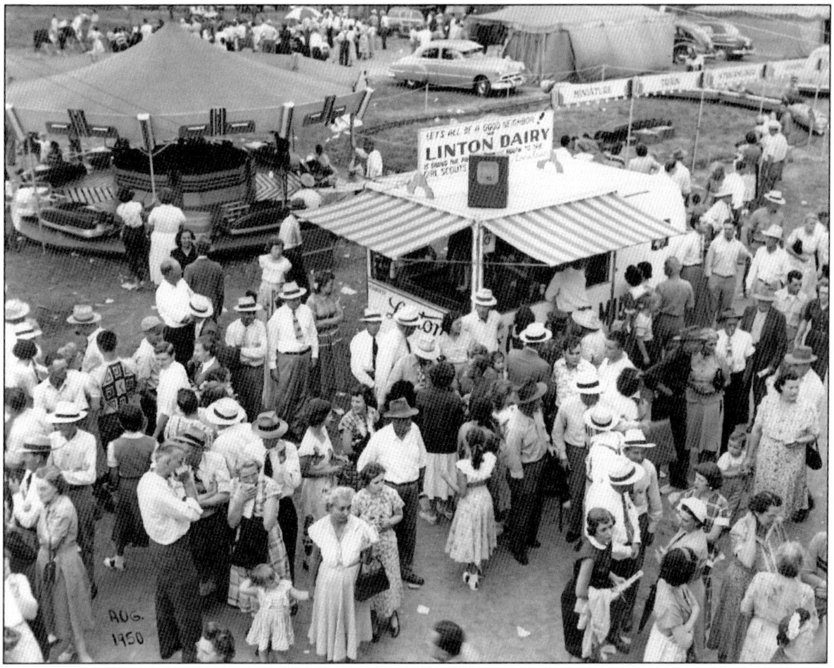

LINTON DAIRY. Wilmington's Linton Dairy operated a booth at the Clinton County Fair in August 1950, with profits going to county Girl Scouts and Boy Scouts. Buttermilk, homogenized vitamin D milk, chocolate milk, and Jersey milk were available at the popular booth. Linton Dairy was started in 1922 between the General Denver Hotel and the Wilmington Friends Meeting. There were approximately five other creameries in Wilmington. Area farmers sold milk to Linton Dairy, which produced and delivered dairy products. Pictured below at front left is where cottage cheese was made at Linton. Milk bottling happened at right, in front, and milk was homogenized in the back. Homogenization was widespread in the United States in the 1930s and nearly universal by the 1940s.

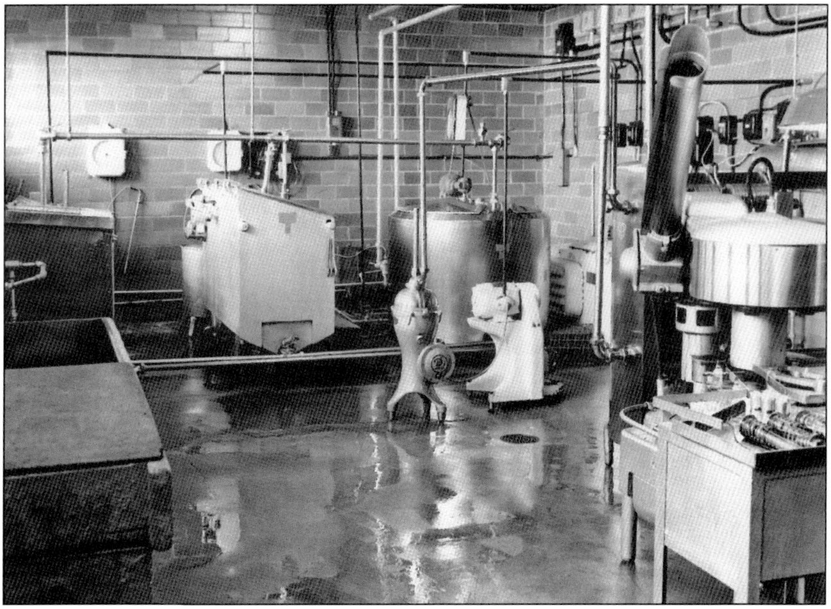

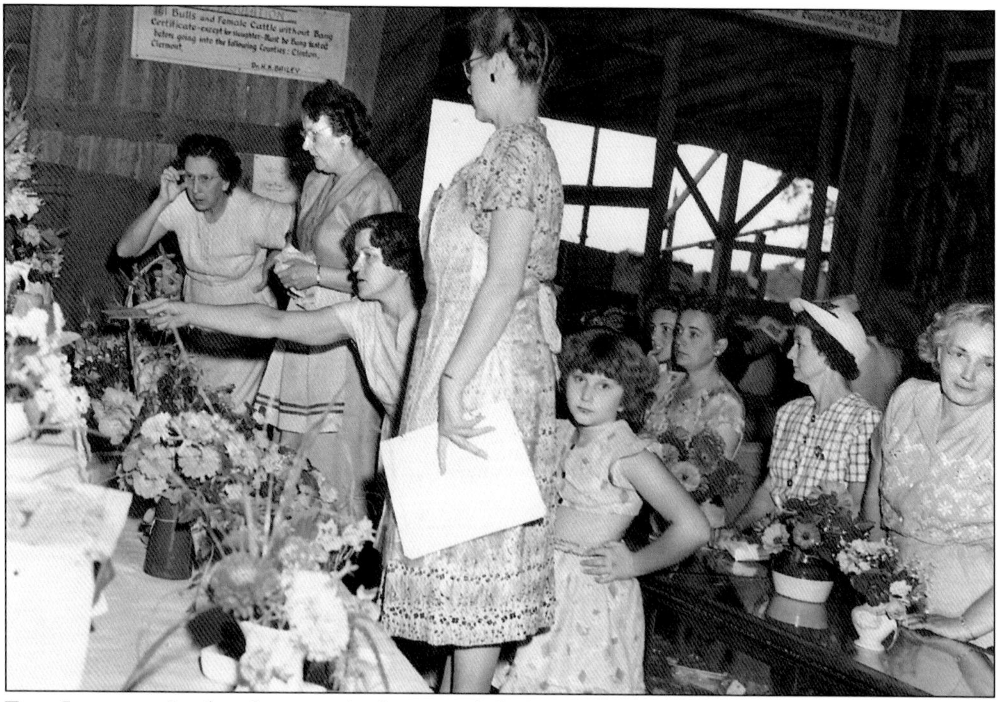

FAIR JUDGING. In the photograph above, at left, Mrs. Isaac McMillan, superintendent of the women's department at the Clinton County Fair, judges flowers on August 11, 1948, along with Mrs. C. L. Ford, Mrs. Eddie Ellis, and Mrs. E. J. McMillan. Since its inception, the fair has been located in at least five places, including on land where Peterson Place subdivision and Wilmington College are currently located. Juanita Bernard (pictured below) showed the champion ewe at the fair on August 7, 1946. The first "lamb pool" in the state of Ohio was started in 1933 at the Clinton County Fair; instead of selling individual lambs to buyers, a middleman bought groups of them for a set price, as with other commodities.

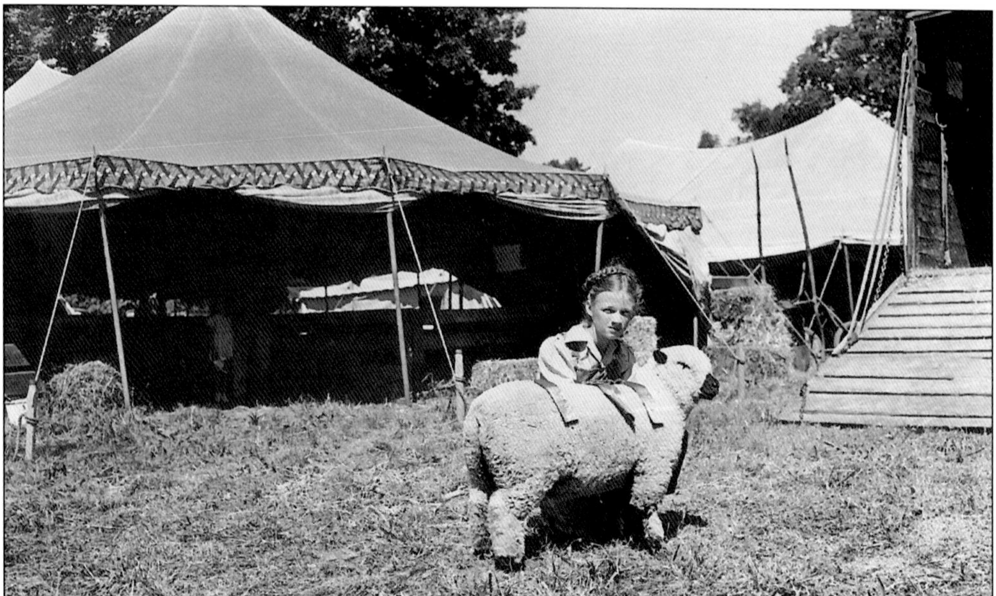

Five

Churches

Although Wilmington has its share of grand church architecture, from the Gothic-style towers and stained glass of St. Columbkille Catholic Church to the stone arches and red doors of the Wilmington United Methodist Church, most churches in town started with humble beginnings.

Many congregations began with a simple conversation among like-minded people, and informal worship was held wherever a place could be found: homes, log buildings, theaters, gymnasiums, and churches of other denominations.

Often, members secured financial pledges even before attempting to construct a permanent structure, and any mortgage was often paid off early, although various economic downturns made for tough times for churches as well.

Whereas the elaborate architecture of Wilmington's early public schools is now lost forever, many churches have meticulously maintained their original buildings, sometimes expanding or remodeling but generally keeping intact the integrity of the original design.

Some churches, such as All Saints Episcopal, have housed various denominations over the years, while others, such as the Church of the Nazarene, have reused building material to create new ones. The Nazarene congregation recycled 39,000 bricks from the demolished Universalist church in Cuba and, using the members' labor, built its first church on Walnut Street.

According to published histories of Clinton County, the Methodist Episcopal Church was the earliest religious organization located in downtown Wilmington, starting in 1813, with its first modest house of worship purchased in 1818. That building and its later incarnations no longer exist, but the group eventually joined with other Methodists, who meet today in a building whose cornerstone was laid in 1928.

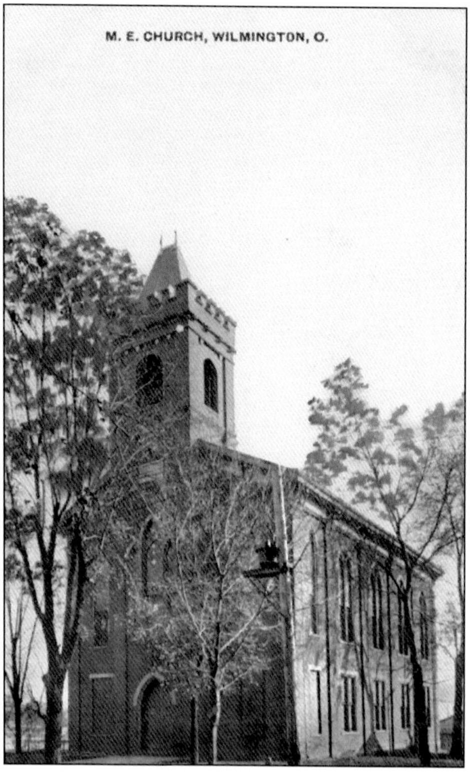

METHODIST EPISCOPAL CHURCH. This church was started in 1813, with minister William Austin. For years, the congregation worshiped in a house converted from a mill. In 1833, a church was built and served the congregation until 1865, when the bricks of the old building were used to construct a two-story church on the original gristmill site. The spire, taken by a cyclone in 1893, was eventually replaced.

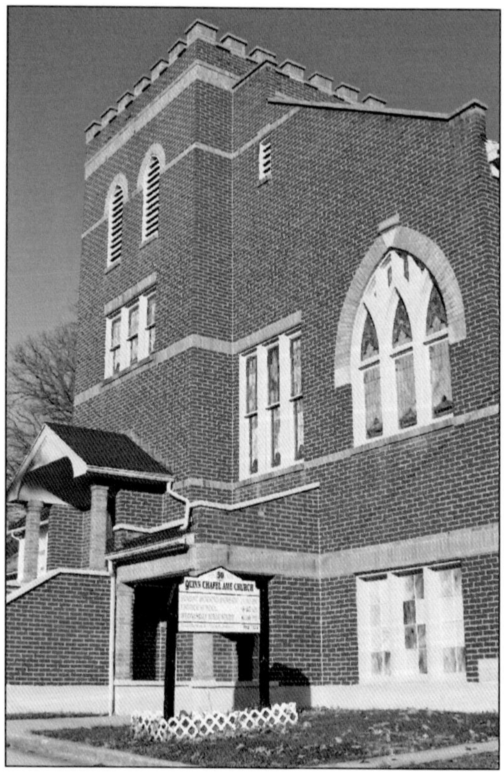

QUINNS CHAPEL AME CHURCH. This African Methodist Episcopal Church was organized in 1833 by Wiley Runnels of Cincinnati at the house of William Brown on the corner of South and Sugartree Streets. The meetings were held at private houses until 1838, when a log church was built on Lincoln Street. It stood until 1852, when the current brick structure was built. (Courtesy of Eileen Brady's collection.)

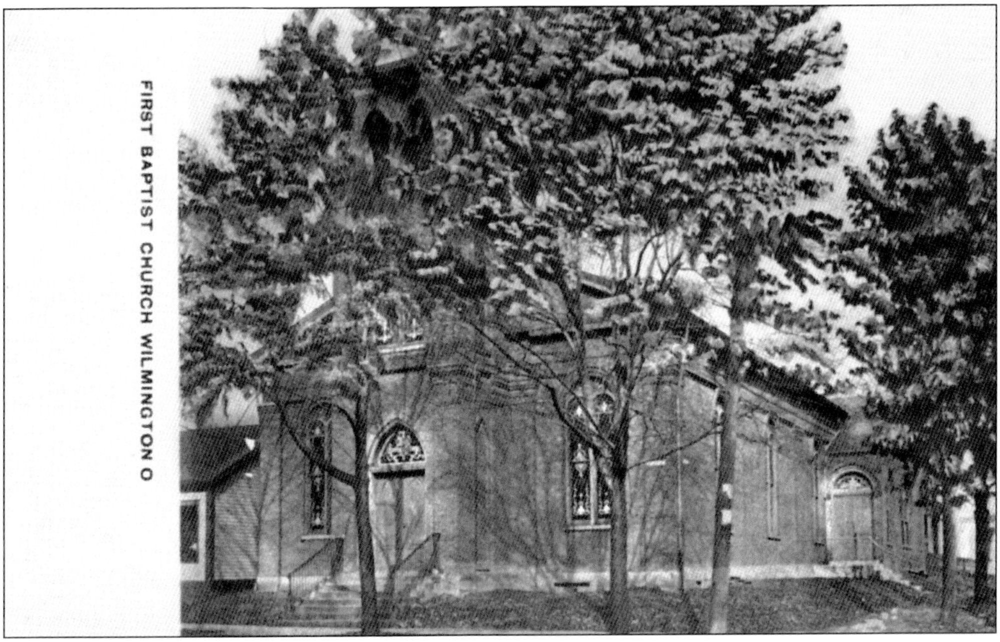

First Baptist Church. The one-story, brick building was dedicated in July 1854. In 1865, a square tower was added. In 1913, bids were received for a new First Baptist Church, to replace the old structure, at the northwest corner of Locust and Walnut Streets, pictured below. The new building cost $27,000. The auditorium could seat 700.

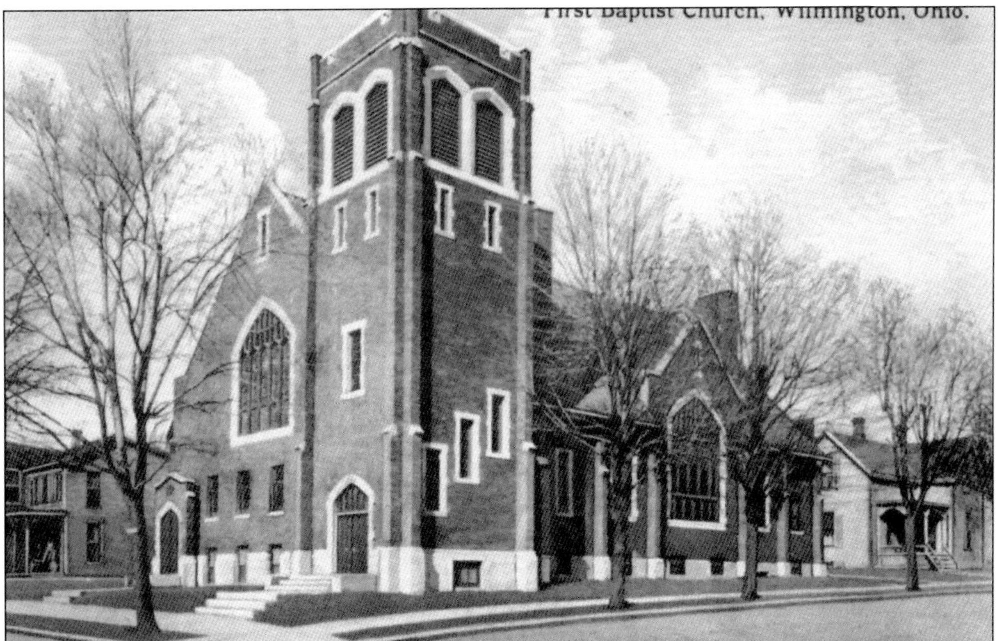

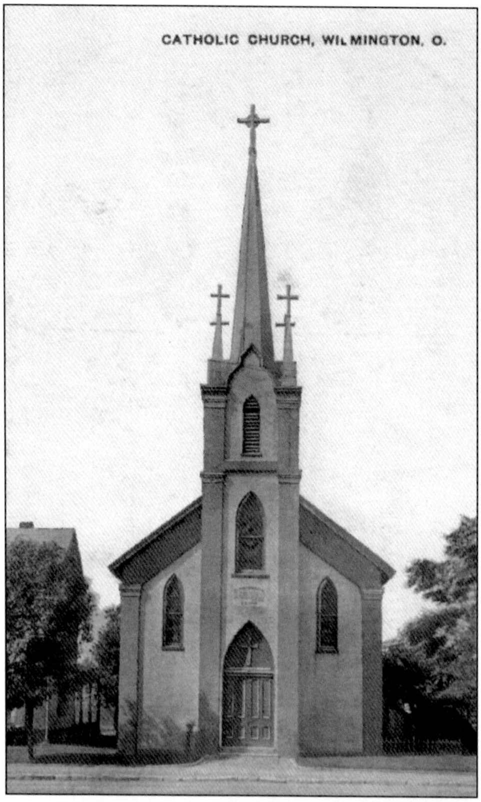

St. Columbkille Catholic Church. Ground was broken for Wilmington's first Catholic church on June 6, 1866, and was officially dedicated as St. Columbkille on October 5, 1870. It stood on the corner of Locust and Mulberry Streets. By 1914, the Catholic congregation had outgrown its church, and the new church was dedicated September 30, 1917. That year, St. Columbkille children received first communion from Rev. Charles Ertel. Pictured below are, from left to right, (first row) Mary Bailey, Nellie Mahoney, Marie Klein, Mary Kuebler, Mary Louise Grogan, Ellen Waldren, and Rose Haley; (second row) James George, William Denehy, William Fealy, ? Klein, Charles Ertel, Alvin Clement, Billy Brown, Ralph Shanahan, and Robert Haley. Ellen Waldren and Robert Haley married in 1934 and are the parents of James Haley, Jack Haley, Rita Haley Butcher, and Pat Haley, as well as the late Kevin Haley. (Below, courtesy of Rita Butcher.)

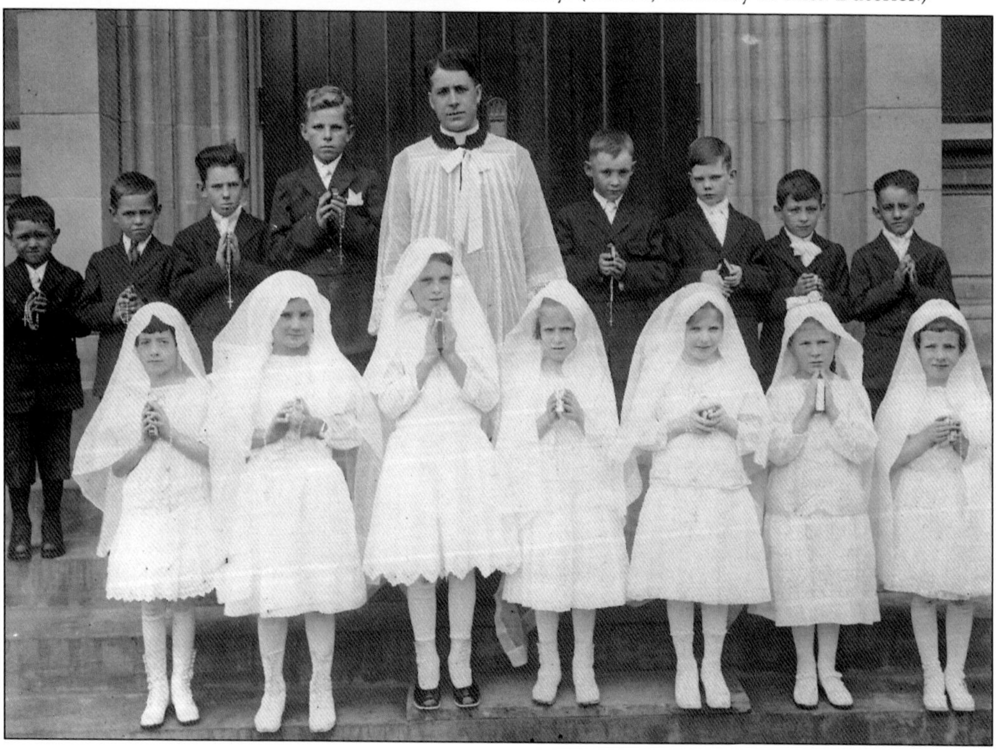

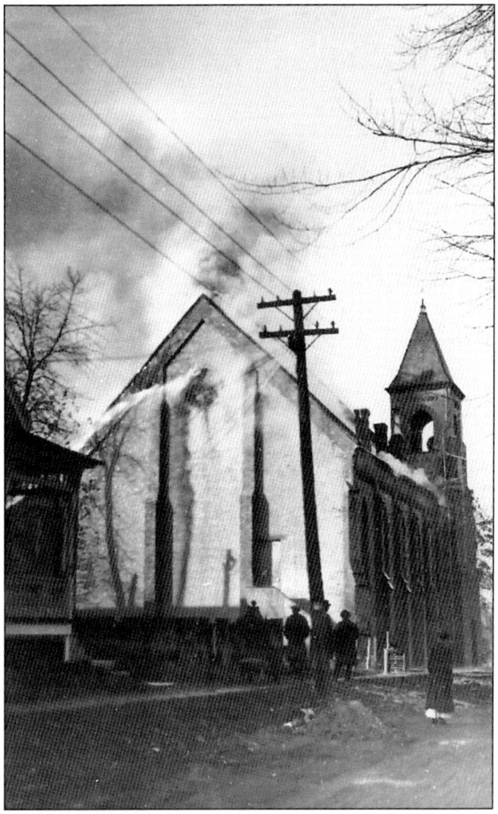

First Christian Church. The Central Christian Church was built in 1882 at the corner of Columbus and South Streets for the First Christian Church (Disciples of Christ), whose members began worshiping in Wilmington in 1828. In 1908, some members formed a new congregation and built the Walnut Street Church of Christ. The two congregations worshiped separately for 13 years but reunited in 1921, using the church on Walnut Street to worship and "Old Central" for education, although that original building was destroyed by fire in 1921 (shown at right). In 1956, the reunited members of Central Christian Church and the Walnut Street Church of Christ, who met in the Walnut Street building that was constructed in 1908, voted to adopt the church's present name, First Christian Church (Disciples of Christ). (Both, courtesy of First Christian Church.)

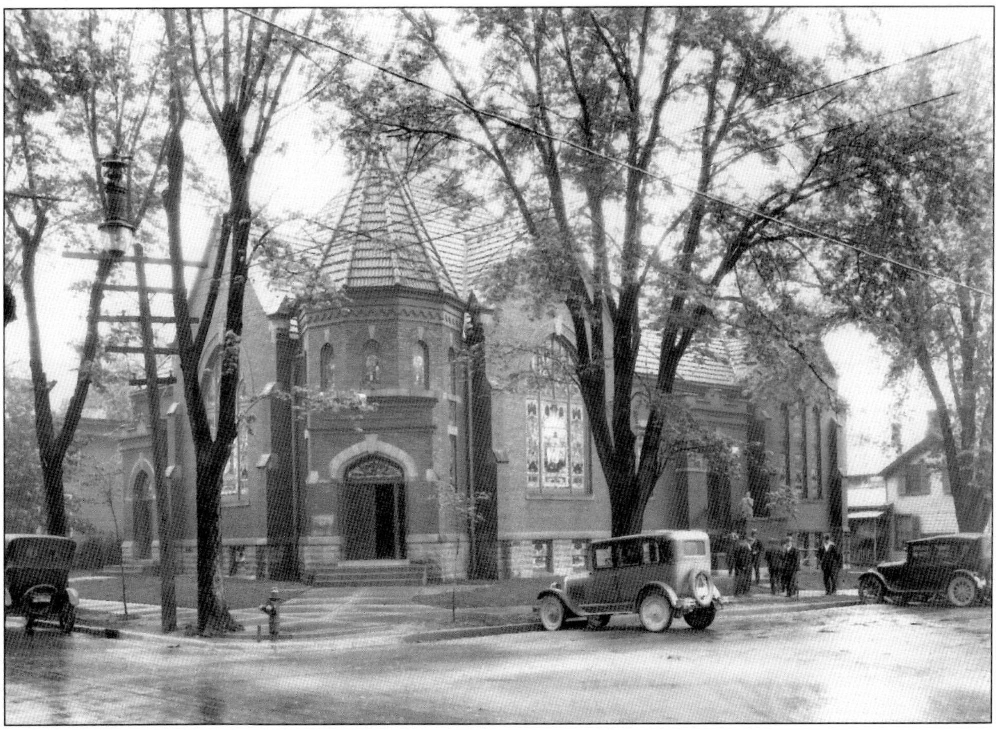

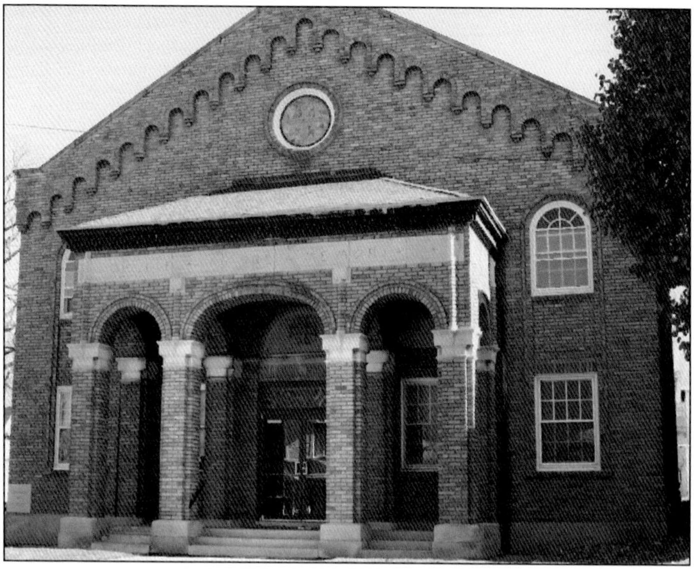

NELLIE MOORE MEMORIAL. N. Huston Moore, a longtime member of Central Christian Church, financed a new education building and gave it to the church in 1924, which used it as an education wing until 1992. Named in memory of Moore's daughter, Nellie, who had been a Sunday school teacher for many years, it currently is used by the nondenominational Dove Church Wilmington. (Courtesy of Eileen Brady's collection.)

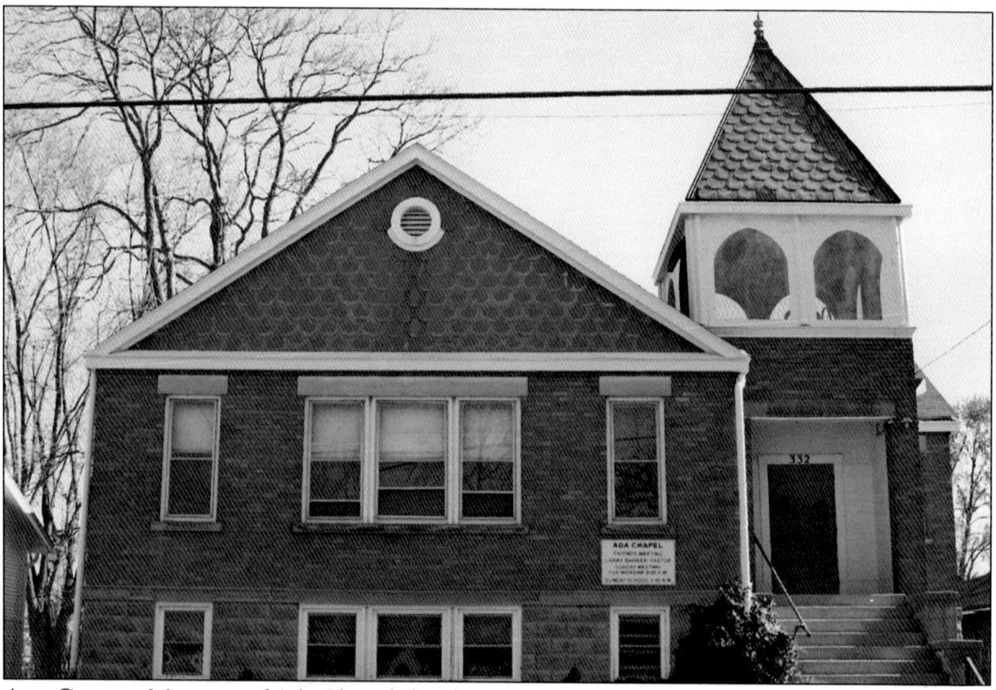

ADA CHAPEL. Meetings of Ada Chapel, first known as the East Wilmington Mission, date back to 1888, when Wilmington teacher Lizzie Harvey obtained permission from the Society of Friends to open a religious meeting in order to help impoverished children. The first building was an 18-by-25-foot chapel. The current building, dedicated in 1911, was named after Ada Jenkins, who financed it. It is currently Ada Chapel Friends Meeting. (Courtesy of Eileen Brady's collection.)

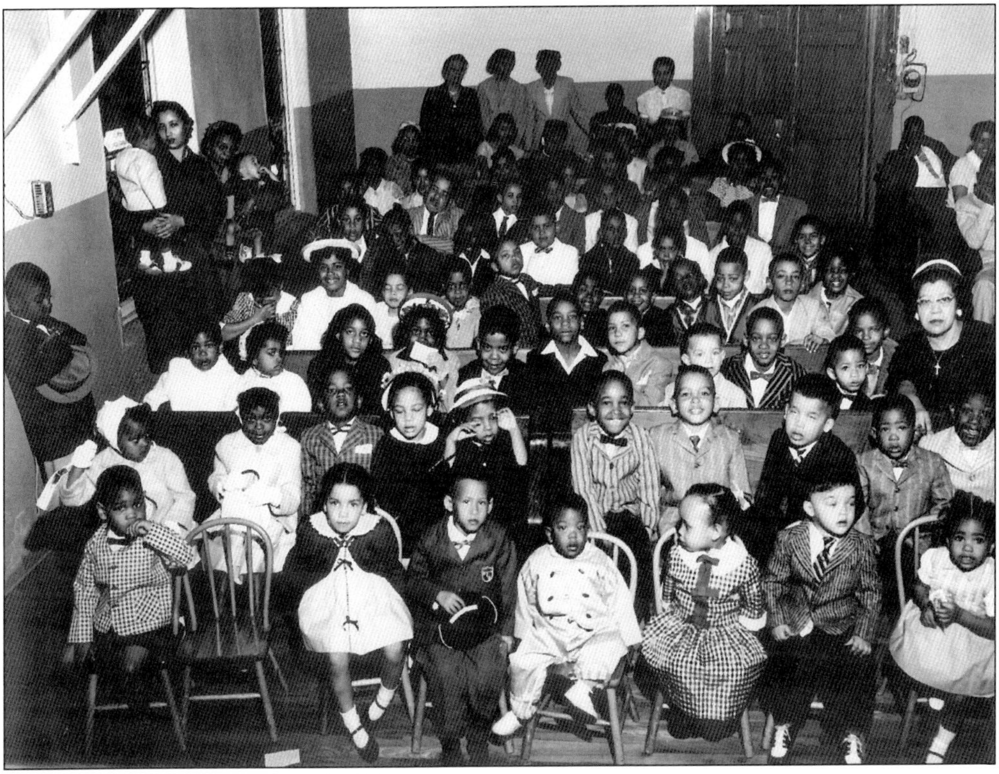

SECOND BAPTIST CHURCH. Called Zion Baptist Church when it was organized in 1854 at the home of Jacob Emmons, services were held in Emmons's home, then in a rented property, and in the Midland School until the current brick church on Grant Street was built for $1,400. The name was changed to Second Baptist in 1862. The above photograph was taken in 1958.

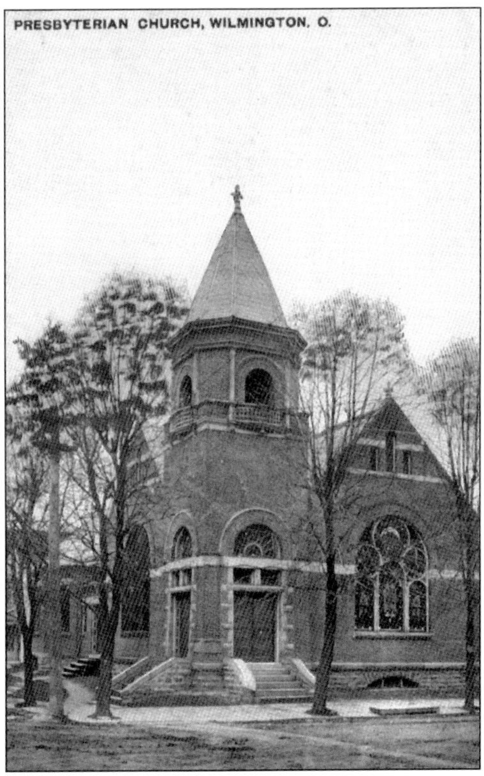

PRESBYTERIAN CHURCH. The first Presbyterian meeting in Wilmington dates to 1823. Members worshiped in homes, then in Wilmington's Baptist Church, until a sanctuary was built in 1830, at the corner of Locust and Mulberry Streets (seen at right). Some of the first Anti-Slavery Society meetings in Clinton County were held at this church in the late 1830s. The church relocated in 1965 to Randolph Street and again in 2000 to Timber Glen Drive.

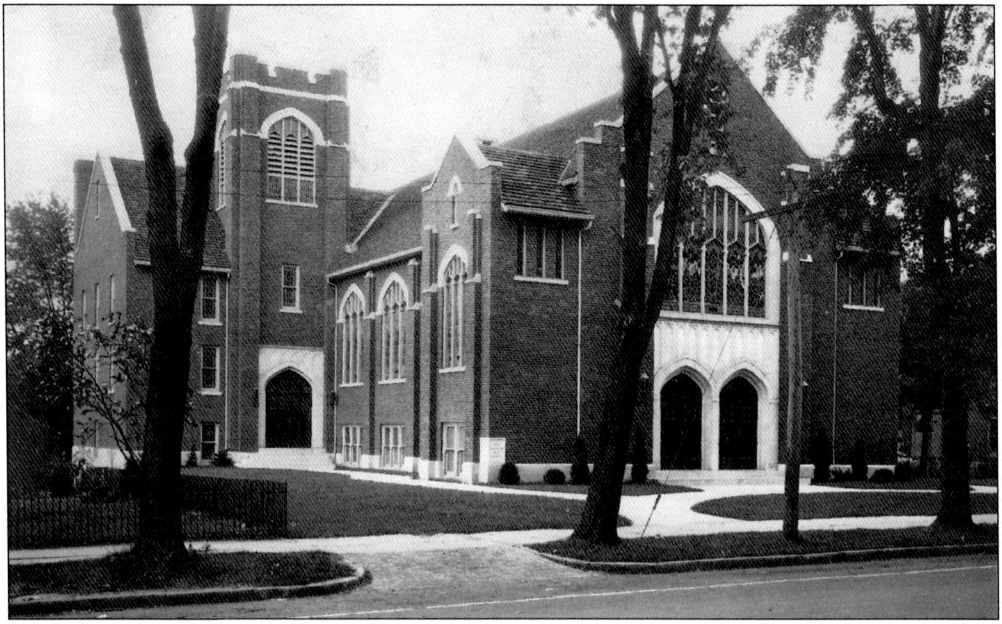

Methodist Church. In 1928, the former church was razed, and the Methodist Episcopal congregation met in the LaMax Theatre during construction of the new (and current) building on East Locust Street, which was dedicated on Easter 1929. In 1939, the Wilmington Methodist Church was born from a national uniting of the Methodist Episcopal Church North, the Methodist Episcopal Church South, and the Methodist Protestant Church.

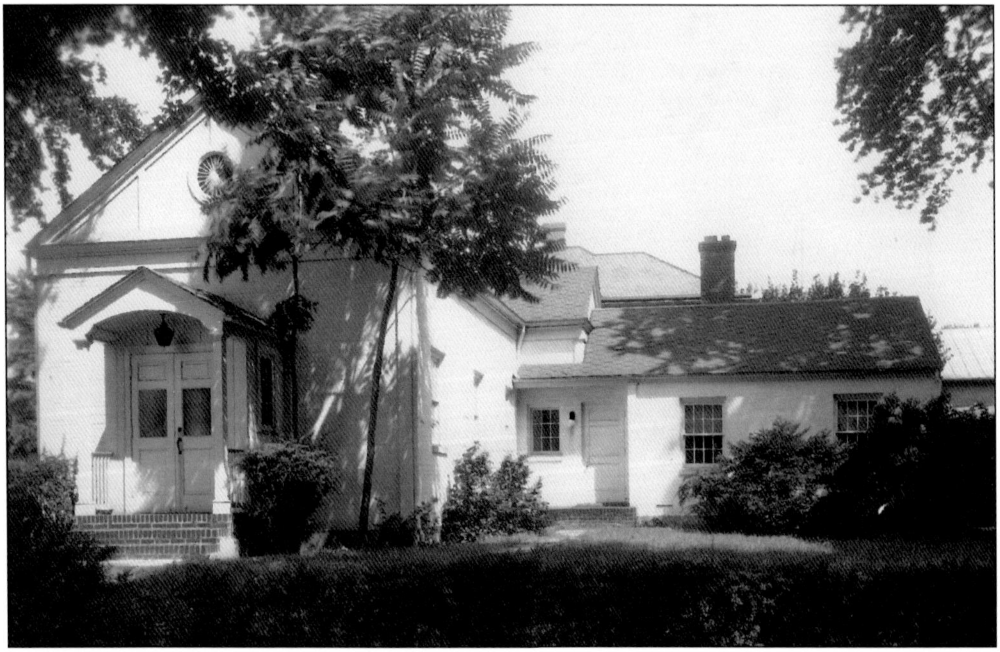

All Saints Episcopal Church. At the corner of Locust and Walnut Streets, the cornerstone of the All Saints Episcopal Church was laid on December 2, 1928, though it was purchased by the Wilmington Episcopal Church in 1907. It became the Wilmington Seventh-day Adventist Church in 1942, and it is currently Wilmington Zion Hill Church.

CHURCH OF THE NAZARENE. The congregation met with its first pastor, Rev. Ray Beegle, in a rented building on Mulberry Street from 1935 until 1940, when the members moved into the basement of the church being constructed with bricks from a former church in Cuba. The original church at 198 South Walnut Street (shown at right) is now Crossroads Community Church. The Nazarene congregation relocated in 1973 to a new building on State Route 73.

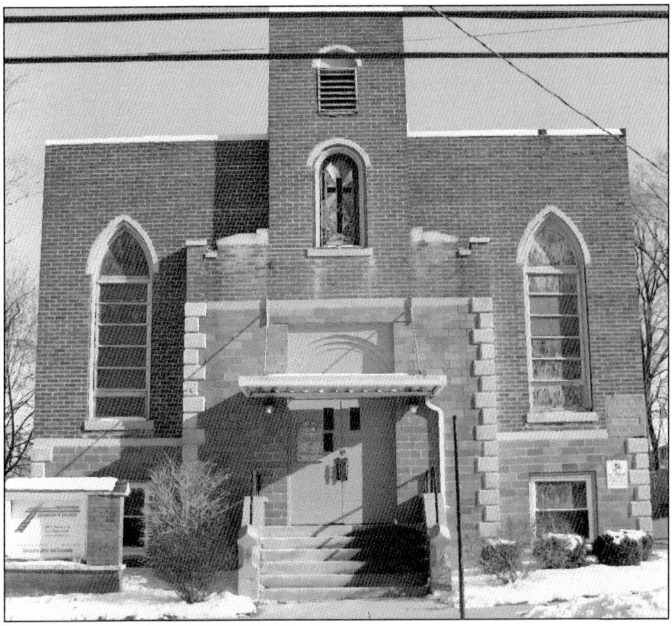

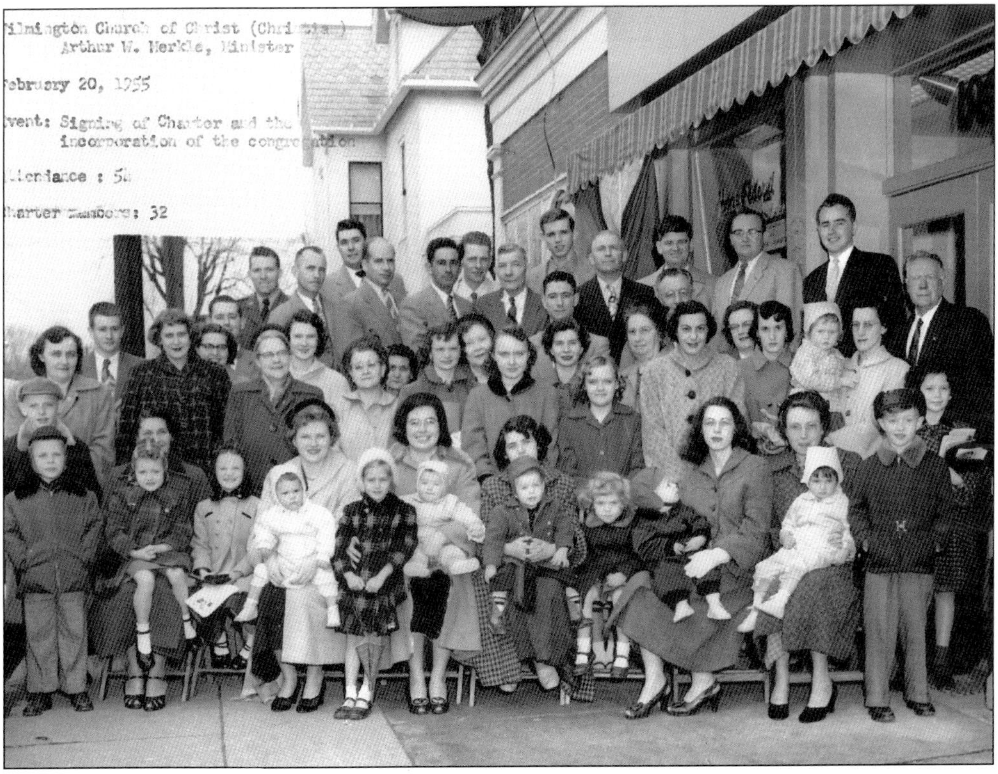

CHURCH OF CHRIST. The charter members of the Church of Christ, shown in this photograph, first met at 106 North South Street, then bought 2.15 acres on West Locust Street in 1955, where a now-annual live, outdoor nativity scene along Locust Street was started even before the building was constructed. The church was organized by Rev. Arthur Merkle (who died in 2000) and his wife, Mabel (Stanforth), of Sabina. (Courtesy of the Church of Christ.)

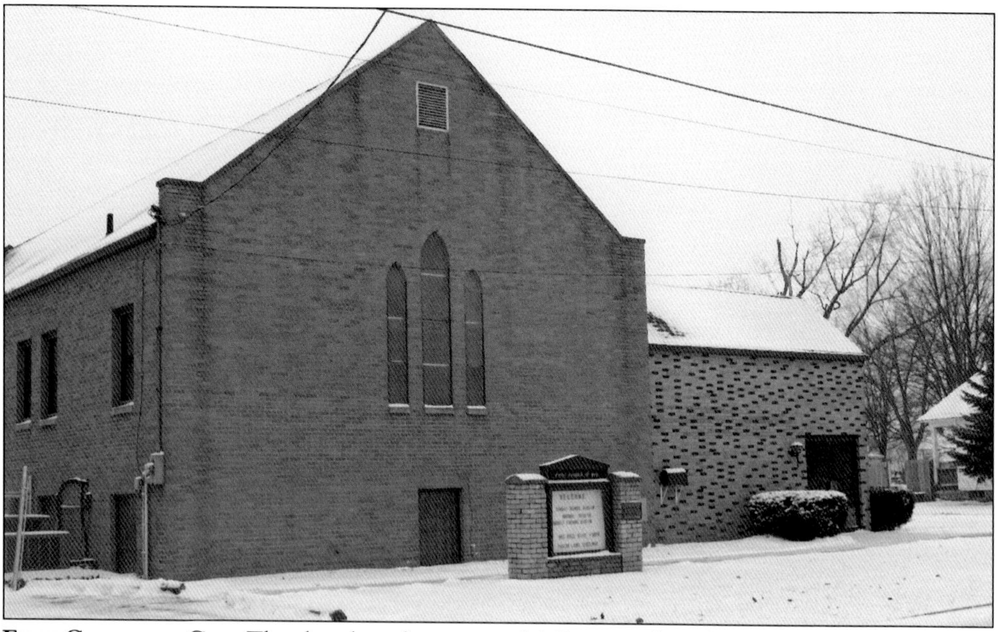

FIRST CHURCH OF GOD. The church at the corner of A Street and Michigan Avenue was dedicated on October 21, 1956, although the congregation was organized in September 1951. The basement was built with a temporary roof to provide a place to worship until construction of the rest of the church could be financed and completed. (Courtesy of Eileen Brady's collection.)

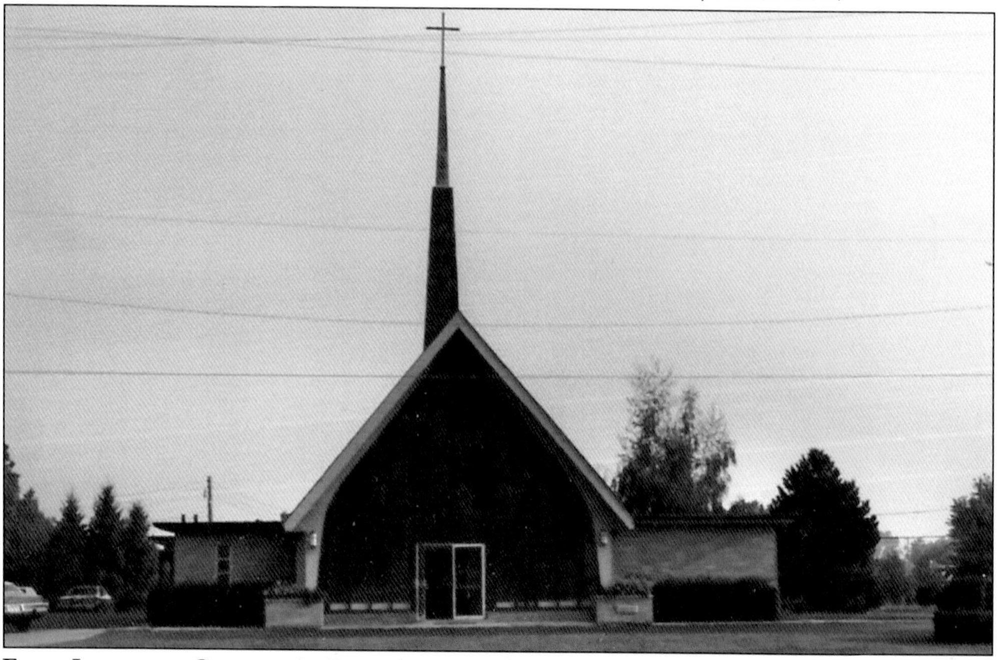

FAITH LUTHERAN CHURCH. In December 1951, the first congregational service of the Lutheran Mission was held at Smith Place's school auditorium. From 1952 to 1956, the group met at the Seventh-day Adventist church, until a chapel was built. A new church on East Vine Street was dedicated in 1960, and in 1988, the sanctuary was expanded, and a fellowship hall and education wing was added. (Courtesy of Faith Lutheran Church.)

Six

SCHOOLS

The first school in downtown Wilmington was a log schoolhouse built around 1810 by Joseph Doan at the corner of Sugartree and Spring Streets, where students were taught by Isaac Garretson, known to be Wilmington's first teacher. Before public schools started in Ohio in 1825, children were taught at "subscription schools," supported by tuition and donations.

There were about 65 one-room schools in the Wilmington area between the early 1800s and 1914, the year Ohio started centralizing schools.

The Taylor Latin School, Wilmington's first post-elementary school, started in 1820 at the southwest corner of Lincoln and Columbus Streets. Around 1839, the Wilmington Seminary was built at Locust and Mulberry Streets, where the Wilmington Friends meetinghouse stands.

Union School, a public school later known as Main School, was dedicated in 1870. The first high school graduating class, in 1873, had 10 people.

In 1853, Charles Hurd was Wilmington's first African American teacher, and he continued teaching until 1867. In 1854, Old Hill Top one-room school taught African American students at Columbus and Lincoln Streets. There were at least eight additional African American schools scattered throughout the area, including the first built by African Americans in 1852.

By 1884, the Midland School, for younger black students, was built at Sugartree and Grant Streets in Wilmington. In 1915, enrollment in Wilmington's African American schools was at 73, although 20 black pupils were enrolled in Wilmington's high school.

The second school that served as Wilmington High School, known later as Smith Place, was built in 1893 at North South Street and East Birdsall Avenue. The third high school, which later served as the junior high, was built in 1911 at 365 West Locust Street.

None of those first large buildings exist today; each was demolished between the 1970s and the 1990s.

East End School, originally built in 1929, and Denver Elementary School, built in 1955, are both still used. The current Wilmington High School was constructed in 1959; its first graduating class was in 1961. It was remodeled in 1964 and again in 1999, and still serves as the city's high school.

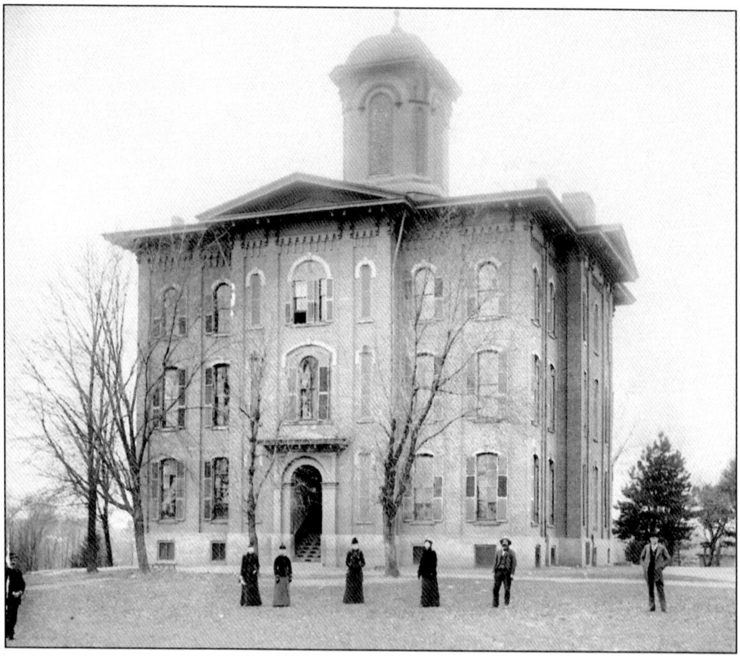

MAIN SCHOOL. Union School, later known as Main School, was built in 1870 on a 5-acre plot on West Sugartree Street. It had 10 large rooms, an assembly hall, and a four-room basement. In this photograph, Main School superintendent Ed Merrick (far left) stands with (from left to right) teachers Lola Street, Almeda Smith, Carrie Ent, Mary Holaday Harris, unidentified, and Paul Williams.

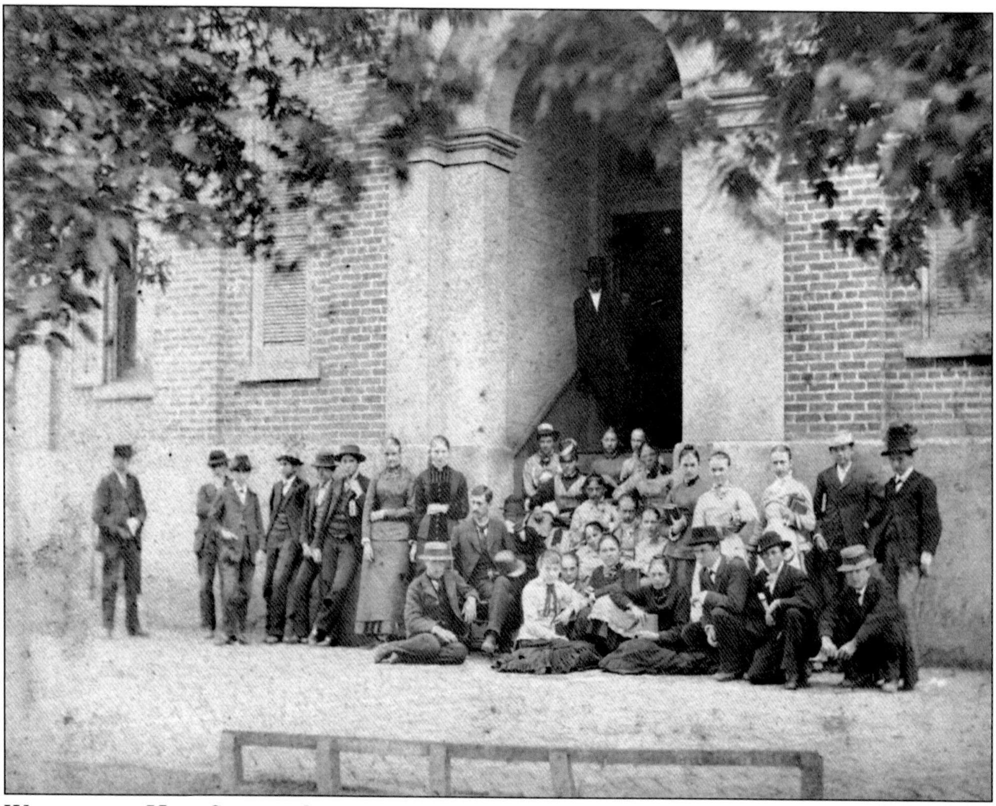

WILMINGTON HIGH SCHOOL CLASS, 1879. Wilmington High School's students at Main Building were photographed in June 1879. Teacher Oliver Thatcher was seated in the middle, holding a hat.

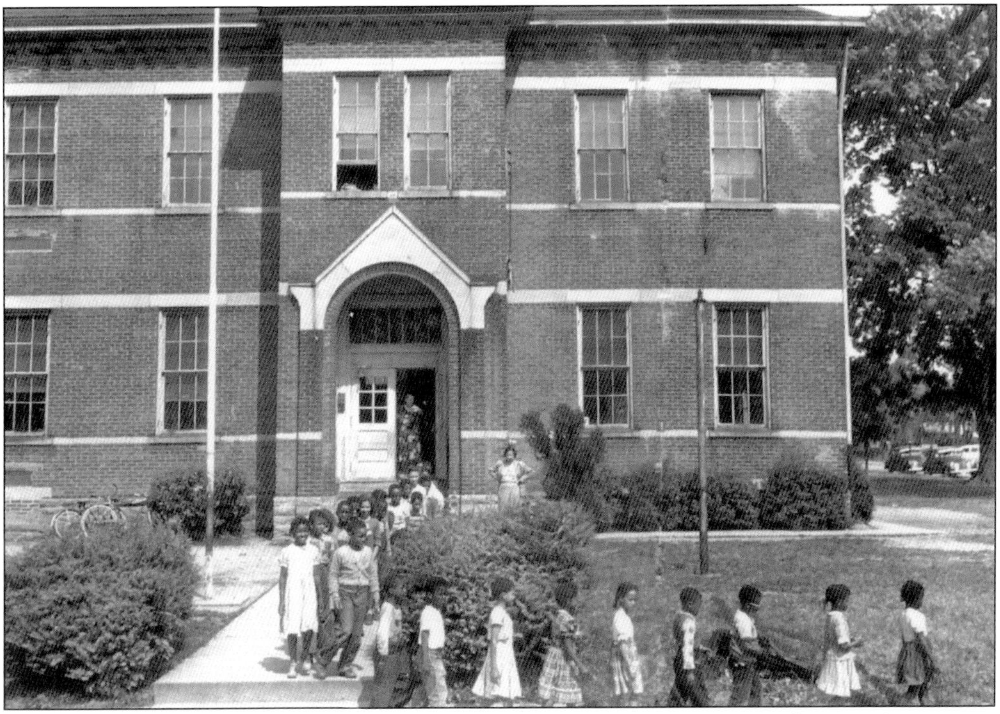

MIDLAND SCHOOL. In 1884, the Midland School was built at Sugartree and Grant Streets as a "colored school." As early as 1895, African American city councilman J. R. Hawley filed suit against the Wilmington school board alleging that it was illegal to maintain a separate and inferior public school for African American children. Midland's last day as a segregated school, shown in this photograph, was not until May 26, 1952.

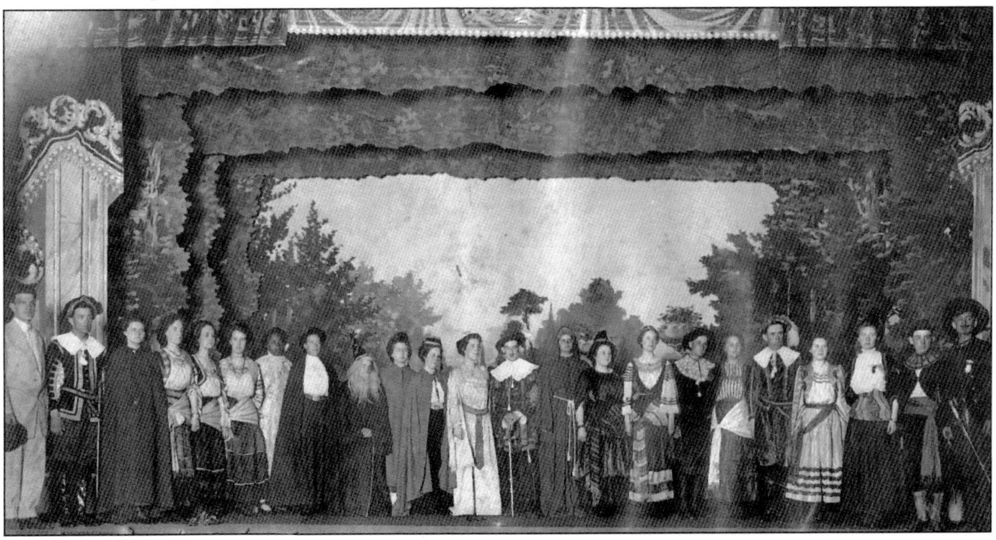

CLASS PRODUCTION. Wilmington High School class of 1909 performed George Eliot's *Spanish Gypsy*, directed by Robert Hocket. From left to right are Hocket, Russell Hiatt, Mary Carey, Mary Vandevort, Hazel Moore, Olive Crary, Glena Emmons, Ivy Edwards, Cora Stoltz, Lettie Clark, Mary Kelly, Faith Austin, March Fisher, Stella Frazier, Carrie Murphy, Lucille Clark, Murray Babb, Fay Hiatt, N. S. Ireland, Mildred Jones, Hazel West, Ray Runyan, and Chas Frazer.

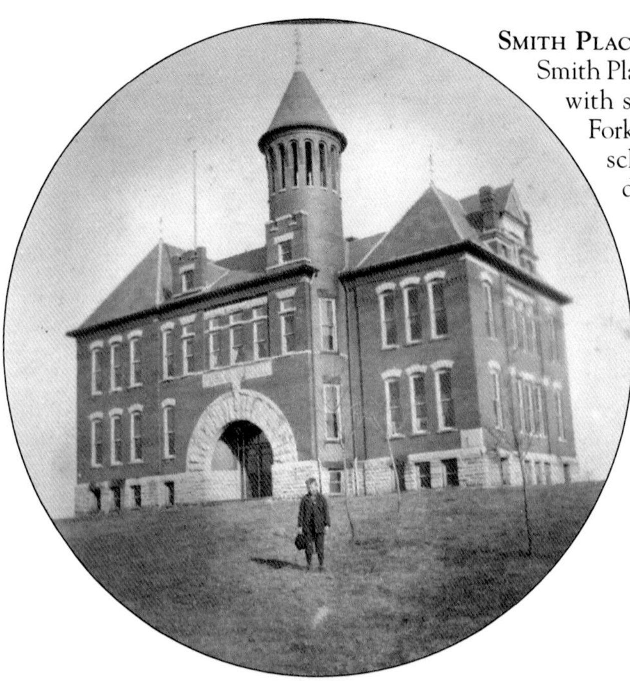

SMITH PLACE. Built in 1893 as a high school, Smith Place featured arched entrances made with stone quarried locally from Todd's Fork. The building, later an elementary school, was closed in 1979 and was demolished in 1984.

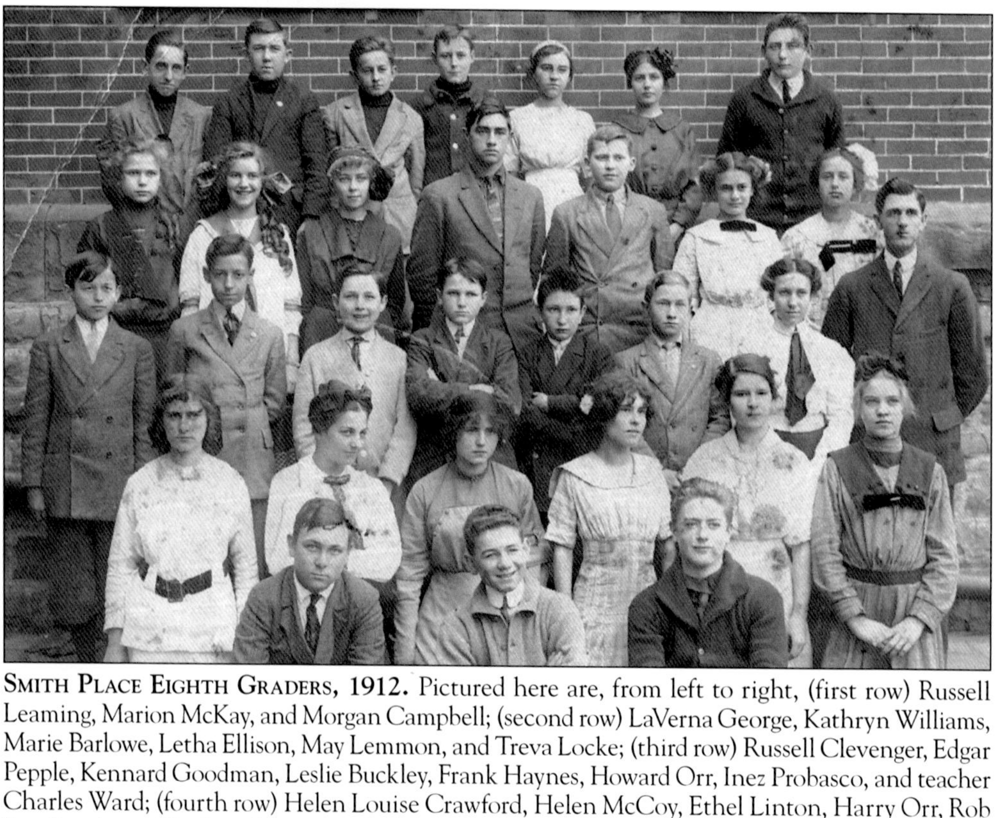

SMITH PLACE EIGHTH GRADERS, 1912. Pictured here are, from left to right, (first row) Russell Leaming, Marion McKay, and Morgan Campbell; (second row) LaVerna George, Kathryn Williams, Marie Barlowe, Letha Ellison, May Lemmon, and Treva Locke; (third row) Russell Clevenger, Edgar Pepple, Kennard Goodman, Leslie Buckley, Frank Haynes, Howard Orr, Inez Probasco, and teacher Charles Ward; (fourth row) Helen Louise Crawford, Helen McCoy, Ethel Linton, Harry Orr, Rob Roy Bangham, Charlotte Martin, and Clara Metzger; (fifth row) Claude Cashman, Huston Talmage, George Bernard, Gale Roush, Lena Howe, Norma Wisecup, and Montgomery Campbell.

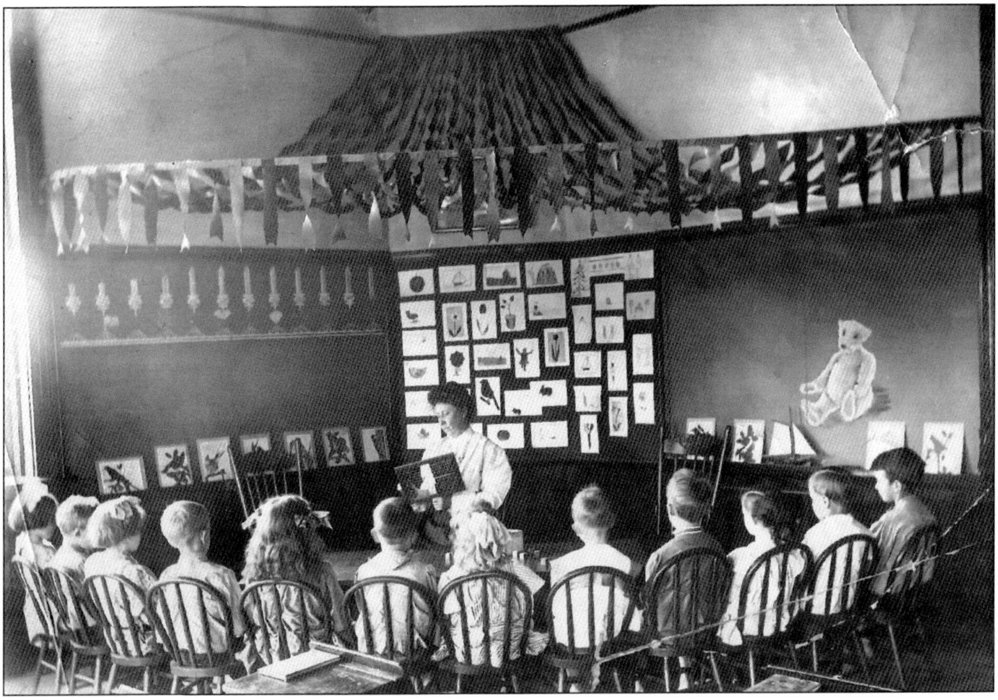

Teacher Lola Street. Lola Street, pictured above with her class at Smith Place, taught first grade for 44 years in the Wilmington schools. The daughter of Charles and Rose Street, she was born in 1868 in Lumberton, moving to Wilmington as a child and graduating from Wilmington High School in 1887. She taught for a year before graduating and worked three years in the county schools before starting as a first-grade teacher in Wilmington in 1890. In 1931, she was a delegate to the National Education Association meeting in Los Angeles. Street, shown below during a class picnic before her California trip, retired in 1934 and died in 1951.

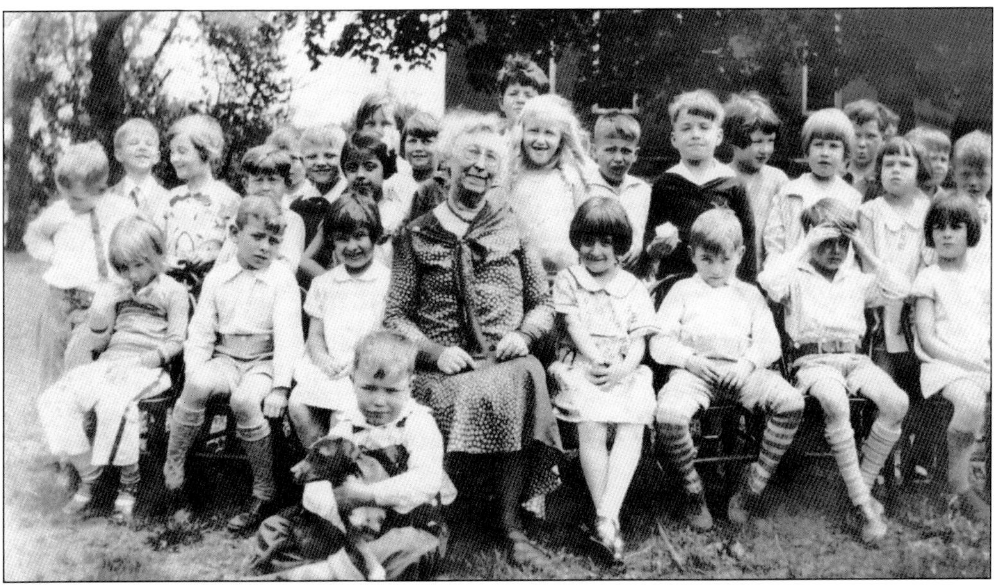

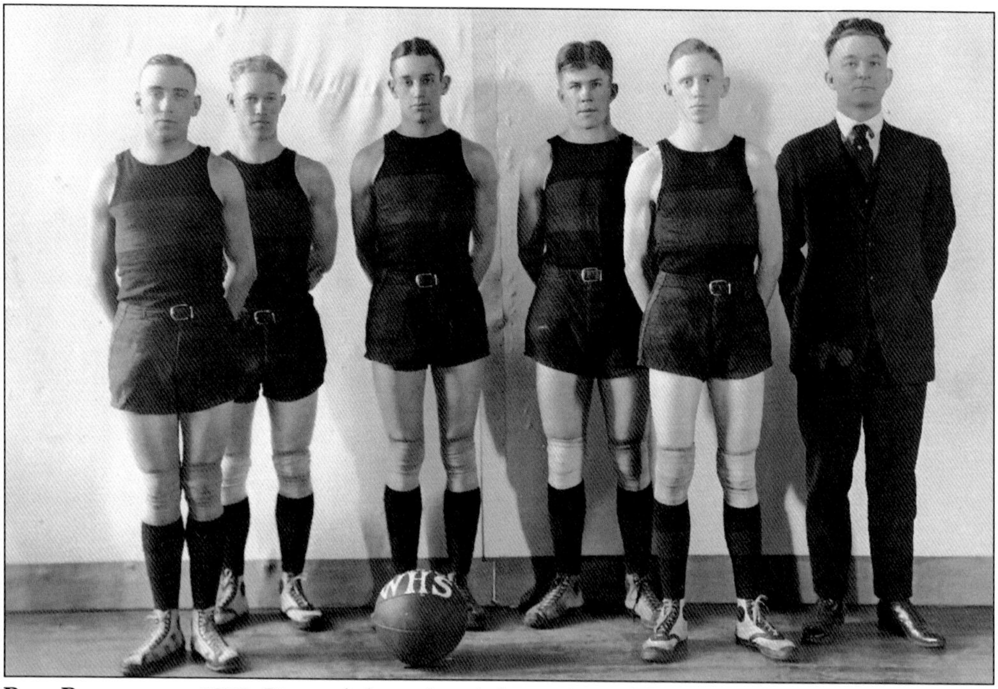

Boys Basketball, 1909. Pictured above from left to right are Elmo Contrill, John Nowold, Elmer Ogden, Robert Stephens, Charles Sapp, and coach Roy Black.

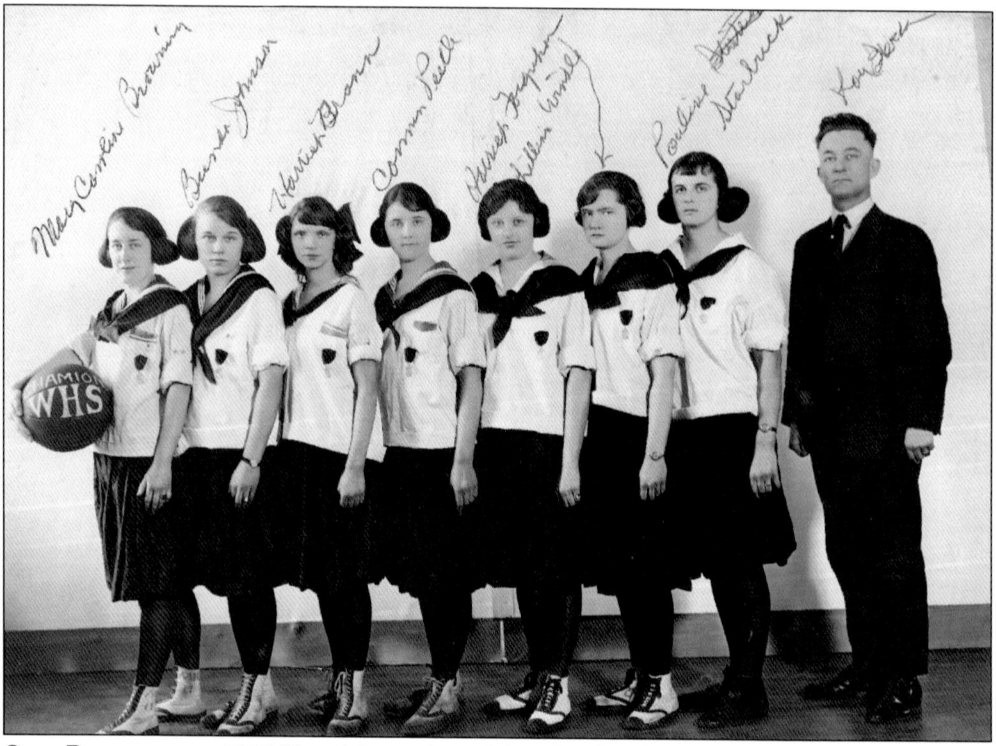

Girls Basketball, c. 1909. From left to right are Mary Coraline Browning, Brenda Johnson, Harriet Bronn, C. Peelle, Lillian Brindle, Harriet Farquhar, Pauline Starbuck, and coach Roy Black.

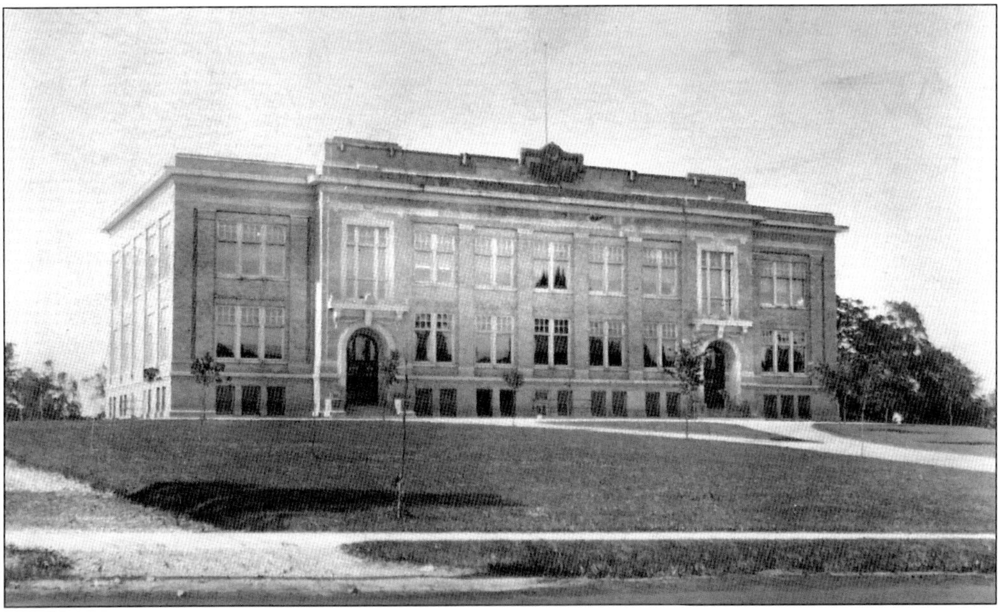

Wilmington High School. Wilmington High School was built in 1911 on Locust Street. It later became the junior high when the high school moved to Richardson Place.

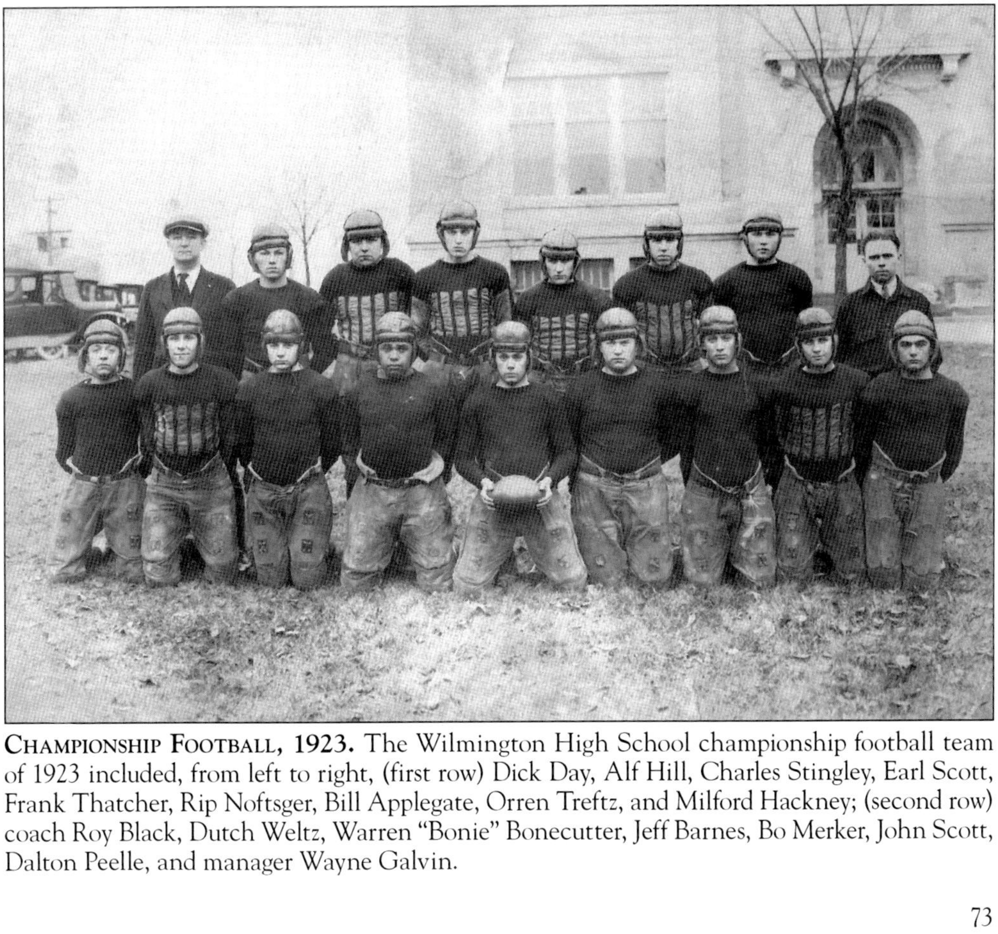

Championship Football, 1923. The Wilmington High School championship football team of 1923 included, from left to right, (first row) Dick Day, Alf Hill, Charles Stingley, Earl Scott, Frank Thatcher, Rip Noftsger, Bill Applegate, Orren Treftz, and Milford Hackney; (second row) coach Roy Black, Dutch Weltz, Warren "Bonie" Bonecutter, Jeff Barnes, Bo Merker, John Scott, Dalton Peelle, and manager Wayne Galvin.

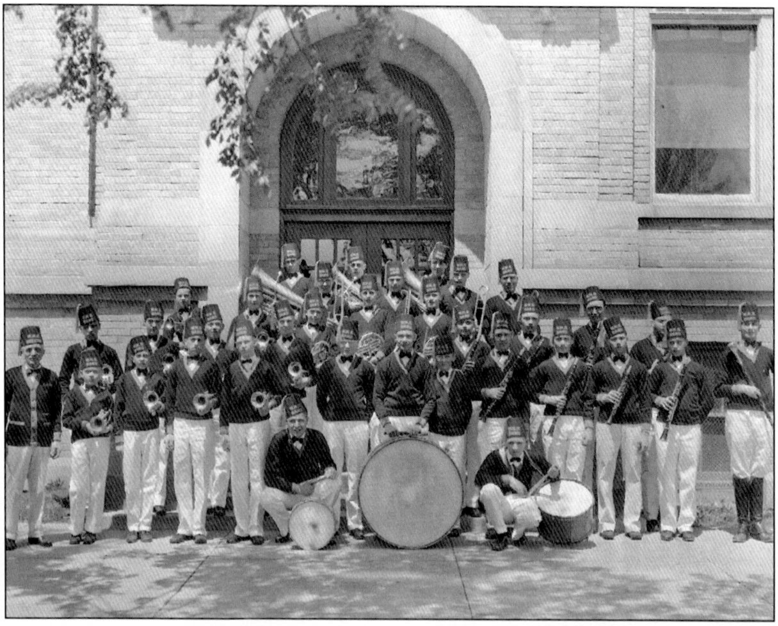

MARCHING BAND, 1928. Wilmington High School's 1928 marching band included about 35 members. The band has had a long tradition of excellence, and it was later directed for many years by Rodger O. Borror, who became superintendent of the Wilmington city school district in 1972 and is the namesake for the current middle school.

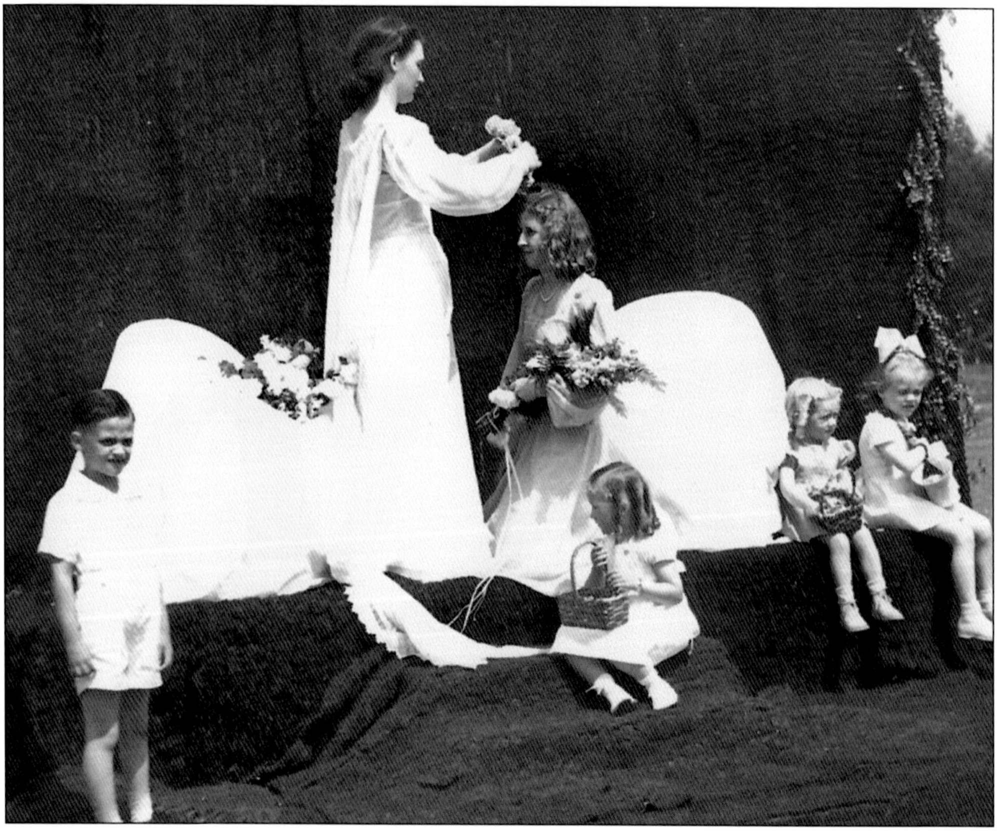

MAY QUEEN, 1941. Judith Simmons crowned Mary Ruth Boyd the new May queen at Wilmington High School on May 15, 1941. Traditionally a May queen is a girl who is selected to participate in May Day celebrations while wearing a white gown to symbolize purity.

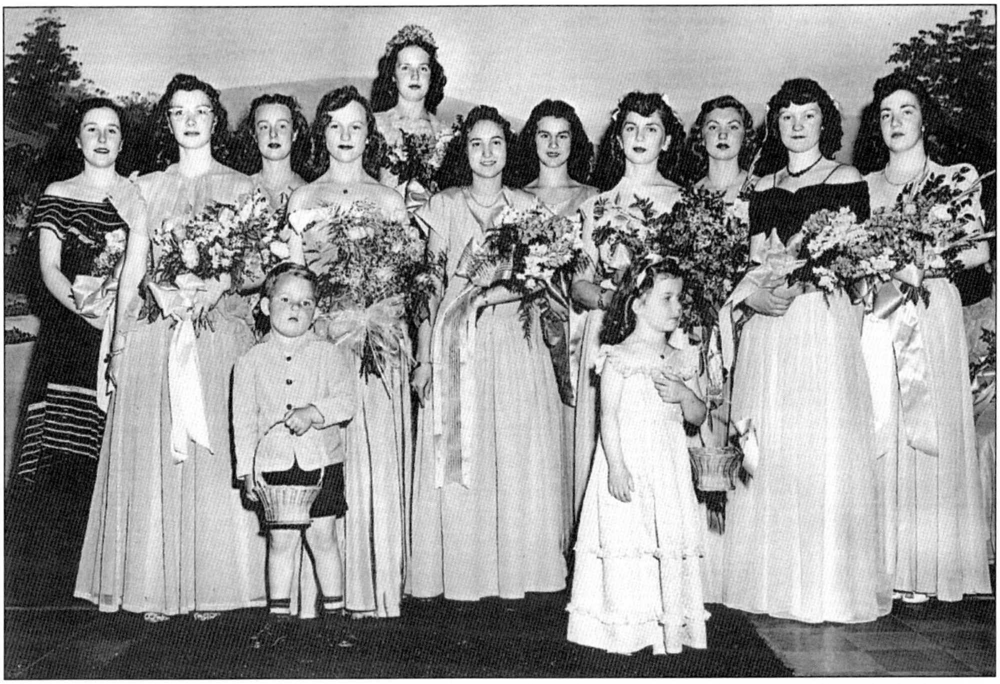

Junior Class, 1947. Members of Wilmington High School's junior class in 1947 included queen Marjorie Haidet and her attendants. Pictured from left to right are (first row) flower boy Eddie Rulon and flower girl Mary Ann Gordon; (second row) Joy Hale, Shirley Dolphin, Evelyn Finney, Madgeanne Cotner, Geraldine Carmen, and Barbara Miller; (third row) Patricia Feike, Barbara Marshall, Wilhelmine Sievers, and Velma Miller; (fourth row) queen Marjorie Haidet.

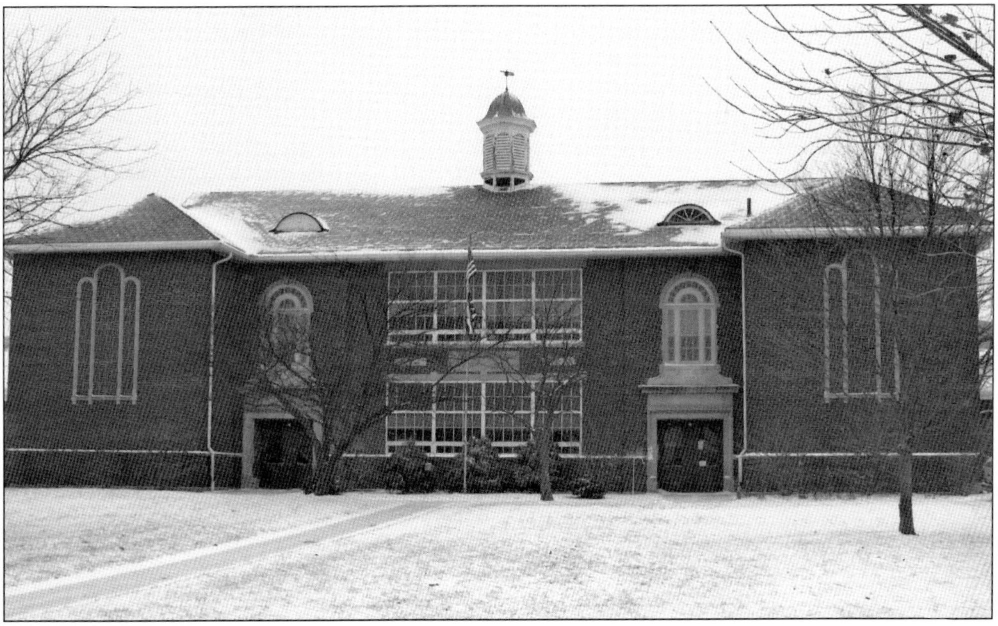

East End Elementary. Located at 769 Rombach Avenue, East End Elementary was built in 1929 and was remodeled in 1993. Today the school educates approximately 300 students in kindergarten through fifth grade.

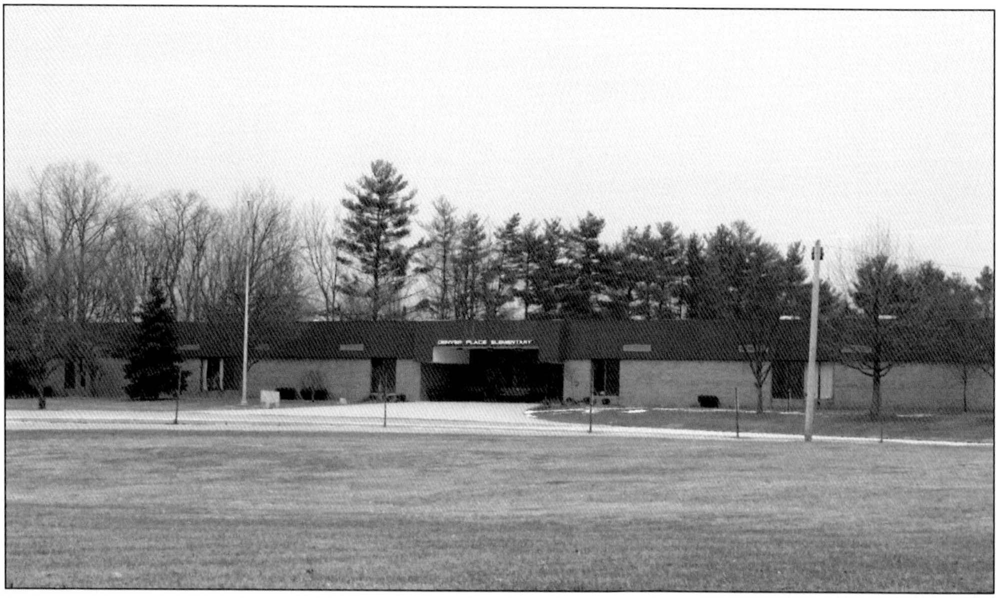

DENVER ELEMENTARY. Denver Elementary School, 291 Lorish Avenue, was built in 1955 and still serves as a school today. It has about 675 students in kindergarten through fifth grade.

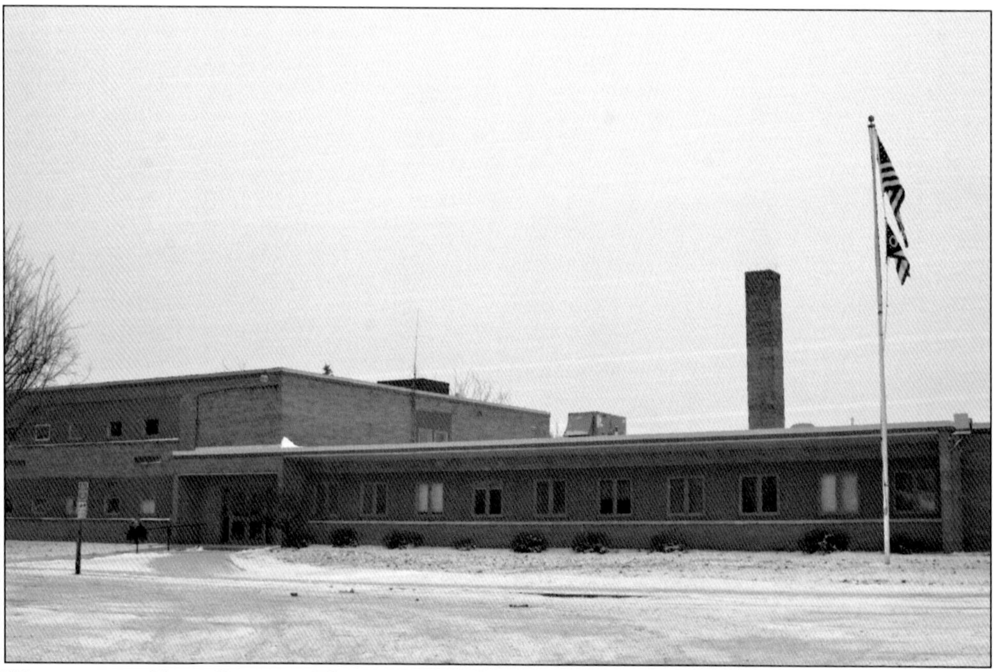

WILMINGTON HIGH SCHOOL. The current Wilmington High School, at 300 Richardson Place, was built in 1959; it was remodeled in 1999 and serves ninth through 12th grades, with about 950 students.

Seven

Wilmington College

Located on a pastoral campus, Wilmington College is close to the heart of downtown Wilmington. In 1866, the owners of Franklin College near Athens, Ohio, relocated the college to Wilmington. After building what became College Hall, they ran out of money during the post–Civil War depression. In 1870, local Quakers raised funds and bought the partially completed building and grounds at what was essentially a fire sale for $11,334. Completed in 1871, College Hall opened its doors to traditional college students as well as to students in the preparatory program, which was designed to equip students for either college or commerce, as there were not many high schools in the area at that time.

Wilmington College has always incorporated its Quaker heritage in its administration, teachers, and programs. During the early years, chapel attendance and Bible study were mandatory. The college also played host to the first Wilmington Yearly Meeting in 1896 and has continued to hold these meetings throughout the years. The college now has its own Friends Monthly Meeting on campus.

The principle Quaker teachings have remained intact, especially the testimony of equality and the testimony of peace. The testimony of equality was apparent in the college's first class, which was composed of three women and one man. From the beginning, women have been an important part of the student body and faculty. The college's commitment to the Quaker testimony of peace has been amply demonstrated by the actions of its faculty and students. Several faculty and administrative leaders have been at the forefront of the conscientious objector movement, including Luther Warren, T. Canby Jones, and Larry Gara. Thomas Kelly, a well-known Quaker theologian, graduated from Wilmington College and was a professor from 1919 to 1921. His treatise *Testament of Devotion* was a compilation of spiritual essays that is still well regarded today.

Wilmington College's course of study has changed dramatically from the classical studies of Latin and Greek toward more modern courses that include the study of agriculture and theater. But the college's commitment to its Quaker roots and to its liberal arts education still draws students to its campus.

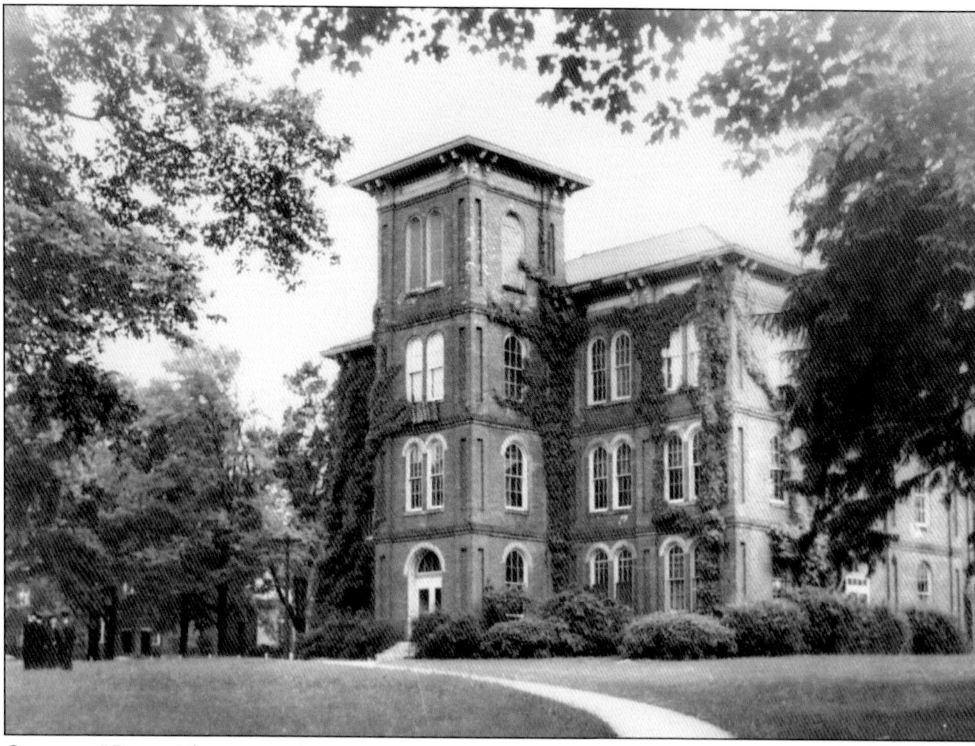

College Hall. The original owners of Franklin College started building College Hall in 1866 but had to sell the college before the building was completed. During the early years, College Hall served all the needs of the college. Renovated in the 1970s, the building was placed on the National Register of Historic Places in 1972. It remains in use for classrooms and administrative and faculty offices.

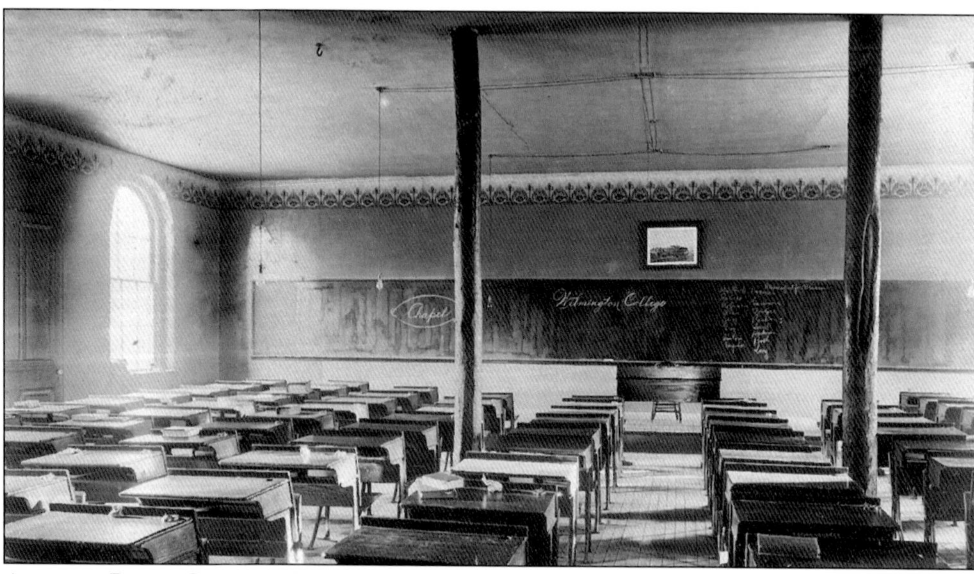

Assembly Room, College Hall. During its early years, College Hall housed classrooms, offices, living quarters, an auditorium, a library, a museum, a parlor, a chemical laboratory, a gymnasium, the office of the president, and the assembly room pictured here.

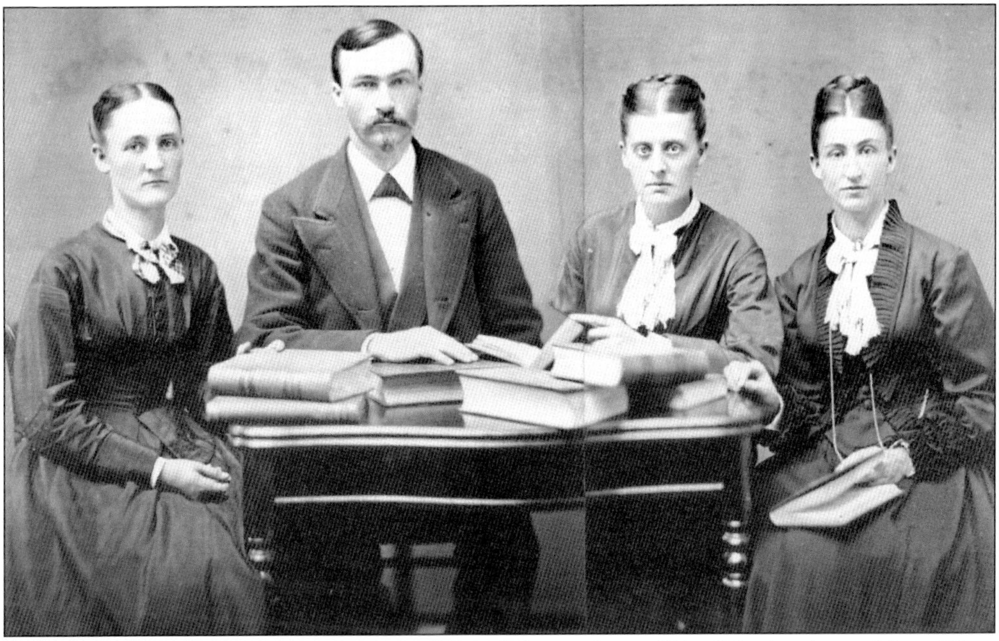

FIRST GRADUATING CLASS, 1875. Pictured from left to right are Ellen Wright, Aaron Hunt, Elma Doster Cook, and Hannah Lewis Smith. Ellen Wright became a legendary teacher, mentor, and friend to many in the Wilmington College community. She began teaching Latin and Greek immediately upon graduation and added composition, debate, and rhetoric, and eventually worked as the librarian and faculty secretary. (Courtesy of Wilmington College.)

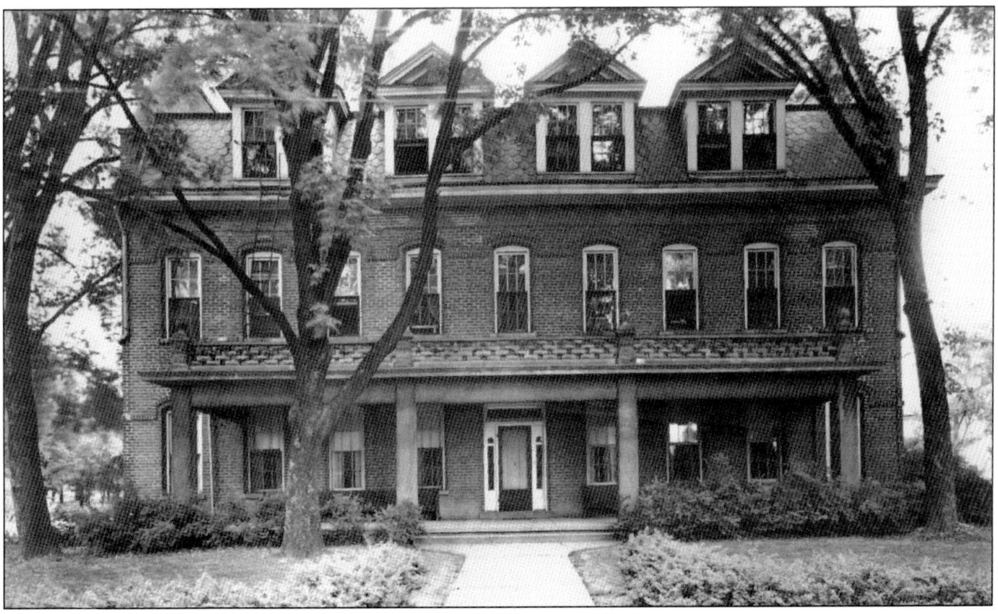

TWIN ASH HALL, 1872–1984. Built in 1872, Twin Ash Hall began as a privately run boardinghouse for girls. Purchased by the college in 1904 for $4,000, the building served the college for more than 100 years. The dining room was turned into a recreation room and greatly enhanced the social opportunities for the students. A third story was added in 1920. (Courtesy of Wilmington College.)

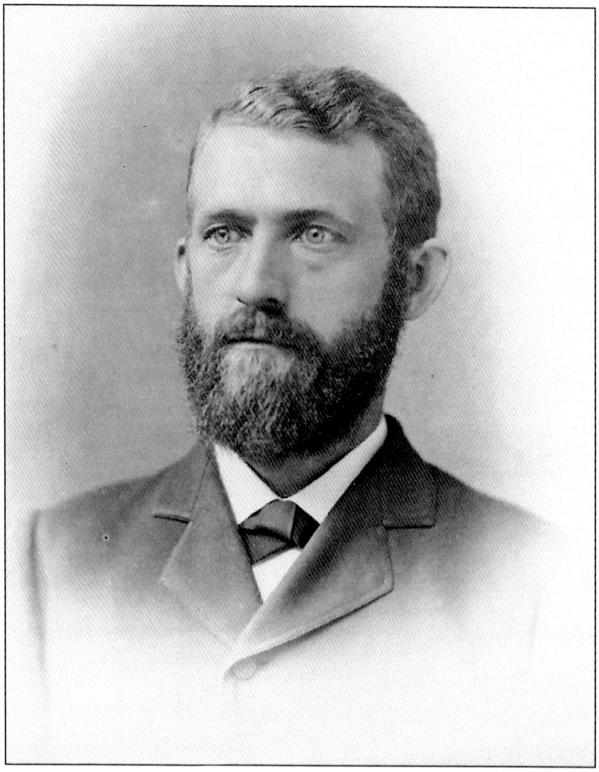

JAMES UNTHANK, PRESIDENT 1881–1903. President Unthank first came to the college as a professor. Known as a scholar, he continued to teach a full course schedule while performing his presidential duties. Unthank tirelessly nurtured ties between the Quakers and the college while seeking contributions from the Friends meetings.

WHITTIER AUDITORIUM, 1896–1967. The Wilmington Yearly Meeting met for the first few years in large tents on campus. After a downpour one year, funds were raised to build the auditorium for $4,500. In 1896, the auditorium was built to hold nearly 2,000 attendees. The building was remodeled in the 1920s to accommodate the college gymnasium.

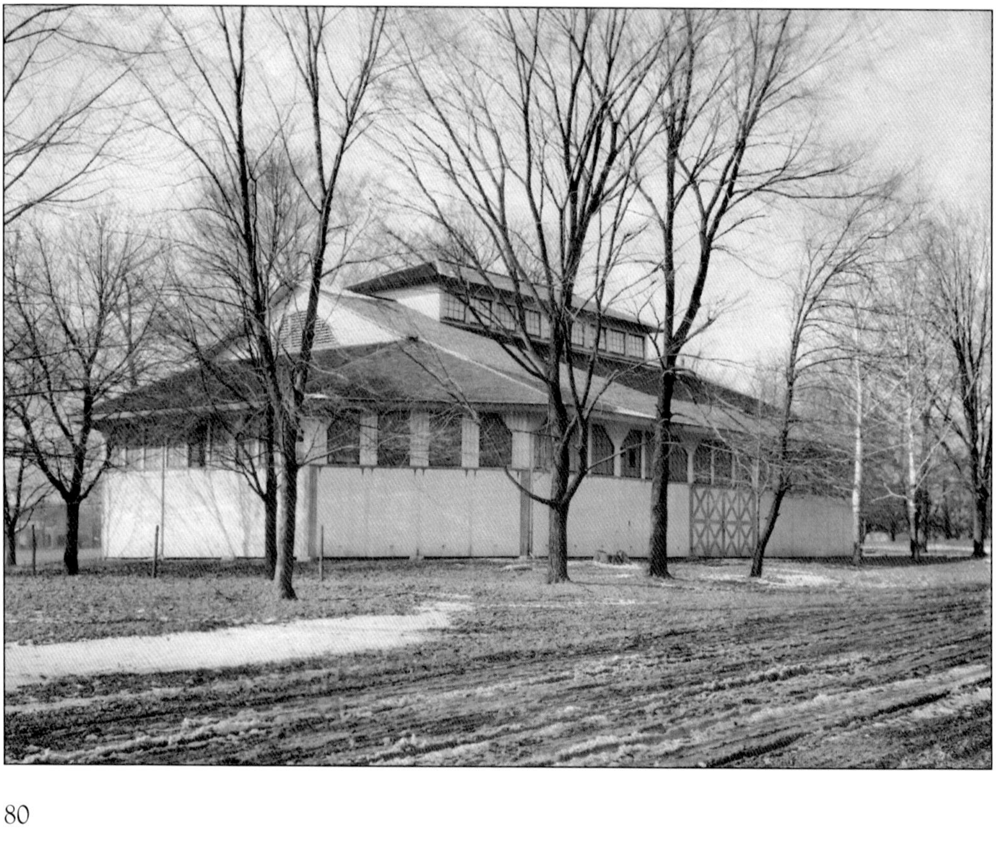

DR. ELIZABETH SHRIEVES. Shrieves graduated from Wilmington College in 1884 and became the first female physician in Wilmington after receiving her medical degree. She attended clinics throughout Europe and equipped the infirmary in Denver Hall.

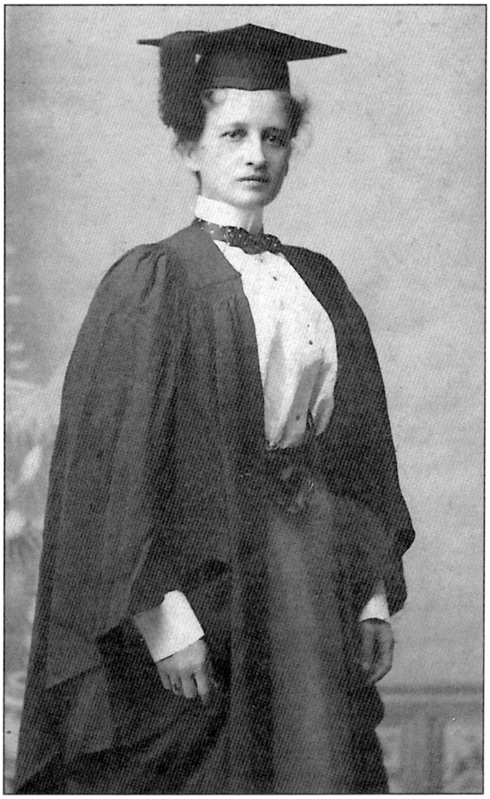

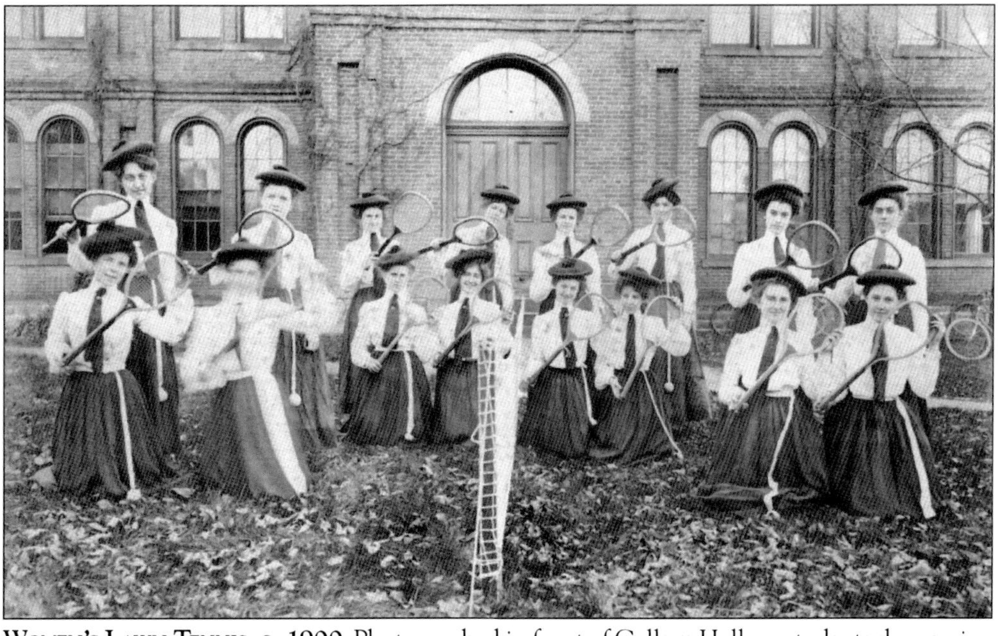

WOMEN'S LAWN TENNIS, C. 1900. Photographed in front of College Hall are students showcasing one of the earliest intramural sports on campus. Intercollegiate sports did not start until 1900, with men's football. Other early intramural sports included baseball, croquet, and horseshoes. (Courtesy of Wilmington College.)

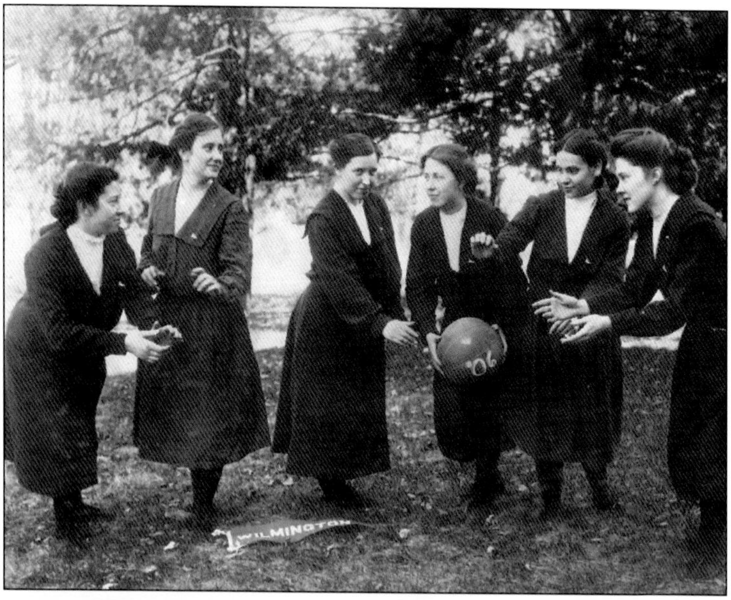

WOMEN'S BASKETBALL, 1906. Pictured are Ethel Hawkins Wall, Pearl Peelle Hiatt, Nellie Thornburg, Carrie Thornburg, Daisy Wright Rannells, and Ila McKay Haworth. The 1907 team was noteworthy for defeating Ohio State University. (Courtesy of Wilmington College.)

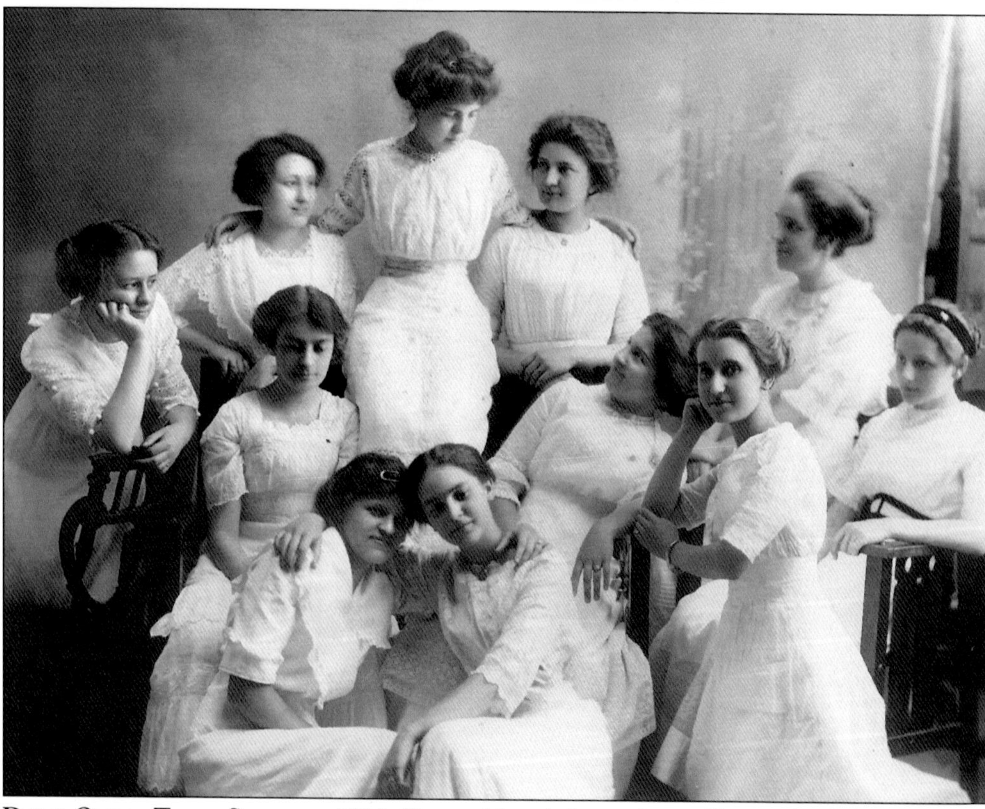

DELTA OMEGA THETA SORORITY, 1912. Pictured from left to right are (first row) Edith Hiatt Frazer and Alice Kerns; (second row) Ruby Fisher Evans, Faye Hiatt Hunt, Esther Doan Starbuck, Sylvia and Sanders Miars; (third row) Mary Kelly Farquhar, Ethel Thompson Wildman, Esther Malone, Lovena Bales Elliot, and Faith Austin Terrell. The president of the college allowed the women from town to form the college's first recognized Greek society in 1907.

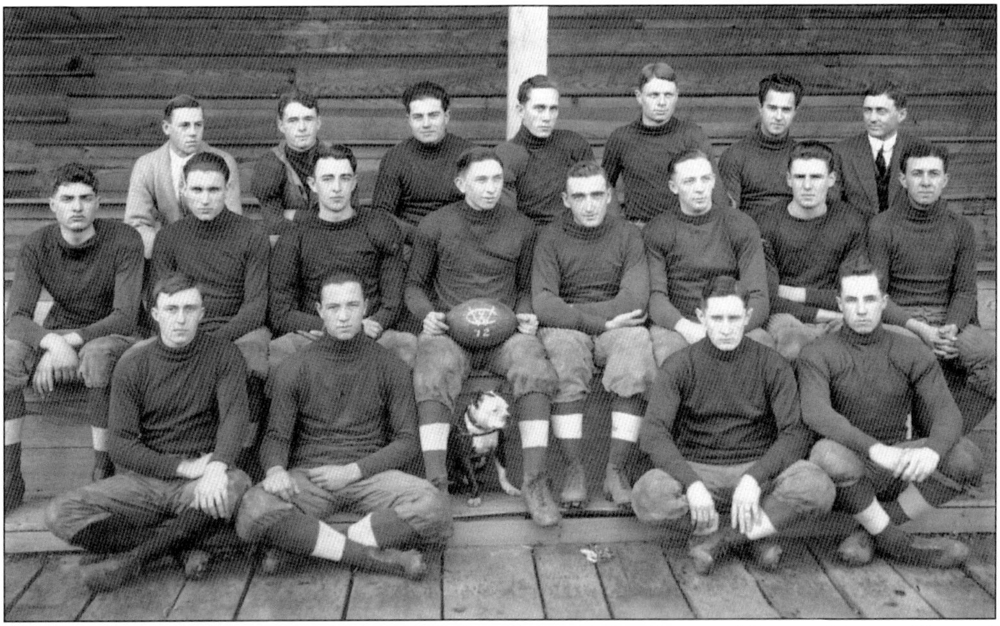

Football Team, 1912. The team included, from left to right, (first row) Everett Haines, Howard Falkner, Clarence Renner, and Willard Stowe; (second row) Sidney Brown, Frank Truitt, Howard Holliday, Ralph Miars, John Lewis, Frank Oren, Pliny Powers, and Hermann Tenner; (third row) Tasso Morgan, Thomas Kelly, Gail Clevenger, Willard Wildman, Ralph Thornburg, Denver Williams, and Tom Bales. The first intercollegiate football game was played in 1900 against Lebanon Normal College. Wilmington won 6-0. (Courtesy of Wilmington College.)

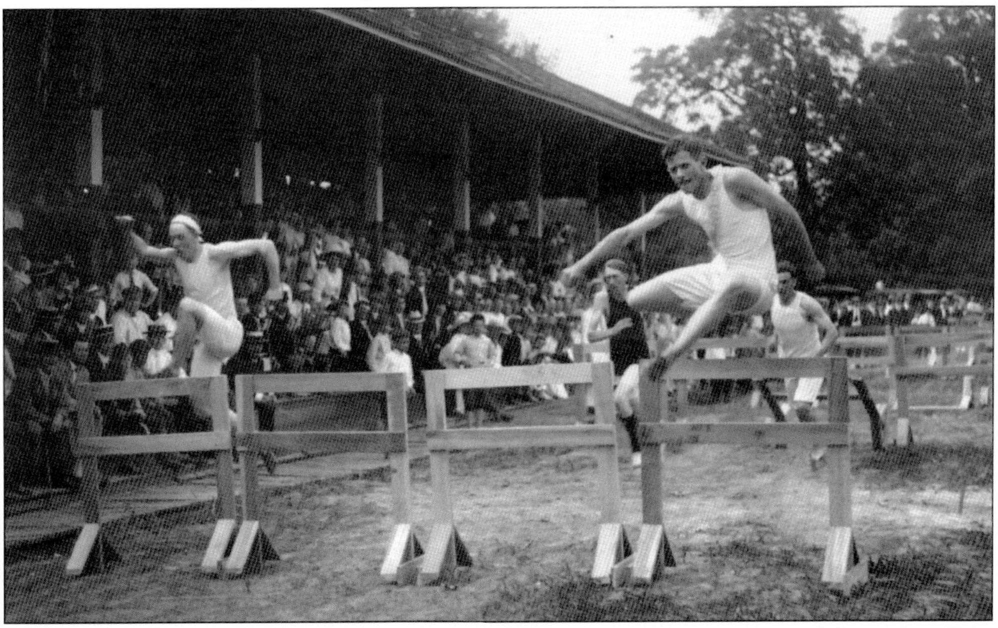

May Day Track Meet, 1915. Track and field events were an important part of the early college years, despite the lack of a suitable track. In 1905, Matthew Rombach Denver offered a trophy to the outstanding track star of the year. The Denver Field Day was held annually from 1905 to 1917. (Courtesy of Wilmington College.)

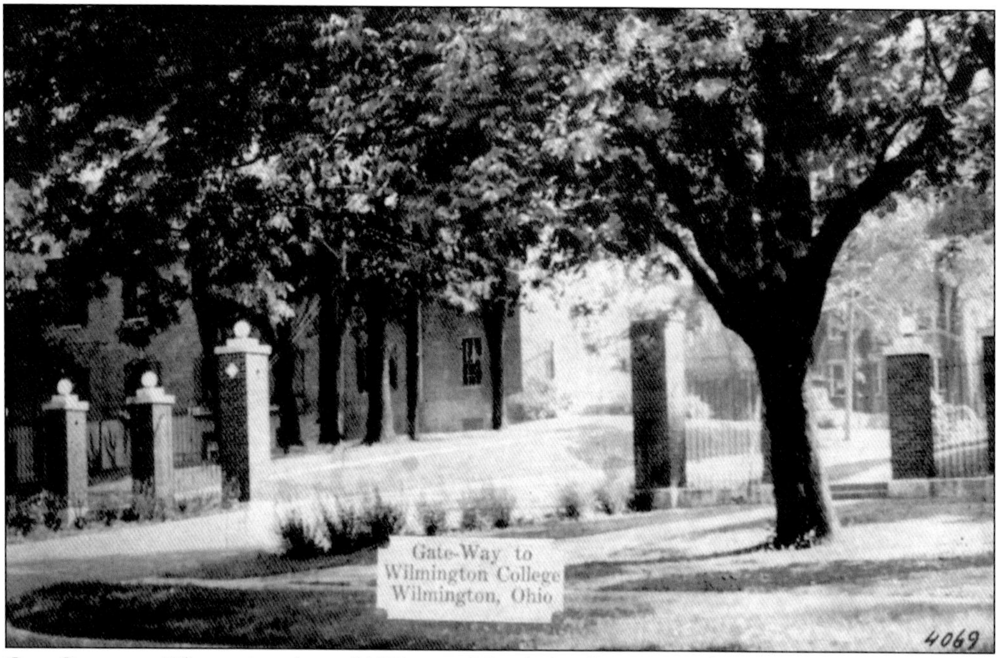

OLD GATEWAY. The senior class of 1919 raised funds for the gateway located at Whittier Place to enhance the entranceway to the college. Whittier Place was closed in 1958 as a safety measure to protect student pedestrians.

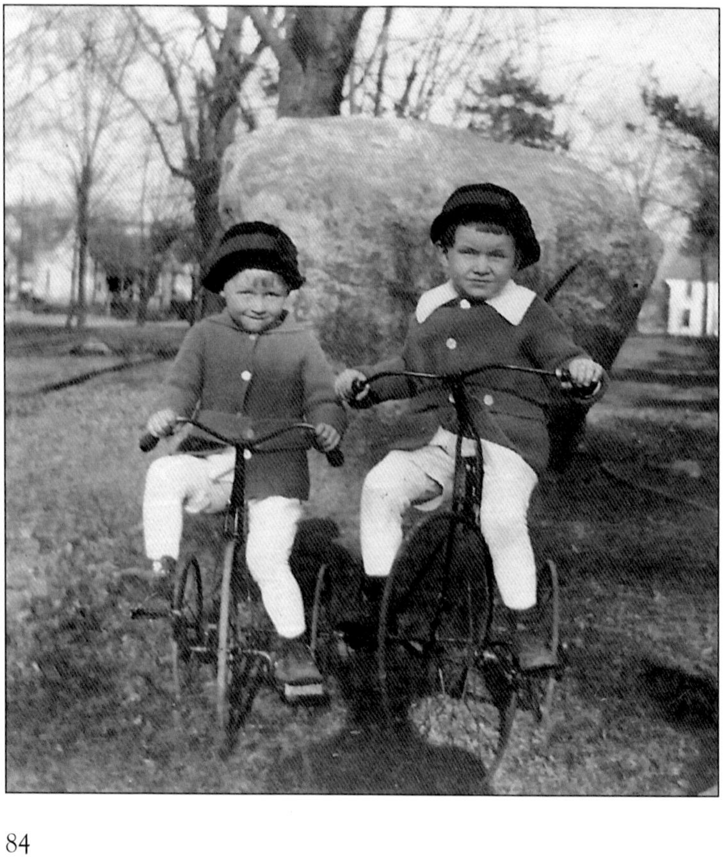

COLLEGE ROCK, 1920. This college landmark is composed of metamorphosed granite from the Wisconsin glacial period and contains red garnets. The class of 1906 doggedly moved the rock from its location at the infirmary to the front of the college. Pictured are Joe Brann (left) and Dick Bath. Legend has it that a couple who kisses for the first time by the rock will marry. Another college tradition is the painting of the rock by school organizations.

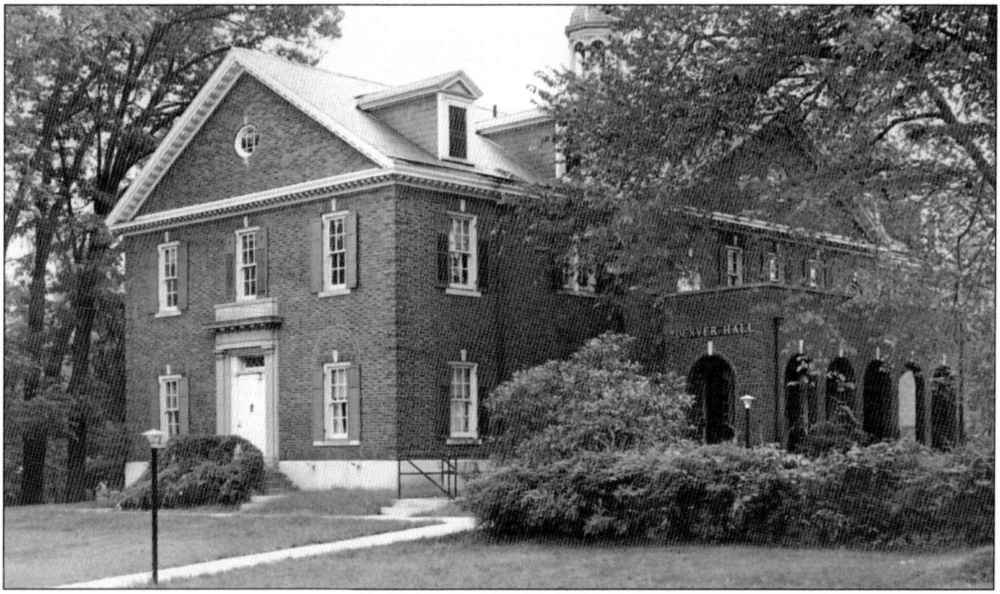

DENVER HALL. Built in 1925, the funds for this building were donated by Matthew and Veda Denver to honor their daughter Kathryn, who was killed by a train. It became a women's dormitory and dining room. The dining hall remained here until 1958, when the Pyle Center opened. It is the third oldest building on campus today after College Hall and Bailey Hall. (Courtesy of Wilmington College.)

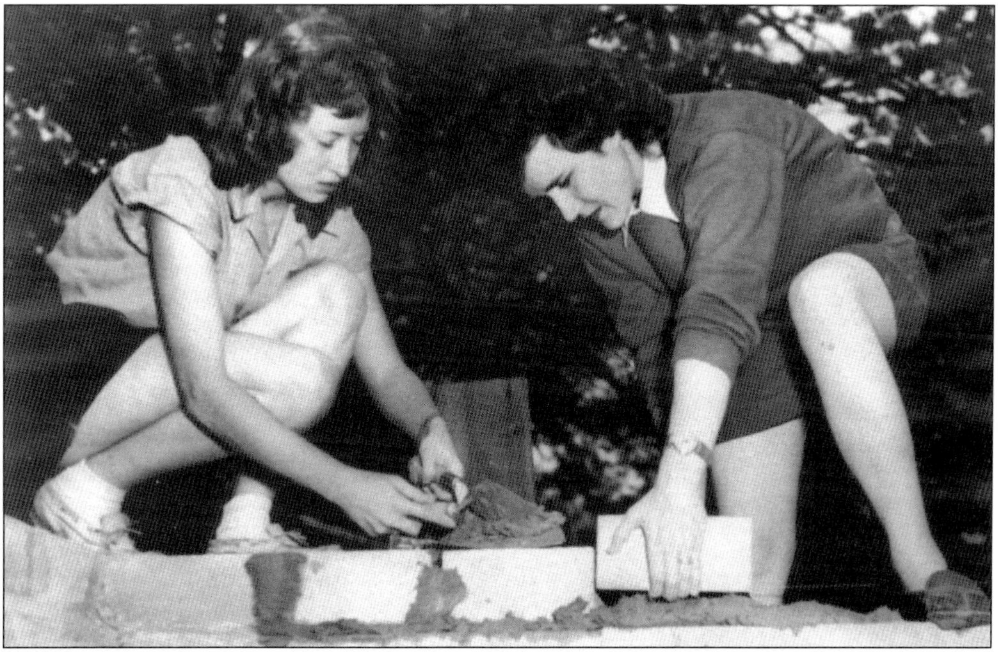

MARBLE HALL, 1940S. Faced with a staggering influx of World War II veterans, enrollment skyrocketed from 105 students in 1944 to 550 in 1946, and the college faced demand for new dormitories. Pres. Samuel Marble challenged students and faculty to build a dormitory. While a professional contractor oversaw the work, students and staff worked on the project for two years. The building is still used as a dormitory. (Courtesy of Wilmington College.)

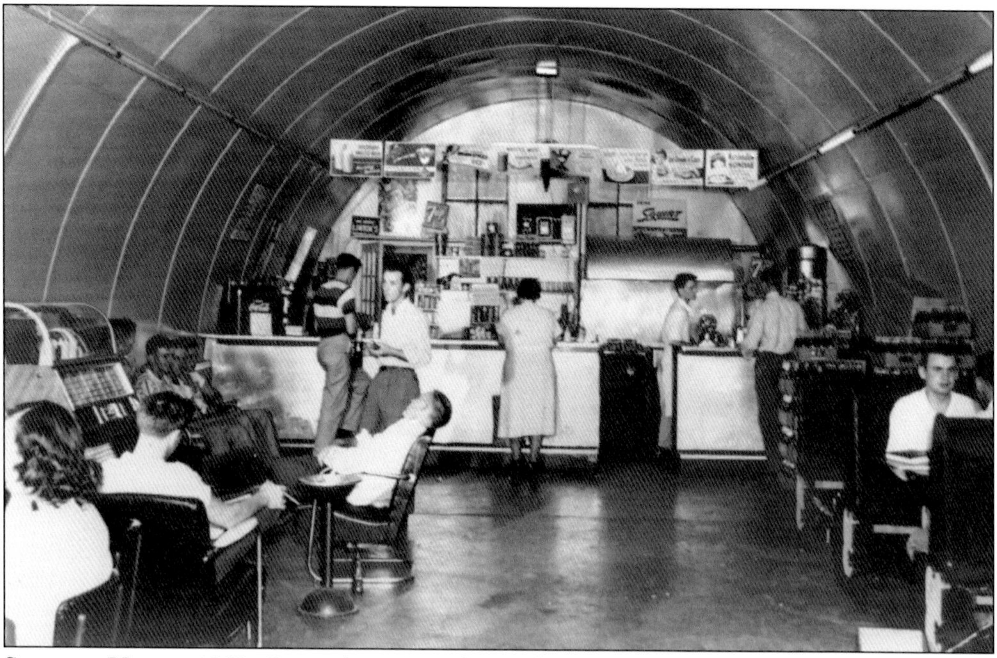

STUDENT UNION, 1953. Opened in 1948, the student union, known as the Cove, served the burgeoning student population's appetite for entertainment. The building was a converted surplus Quonset hut that included a jukebox, a dance floor, and a student-run snack bar. (Courtesy of Wilmington College.)

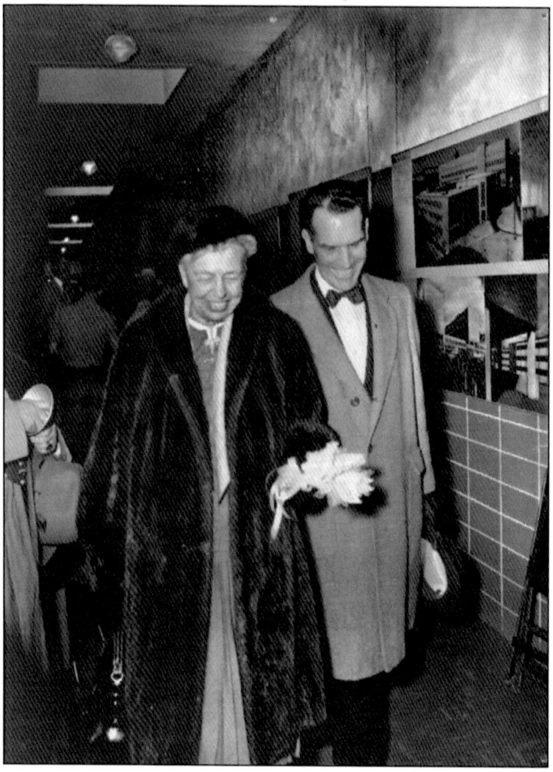

ELEANOR ROOSEVELT, 1958. Roosevelt is pictured here with college president Samuel Marble. Roosevelt attended the annual International Folk and Music Festival, which began in 1948 and continued through the early 1980s. Other famous speakers at the festival have included poet Carl Sandburg, British prime minister Clement Attlee, and author Pearl S. Buck. (Courtesy of Wilmington College.)

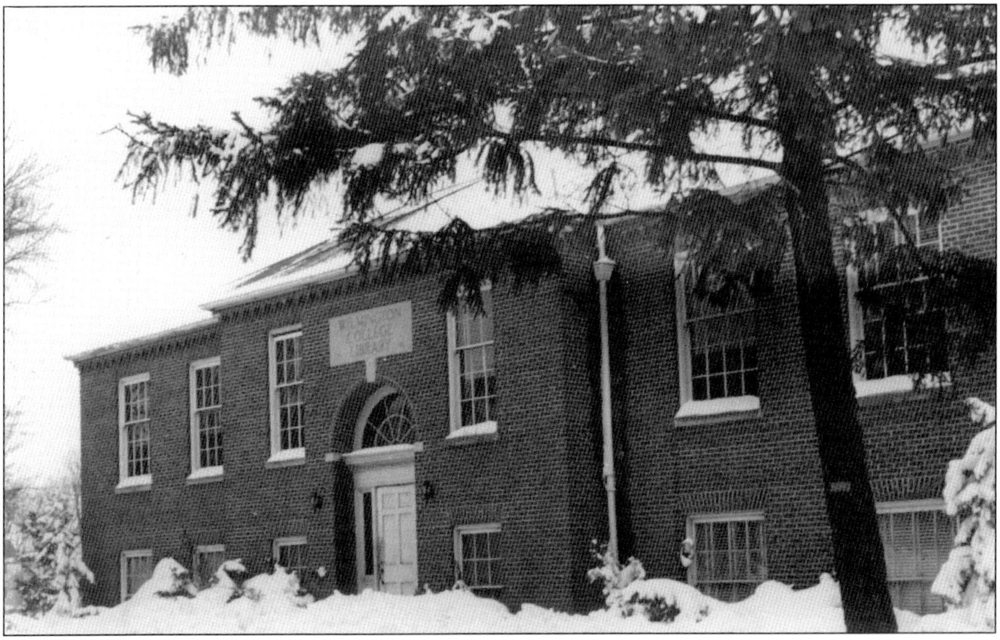

WATSON LIBRARY. The first library was housed in College Hall on the second floor, but college accreditation standards necessitated a new building (pictured above). Constructed in 1941 for $42,000, the library was named after Sheppard Watson, president from 1940 to 1947. The collection contains more than 100,000 titles, as well as a special collection of Quaker books and documents, and items housed at the Peace Resource Center. (Courtesy of Wilmington College.)

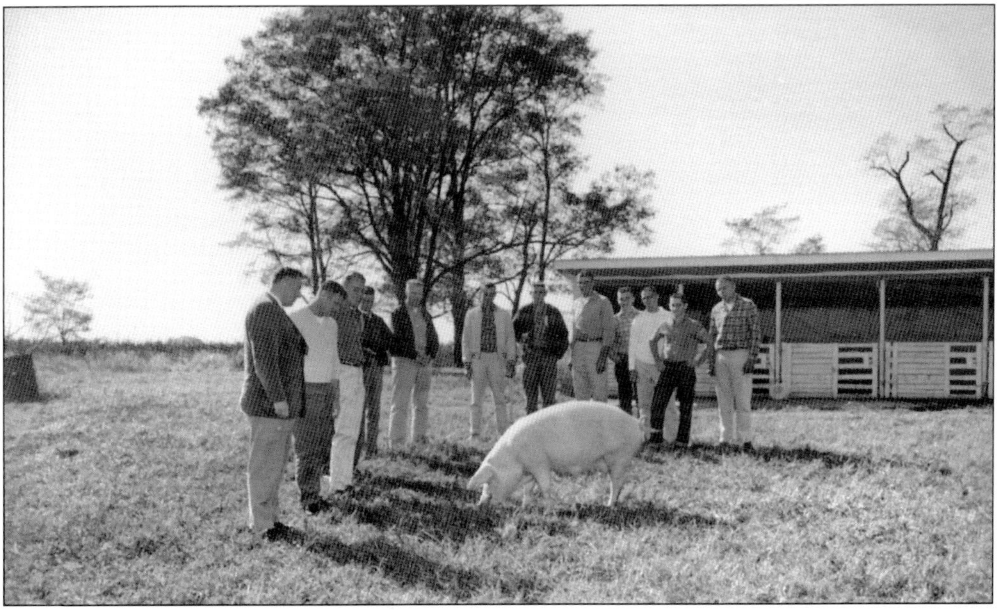

AGRICULTURE DEPARTMENT, 1954. Roy Joe Stuckey (standing at far left) established the agriculture department in 1948. It is currently one of only two baccalaureate programs in agriculture in the state. The college owns more than 1,300 acres of farmland, which is used by the students for educational and research purposes or is leased to other farmers. Stuckey served as a farm manager, professor, and trustee. (Courtesy of Wilmington College.)

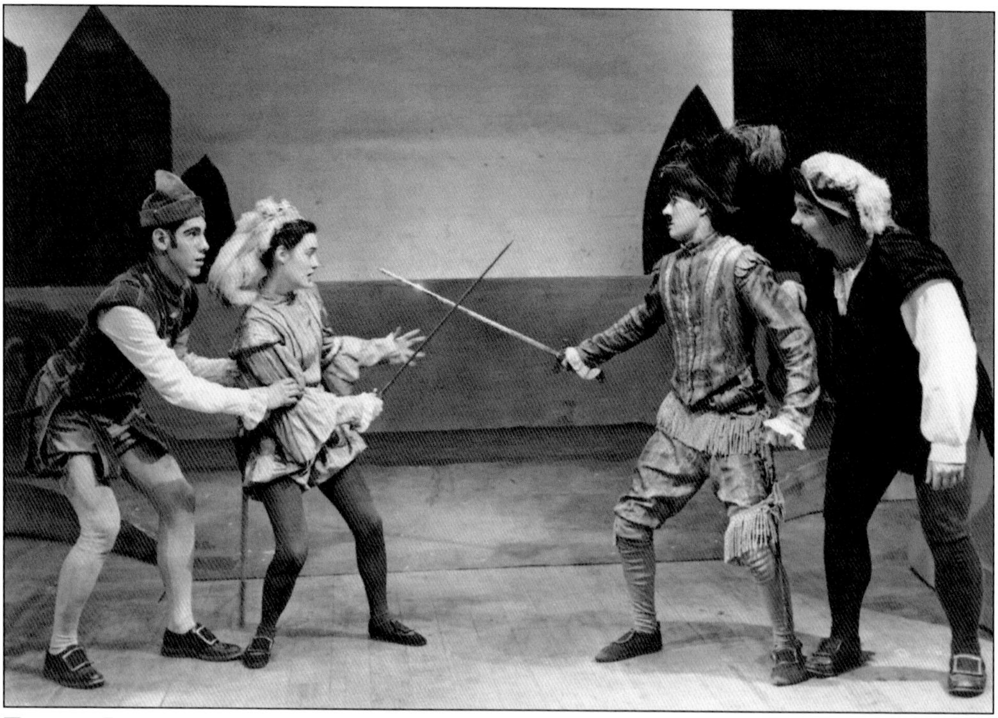

Theater Department, 1958. While the college did not include a formal study of the arts during its early years, it eventually became well known for its theater productions. *Twelfth Night* was directed by Lewis Marcuson, and the sets were designed by Hugh Heiland. Perhaps the theater department's best-known student was Gary Sandy, who starred in *WKRP in Cincinnati* in the late 1970s and early 1980s. (Courtesy of Wilmington College.)

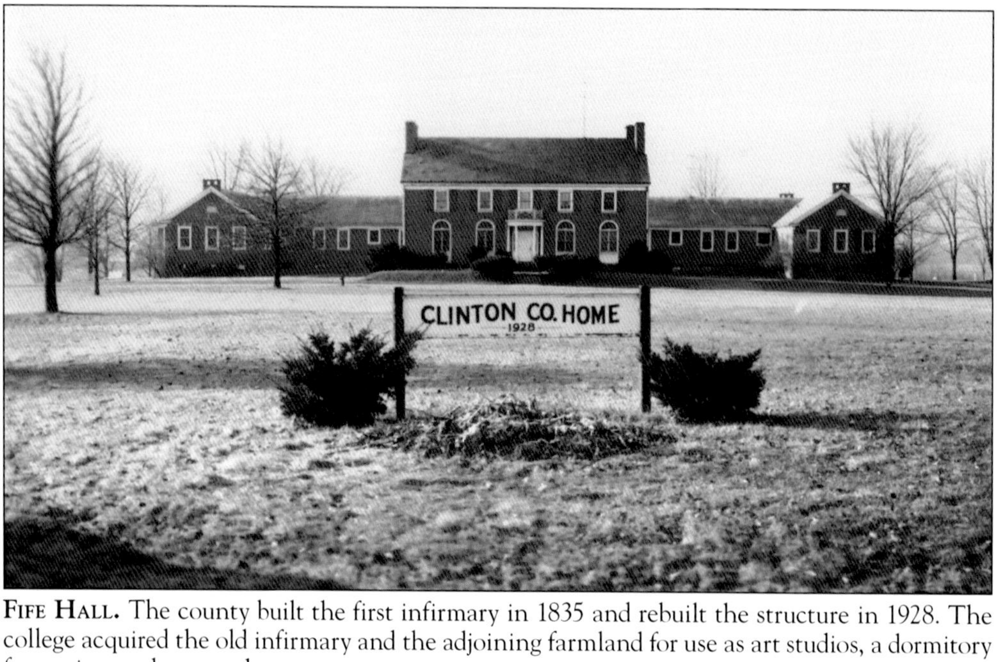

Fife Hall. The county built the first infirmary in 1835 and rebuilt the structure in 1928. The college acquired the old infirmary and the adjoining farmland for use as art studios, a dormitory for equine students, and as storage space.

Eight

Commerce

Much of Wilmington's contemporary downtown remains a manifestation of Wilmington's past, as numerous original buildings and storefronts still stand. The tenants may have changed over the years, but Wilmington's citizens can still walk downtown to a bank, a restaurant, an inn, or a theater, along with stores and government offices, just as they have been able to do during the city's 200-year history.

A few of Wilmington's earliest businesses are still crafting quality products, whether they continue to operate in the area, such as Champion Bridge, or whether they have moved to other locations, such as Farquhar Furnace or Irwin Auger Bit. The descendants of the man considered the town's first permanent merchant, Warren Sabin, continue to run a wholesale distributorship on Main Street—almost 200 years after the entrepreneurial spirit moved the original Sabin to open his doors.

Some of the businesses in Wilmington's past have gained national attention over the years, such as Hygienic Productions film production company or Ernest Hazard's Café, which many consider the birthplace of the banana split.

Various industries have come and gone, but family-run businesses have long pushed Wilmington's economy forward and continue to do so today, such as the Roberts family's R+L Carriers or the Ferneau family's Ferno-Washington Company, both of which are headquartered in Wilmington.

Wilmington's businesses have supported the area's farmers since the town began, and today the closest thing to a skyscraper in town belongs to Buckley Brothers, at 320 East Main Street. Brothers George and Parker Buckley began their grain and feed business in 1904, and it remains a family-owned operation.

In a town where bankers still know customers by name, where doctors have treated generations within families, where photographers capture weddings of those whose baby portraits they created, and where family-run florists provide flowers for the grandchildren of original customers, commerce has always had a personal touch.

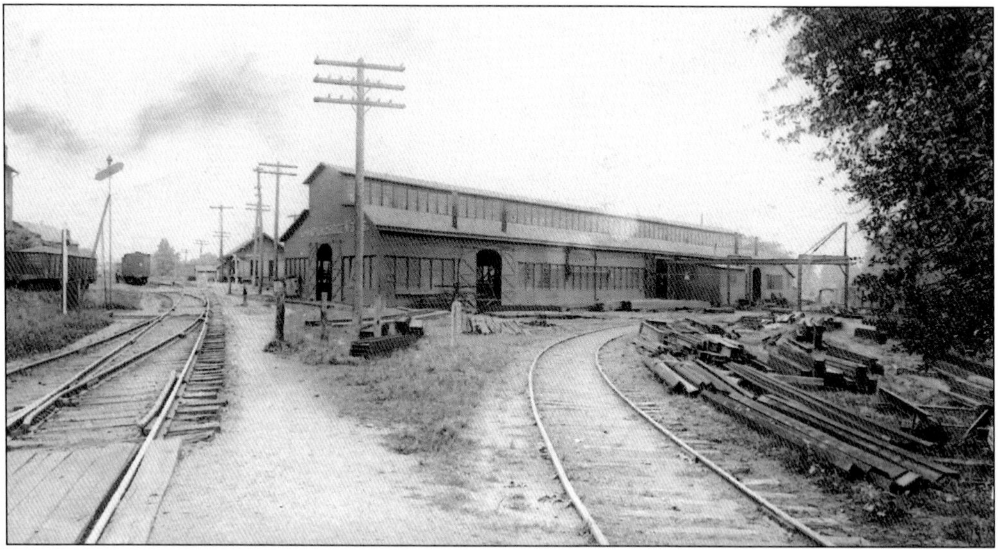

Champion Bridge. In 1860, when Zimri Wall was 24, he built timber bridges across Clinton County, although the Civil War brought road and bridge construction to a halt. Zimri Wall and Company built the Martinsville Road covered bridge, with the final payment made in 1871, and it is known as the oldest "Champion Bridge" because Wall later founded the Champion Bridge Company with his brother, Jonathan, and Albert Bailey in 1872. It is the oldest continuously operating business in Wilmington. Pictured below is the metal arch bridge at J. W. Denver Williams Jr. Memorial Park. The bridge was one of the first such bridges manufactured by Champion and is located near a popular duck-feeding area. It was relocated from Laymon Road. (Below, courtesy of Eileen Brady's collection.)

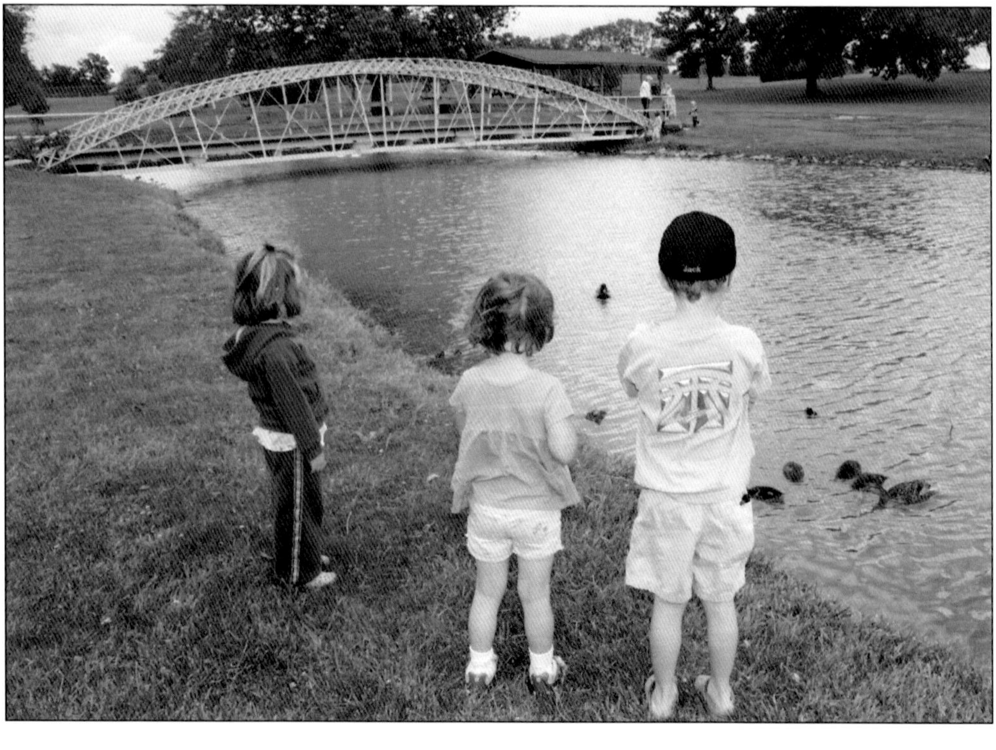

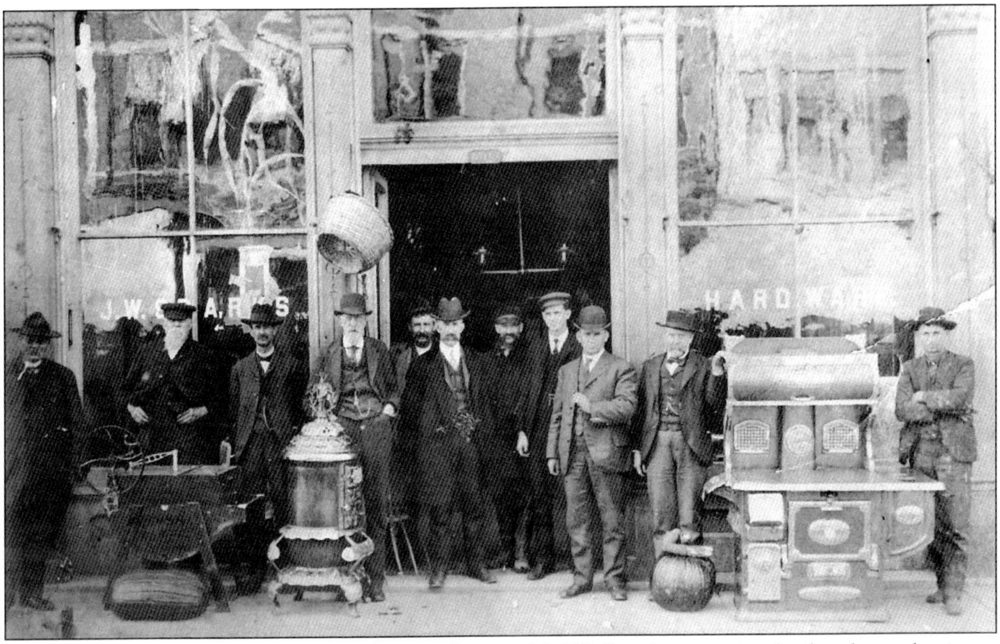

SPARKS HARDWARE, C. 1880. Frank Farquhar and J. W. Sparks were in the hardware business together when they started a galvanized iron business and began to install roofs, ceilings, and cornice work. Later the businesses were separated; Sparks continued with hardware until 1915, and Farquhar, along with sons Henry and Milton, took over the galvanized iron business, eventually patenting a furnace sold through Farquhar Furnace.

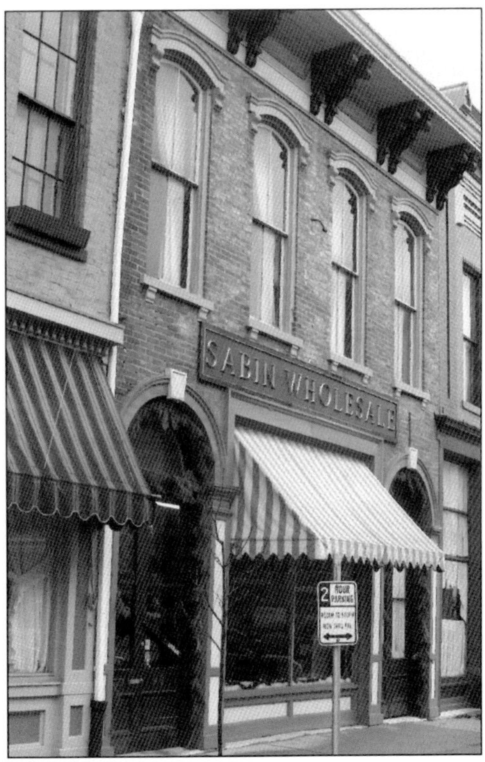

SABIN LEGACY. The first permanent merchant in Wilmington is generally considered to be Warren Sabin, who kept a tavern and inn in a log building on North South Street; his license (the first was issued to Larkin Reynolds) was granted on October 10, 1811, and Sabin's sign hung for nearly 40 years. The current Sabin Wholesale on Main Street, owned by descendants of Warren Sabin, represents Wilmington's longest existing entrepreneurial family. (Courtesy of Eileen Brady's collection.)

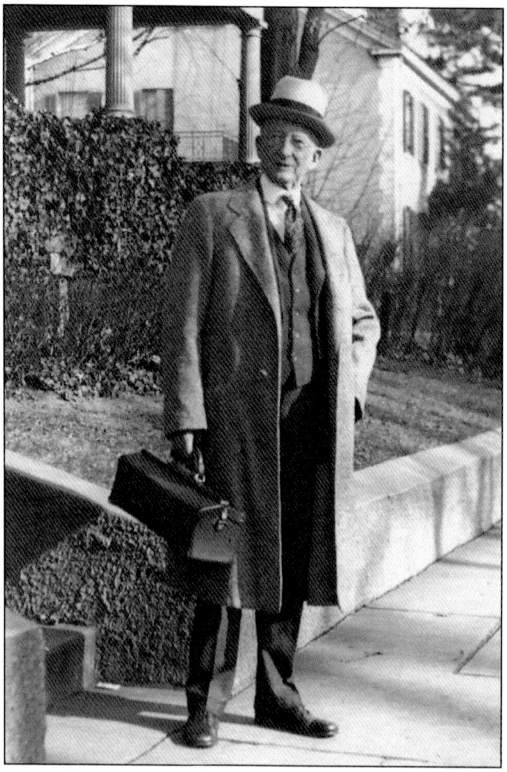

Dr. George Wood (1856–1935). Wood practiced medicine in Wilmington for nearly 50 years, beginning in 1886. His obituary stated, "Dr. Wood was known to almost everyone in Wilmington and Clinton County" because of his continuous service, broken only during three months' service at the Ohio Soldiers' and Sailors' Orphans Home in Xenia.

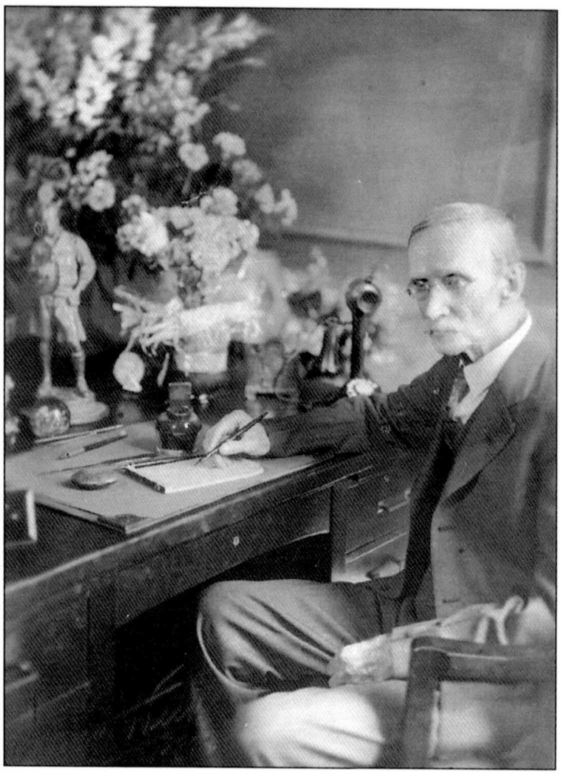

Flag Tower Creator. In 1889, Andrew Wilson (1869–1943), married to Hannah Custis, was named vice president of First National Bank of Wilmington. It was Wilson's idea to build, at his own expense, a 150-foot steel tower with a concrete platform 10 feet off the ground. The platform, near the corner of the courthouse, was used for city summer band concerts, and the flag tower was sometimes covered with colored electric lights.

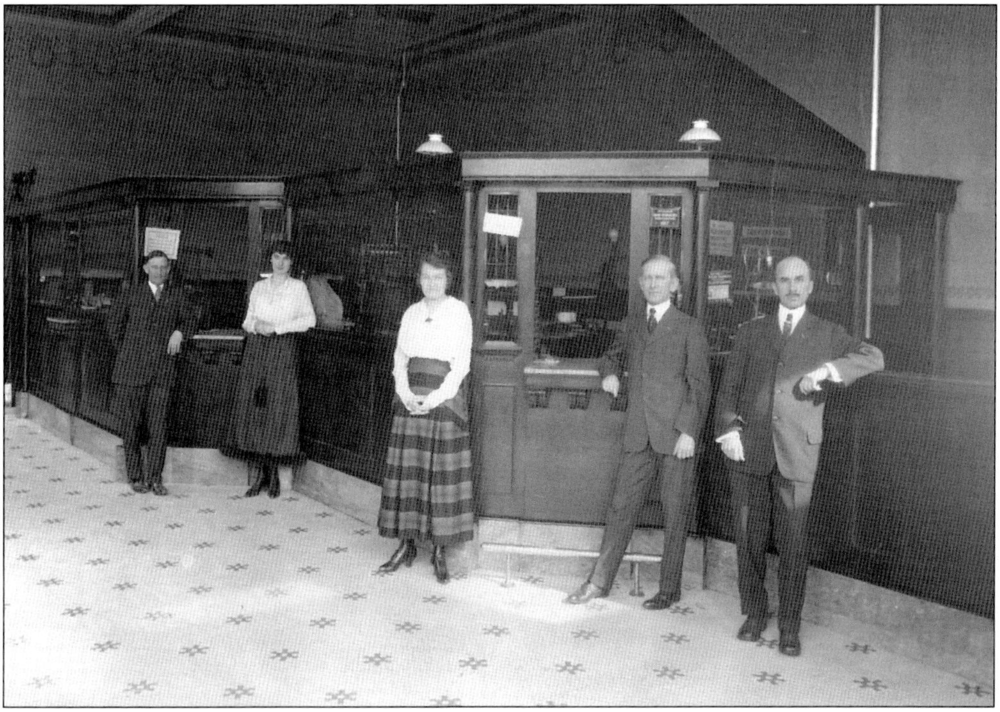

Citizens National Bank. Employees at Citizens National Bank are F. M. Harlan, Della Hadley, Dora Smith, William Fife, and I. N. Nair.

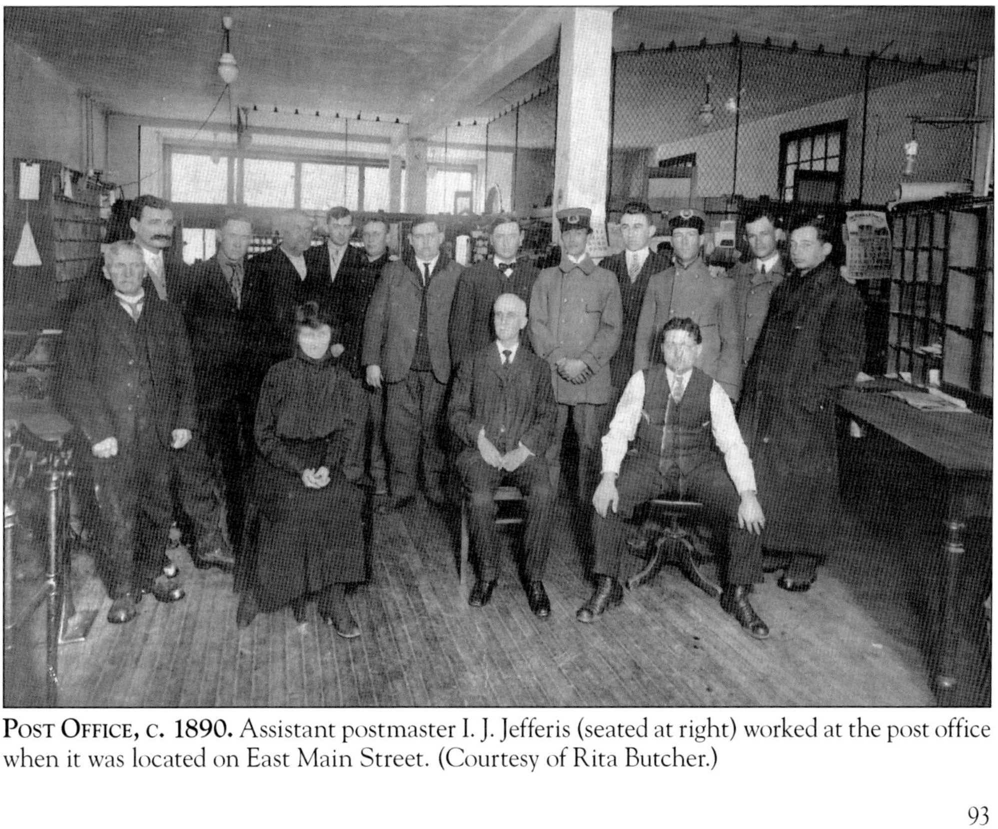

Post Office, c. 1890. Assistant postmaster I. J. Jefferis (seated at right) worked at the post office when it was located on East Main Street. (Courtesy of Rita Butcher.)

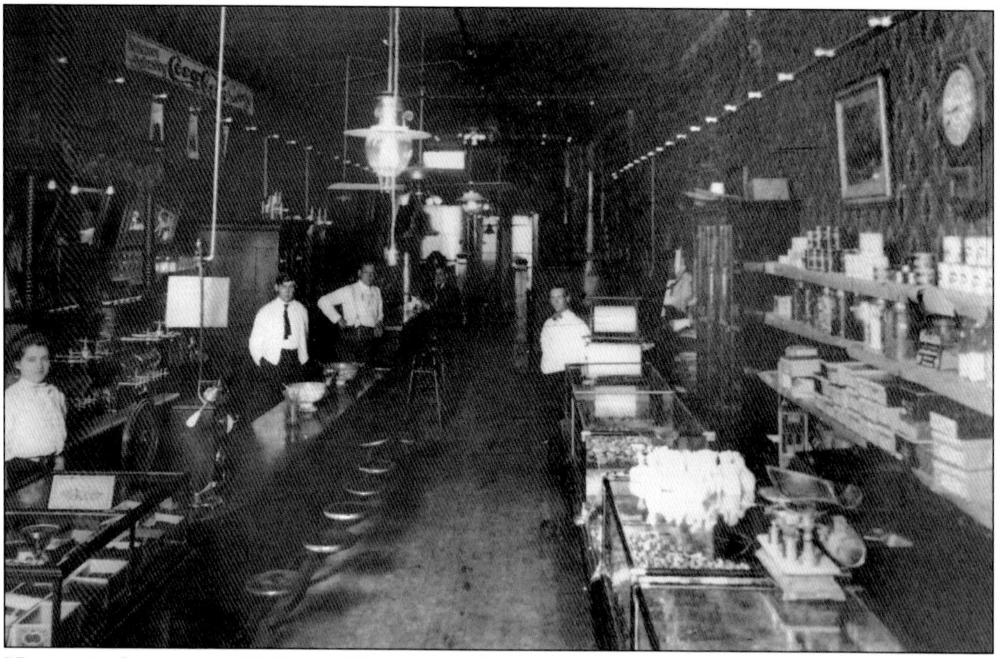

HAZARD'S CAFE, c. 1907. Ernest Hazard (third from left) owned the restaurant on North South Street that many believe served the first banana split in 1907, as a way to attract Wilmington College students. Note the 10¢ price of the banana split. Folks in Latrobe, Pennsylvania, claim the banana split was invented there in 1904.

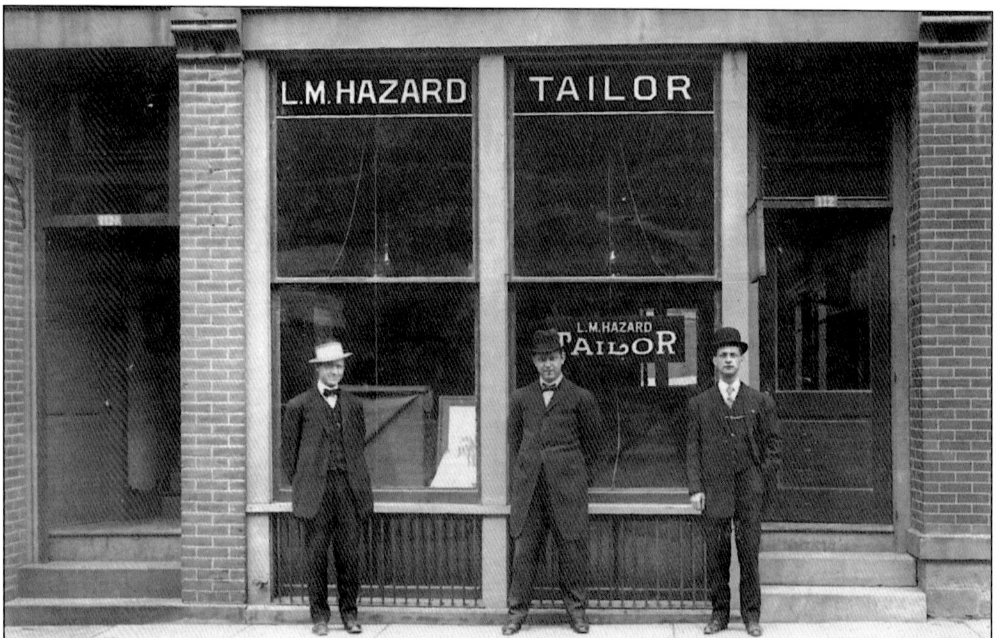

DOWNTOWN TAILOR, 1914. Loren Hazard was the son of Frank and Luella Miars Hazard of Wilmington. Frank was a hardware salesman. Loren Hazard learned the tailoring trade while working for William Sharkey. He then opened his own shop at 112 East Locust Street. Hazard's brother, Ethelbert, owned a laundry.

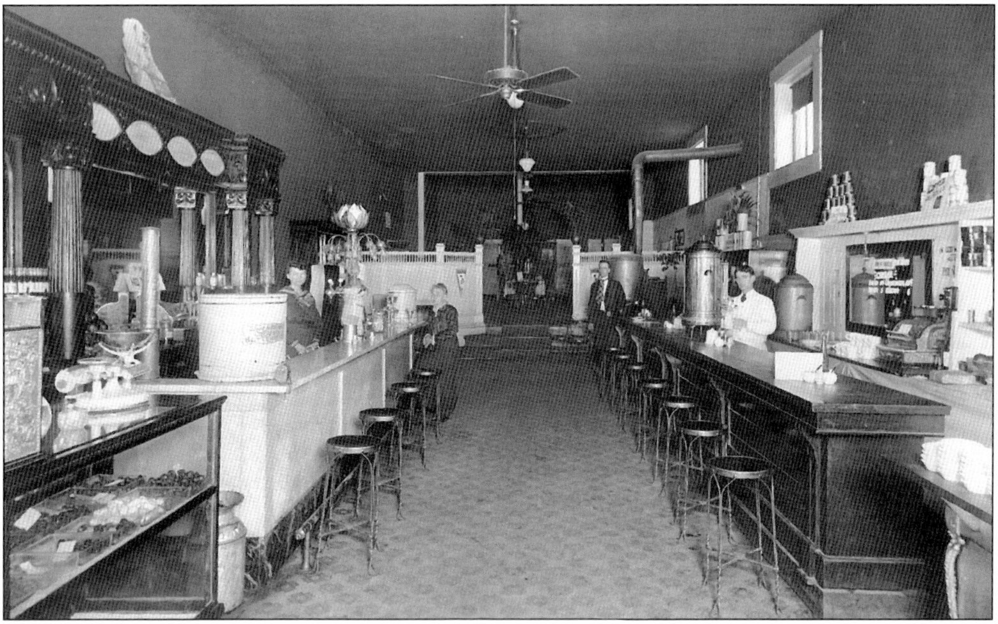

DINNER AT THE PALM. The Palm Restaurant and Confectionery on Main Street was owned by Jim Swisshelm, standing in the background. His wife, Carmen Swisshelm, is shown behind the counter on the left, with his mother, Mary Swisshelm, seated on a stool, and his brother, Charles Swisshelm, behind the counter on the right. Jim and Carmen Swisshelm had two daughters: Regina Swisshelm and Kathryn Moore.

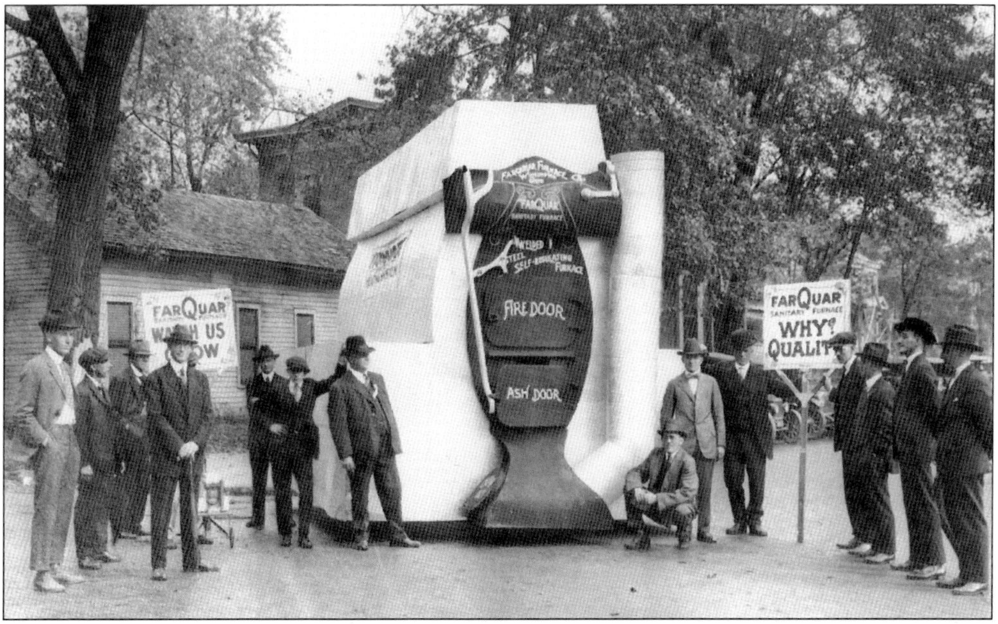

FARQUAR SANITARY FURNACE. The furnace was displayed at Locust and Walnut Streets. Organized in 1887, Farquhar Furnace Company received offers from other cities to relocate, but the directors kept the plant in Wilmington. An advertisement in the May 27, 1922, *National Geographic* magazine touted the "one-piece, electrically welded steel firebox, which positively prevents the escape of gases or the contamination of the warmed air."

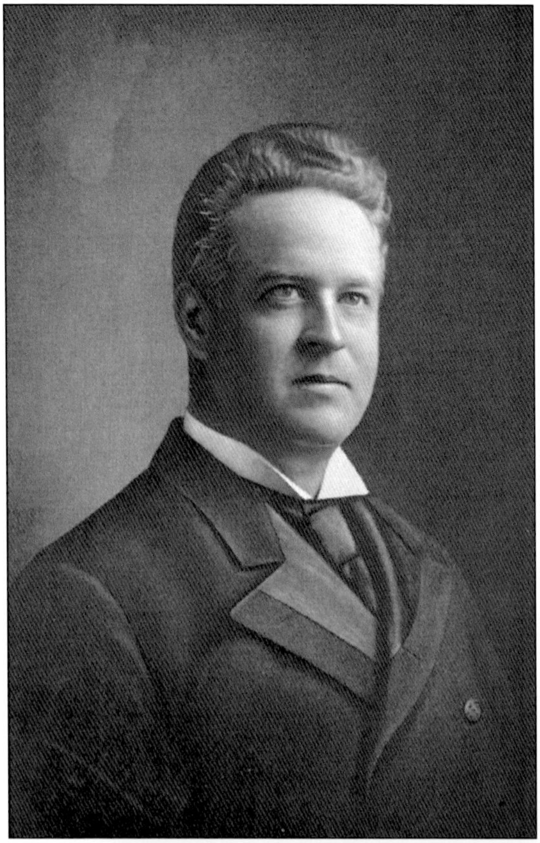

MATTHEW ROMBACH DENVER (1870–1954). The son of Gen. James W. Denver, Denver attended Wilmington public schools and graduated in 1892 from Georgetown University. He was the president of the Clinton County National Bank and was a U.S. representative from Ohio's 6th District from 1907 to 1913. He declined to be a candidate for reelection to the 63rd Congress. He returned to Wilmington to resume banking. He is buried in Sugar Grove Cemetery.

WILMINGTON PAPERBOYS, C. 1920. At one time, Wilmington had several competing daily papers. The Wilmington *Daily News Journal* used newsboys around 1920 for quick delivery. Pictured below from left to right are (seated) Arthur Howe, Lewis Sutton, Roderick Cowgill, Kenneth Probasco, and Maynard Ames; (standing) Dean Wolfe, Max Pemberton, Rollo Dunlap, Paul Pennington, Harold Howe, Glenn Curtis, Mason Dunlap, and Wayland Gillespie. Grace Willett was in charge of distributing papers and collecting money.

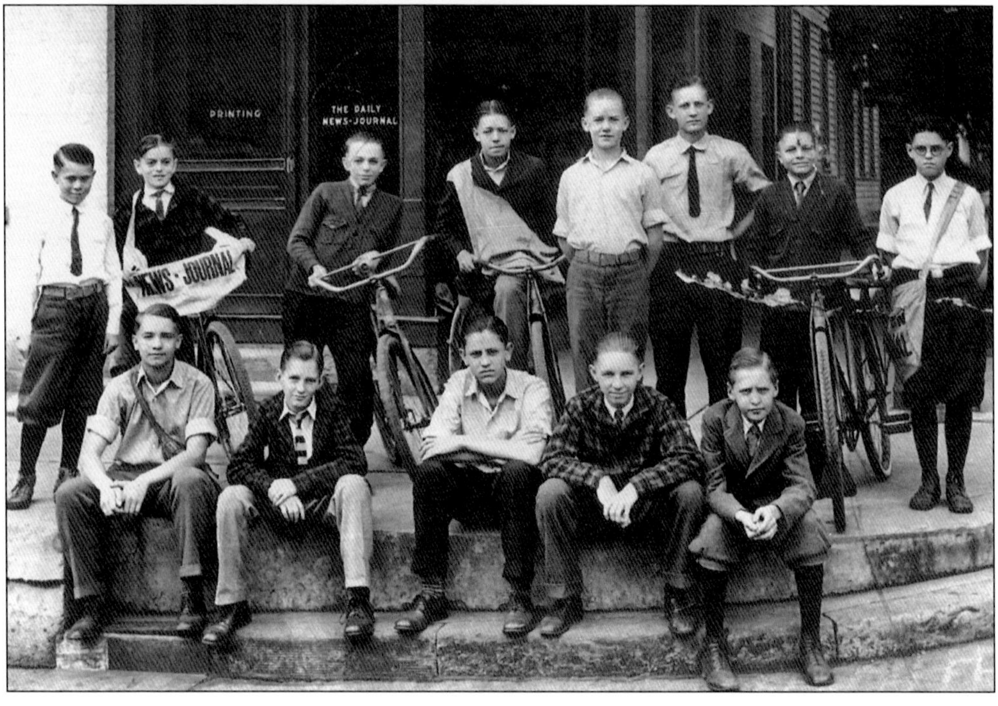

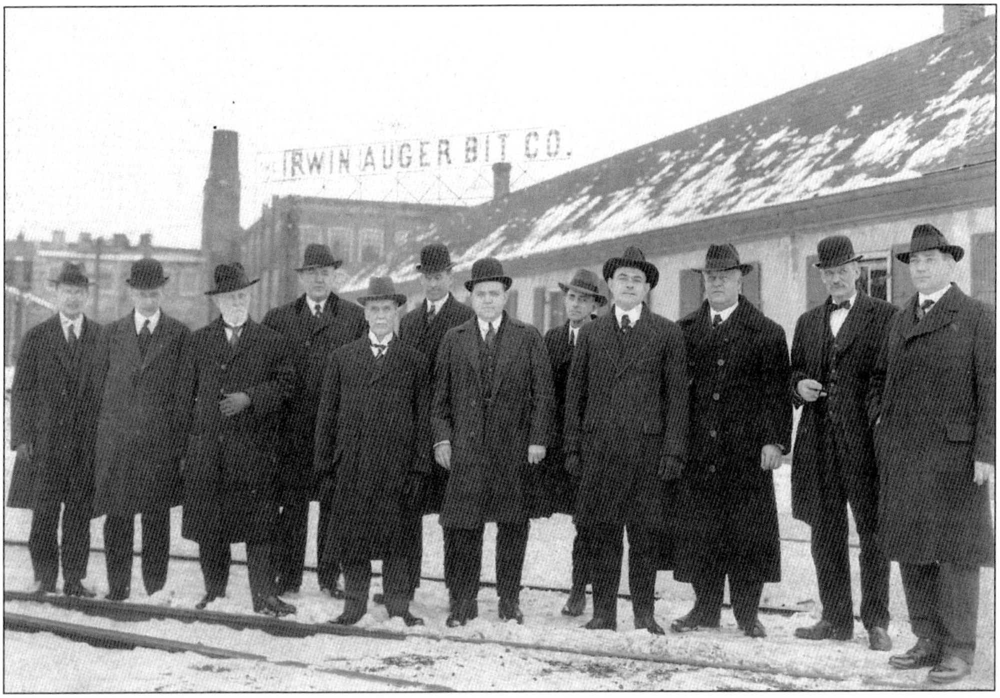

IRWIN AUGER BIT. In 1916, members of the staff at Irwin Auger Bit Company are, from left to right, B. M. Hiatt, Charles Miller, William Vrooman, John Gregg, J. Mortimer, E. L. Culin, G. M. Riley, Scott Molyheaux, L. L. Sullivan, Matthew Rombach Denver, J. R. Clevenger, and S. A. Mitchell. Irwin was the first business in Wilmington to enter the global market. Below, employee Jobe Clevenger was honored in 1943 for 50 years of service at Irwin.

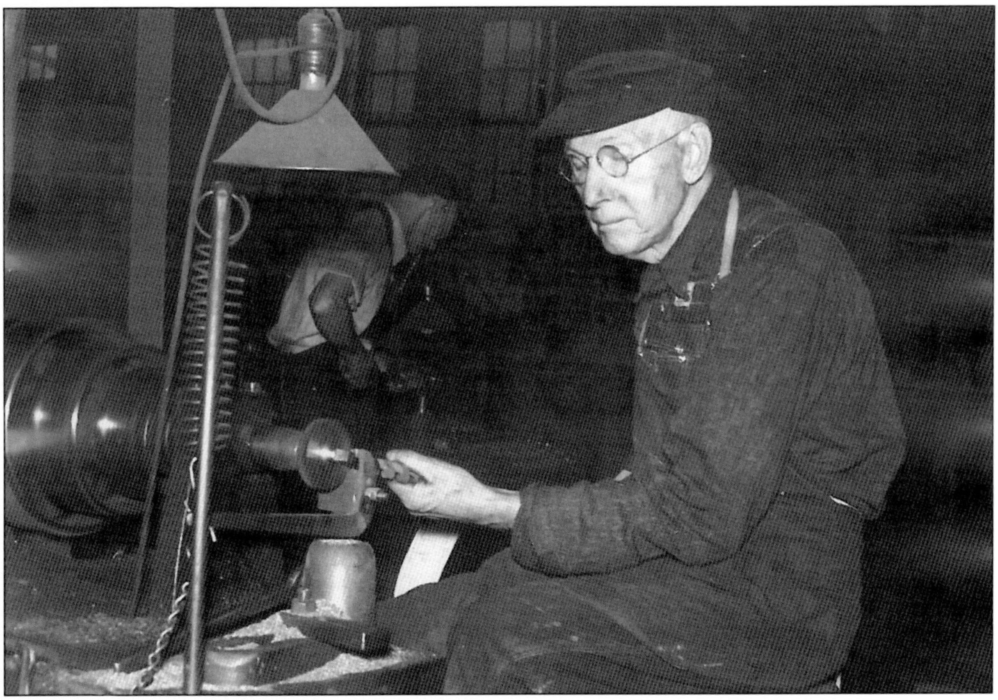

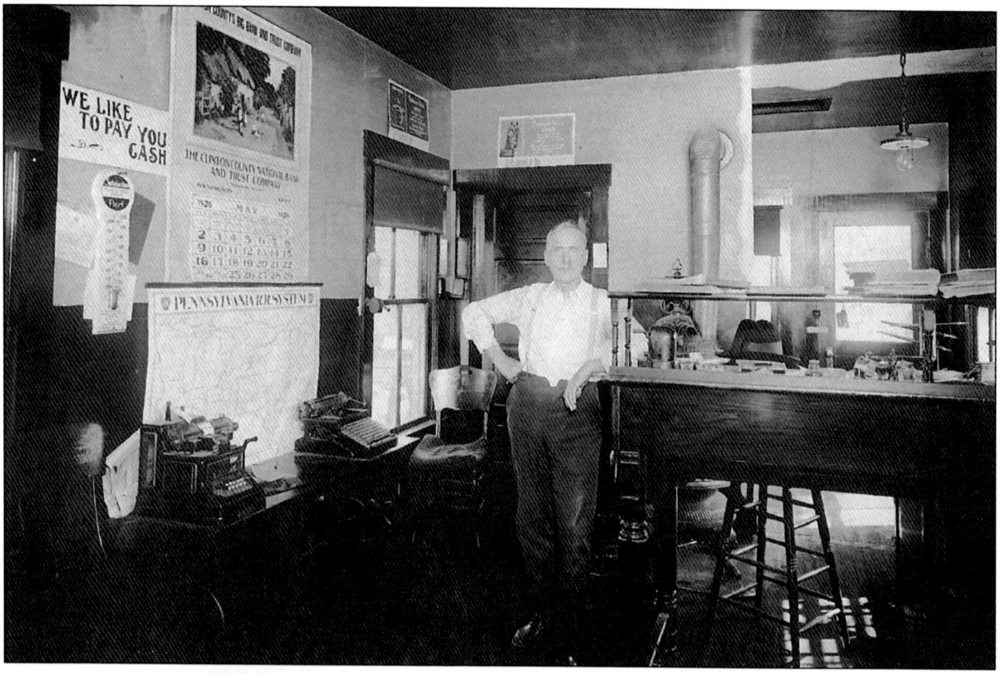

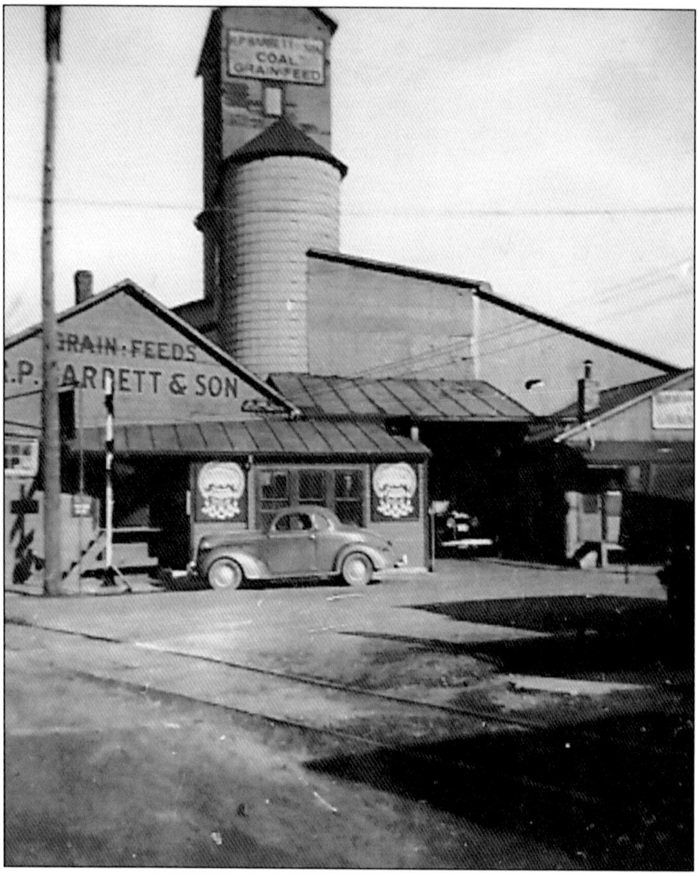

BARRETT AND SONS. Around 1917, Ruben Putnam Barrett (pictured above) built this feed, grain, and coal business, R. P. Barrett and Sons, at the corner of Walnut and Sugartree Streets. R. P. Barrett worked with his son H. A. Barrett and his grandson H. Briggs Barrett but sold the business in 1944. (Both, courtesy of Jean Rachford Barrett.)

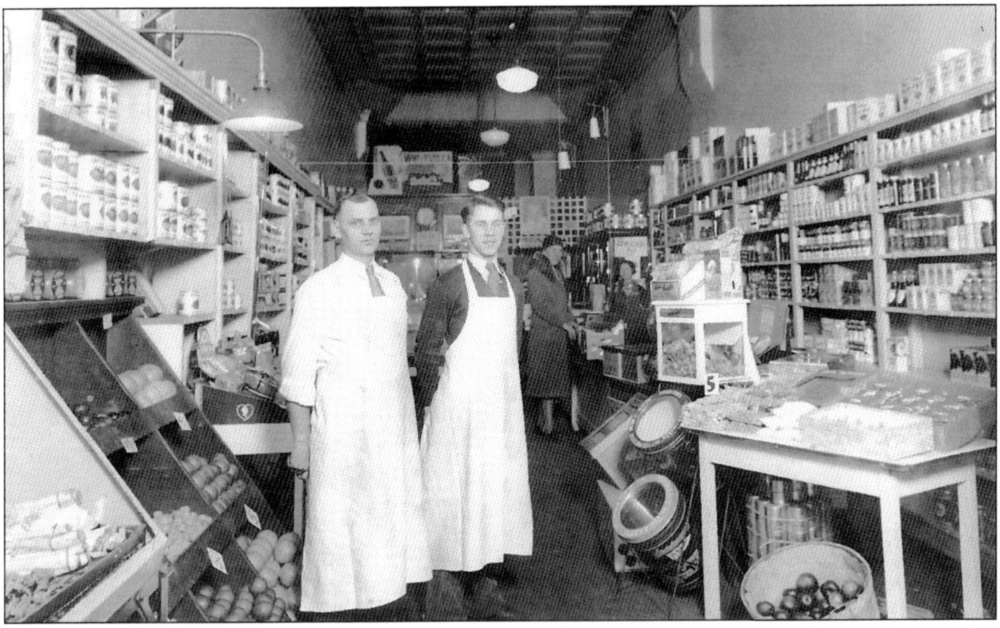

STEWART'S GROCERY, 1932. Lena Sheeter (left) and Cora Stewart are at the counter in the background of Stewart's Grocery at 210 North South Street. Howard Stewart (left) and Dean Wolfe stand in grocer's aprons. Sheeter ran Sheeter's 5 and 10 Cent Store after her husband, Clarence, died in 1923 after eight years in business; the five-and-dime store remained in business downtown until 1984.

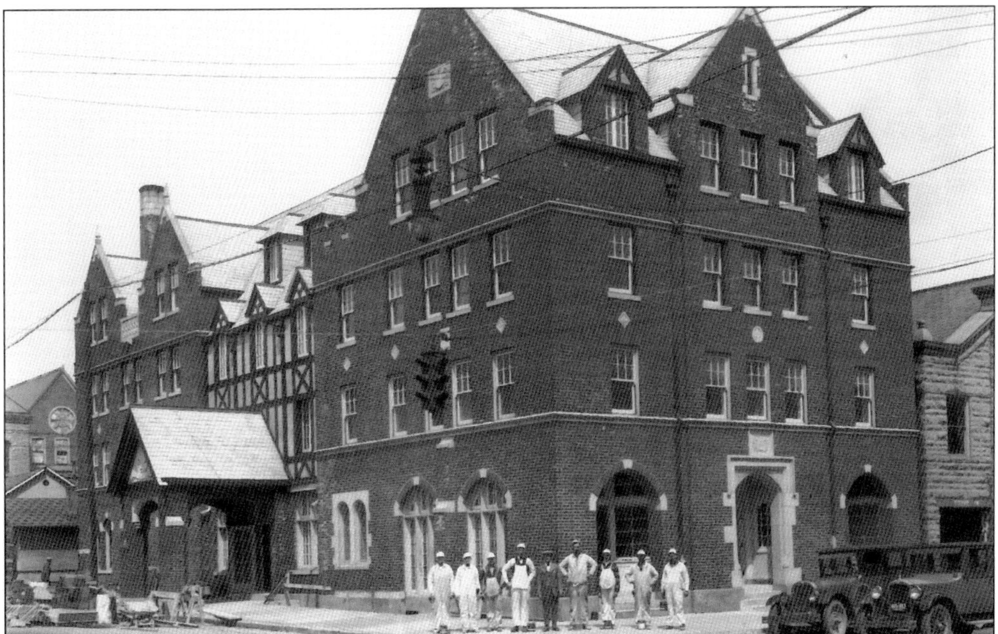

GENERAL DENVER HOTEL. Named for Gen. James W. Denver, the hotel was opened in 1928 after the community determined that there was a need for a hotel with quality dining facilities to cater to automobile travelers. Local citizens bought stock at $1,000 per share to finance the project, totaling $140,000. It is still an inn and restaurant today.

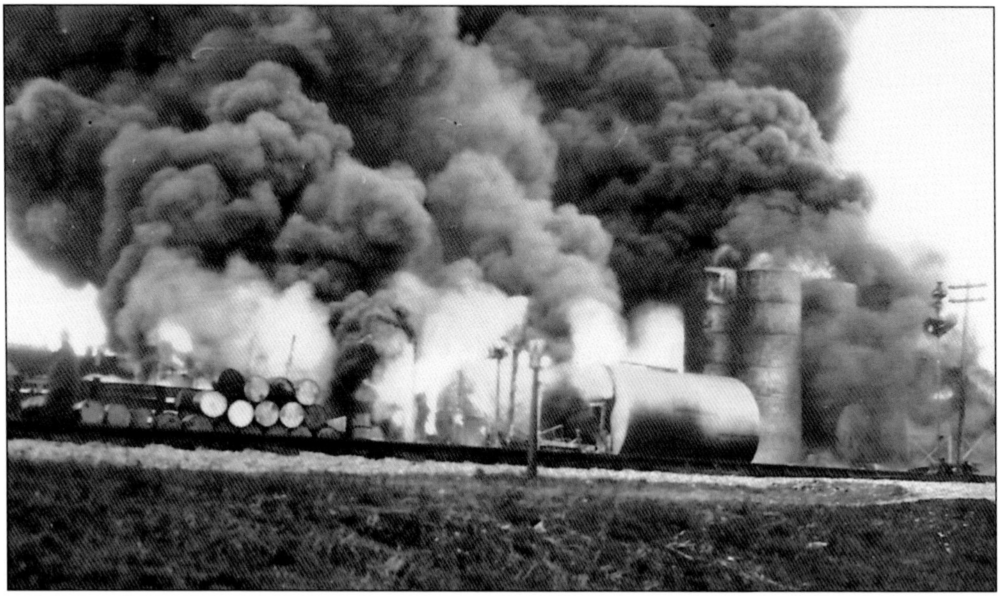

Oil Fire. The Wilmington Oil Company fire on January 26, 1929, was caused when a spark ignited gasoline, which had overflowed when a tanker truck was being filled. More than 12,000 gallons of lubricating oil and four storage tanks holding 22,000 gallons of gasoline were destroyed at the company on Hawley Avenue. One man was killed in the blaze.

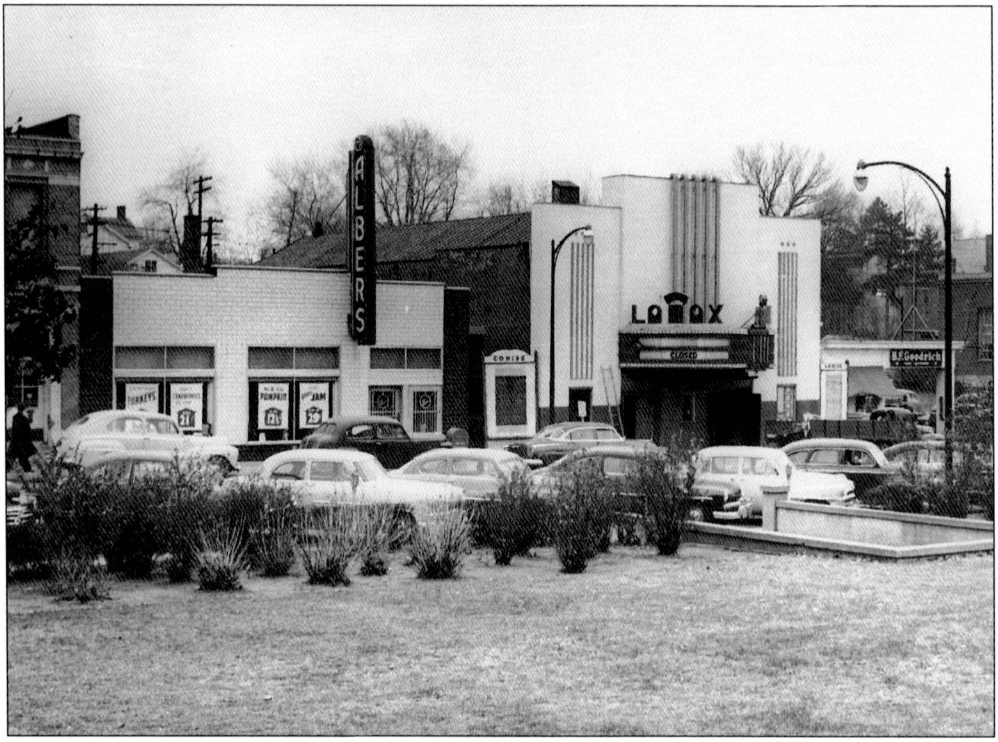

Albers Downtown, c. 1960. Albers offered groceries downtown in the early 1960s on Main Street, next to the LaMax Theatre, which is now a parking lot for the Wilmington United Methodist Church.

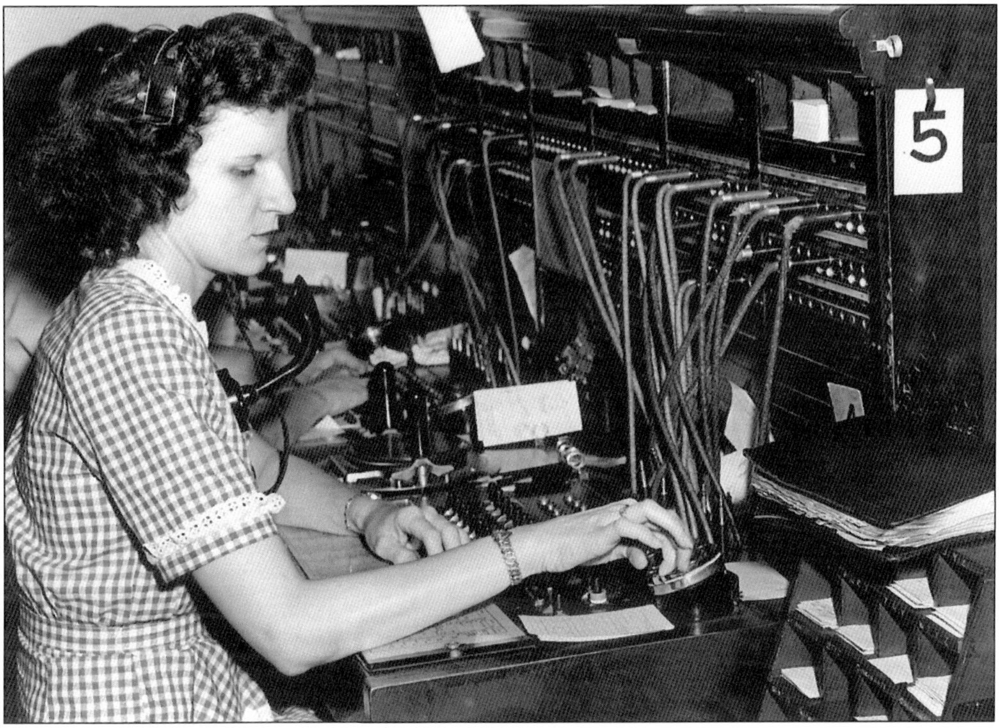

TELEPHONE OPERATOR, 1946. Dorothy Schuer was an operator for Ohio Consolidated Telephone Company in 1946. Wilmington was the first Ohio city to have automated telephones.

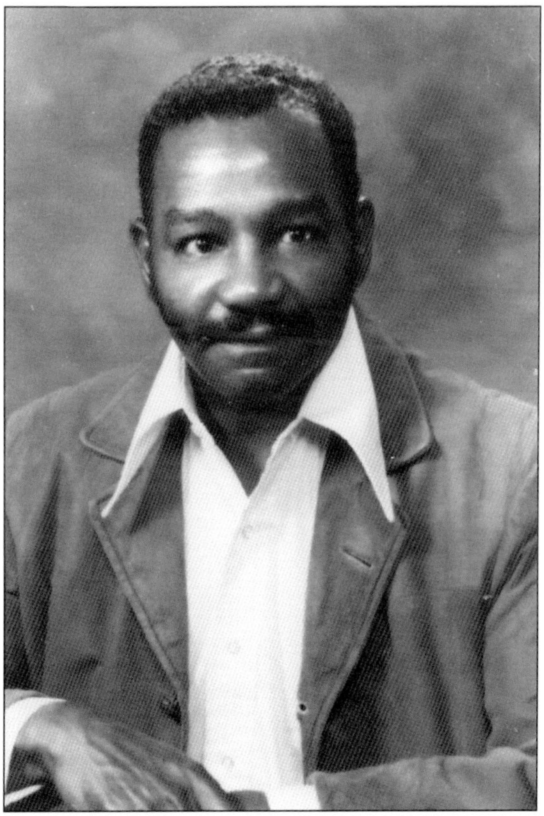

CHARLES GRAHAM (1918–1981). Charles "Hammie" Graham owned a popular restaurant, Hammie's, near the end of World War II. He was instrumental in desegregating the White House Restaurant in downtown Wilmington and eventually desegregating Wilmington's elementary schools, a cause previously taken up by Ted and Mary Elizabeth Lewis of Grove Street in 1939 and by J. R. Hawley in 1895. Graham was a charter member of Homes of Wilmington to eliminate substandard housing.

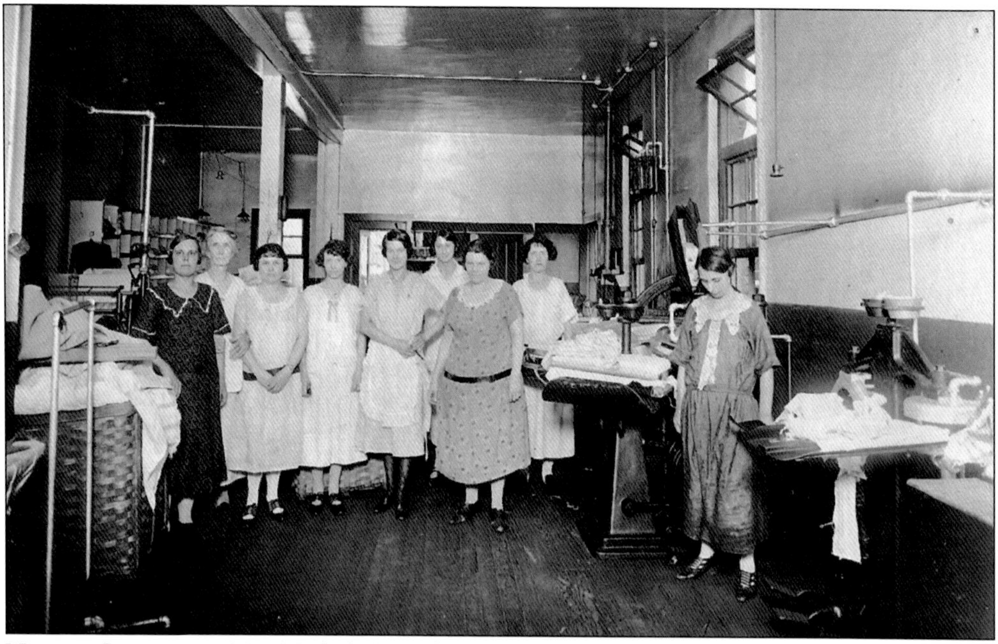

NICHOLS LAUNDRY, 1930. Nichols Laundry was located on West Sugartree Street. Its previous name was Wilmington Steam Laundry. The concept of a public laundry was first seen in the late 1920s and early 1930s. Initially, "take-in laundry" was done by attendants and returned to customers. The coin-laundry concept took off in the 1950s with coin meters added to machines, creating true self-service businesses.

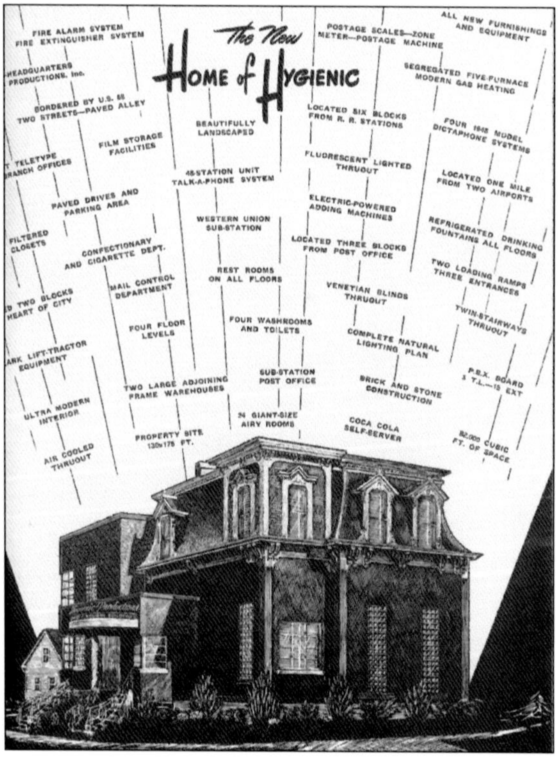

HYGIENIC PRODUCTIONS. Howard "Kroger" Babb (1906–1980) was a movie and television producer who started a production company in 1944 near his childhood home on the corner of North South and Columbus Streets. Hygienic Productions was best known for its 1945 film *Mom and Dad*, a morality tale about an unwed girl who becomes pregnant. The third highest grossing film of the decade, it was estimated that it earned between $40 million and $100 million.

Nine

Community Life

For almost as long as there has been a downtown Wilmington, community members have congregated there for social events such as street fairs and carnivals, operas and plays, movies and music.

Wilmington has been home to several theaters downtown, although only the Murphy Theatre remains. Four different marquees have adorned the Murphy Theatre since it opened in 1918, when Chicago Cubs owner and Wilmington native Charles Murphy spent $250,000, which today would be more than $5 million, to create an elaborate playhouse for his hometown. Murphy knew it was extravagant for such a small town, but he said, "That's not an investment—that's a monument."

A block away, the Wilmington City Hall's middle tower held a clock that was the second largest in the United States at the time it was built in 1878, dwarfed only by the clock on Philadelphia's City Hall. Also known as the "opera house," the Wilmington City Hall housed the fire and police departments and included a well-equipped auditorium on the second floor. It was the place where Sam Lucas, the first African American man to star in the stage and screen versions of *Uncle Tom's Cabin*, launched a minstrel career, later branching out as a comedian and composer. He was known as the most celebrated minstrel in the United States during his time.

Another famous entertainer, Vic Tooker came from a long line of local musicians and was the master of 19 instruments. He performed for five presidents, with bandleader Benny Goodman, and for jazz trumpeter Louis Armstrong's 70th birthday party in Hollywood. Although he traveled extensively during his musical career, he always returned to Wilmington.

Along with its storied theater and arts history, Wilmington residents have valued their social outlets, such as scouting and clubs, with generations of families participating over the years. Like many towns at the beginning of the 20th century, Wilmington's community baseball teams traveled the region, playing for the love of the game.

Wilmington citizens also have benefited from a history of innovative health care that has spanned from the first Hale Hospital, built in 1914, to Clinton Memorial Hospital, built in 1951, to the Foster J. Boyd, MD, Regional Cancer Center, which opened in 2007.

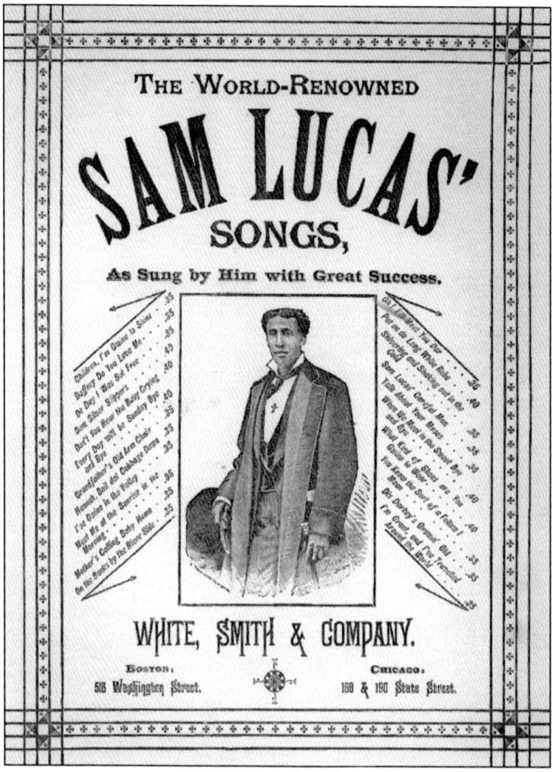

Sam Lucas, c. 1880. African American entertainer Sam Lucas (1850–1916) started performing at the Wilmington "opera house" in June 1880. Although it is widely believed Lucas was born in Ohio, some accounts say he was born on a Virginia plantation. In Wilmington, Lucas launched a minstrel and acting career. In 1890, he worked on the production of the *Creole Show*, which is often cited as the first African American production to break the links to minstrelsy. (Courtesy of Brown University Library.)

Broom Brigade, c. 1880. Members of the Broom Brigade women's organization, under command of Etta Strumm (in front), are (seated) Carrie Hood, Jennie Morgan, Gertie Hoskins, Adda Haines, Jennie March, and Minnie Wire; (standing) Hattie Carol, Lucy Nordyke, Bertha Hill, Laura Swaim, Lona Haworth, and Calista Martin. The drummer is Emma Brown.

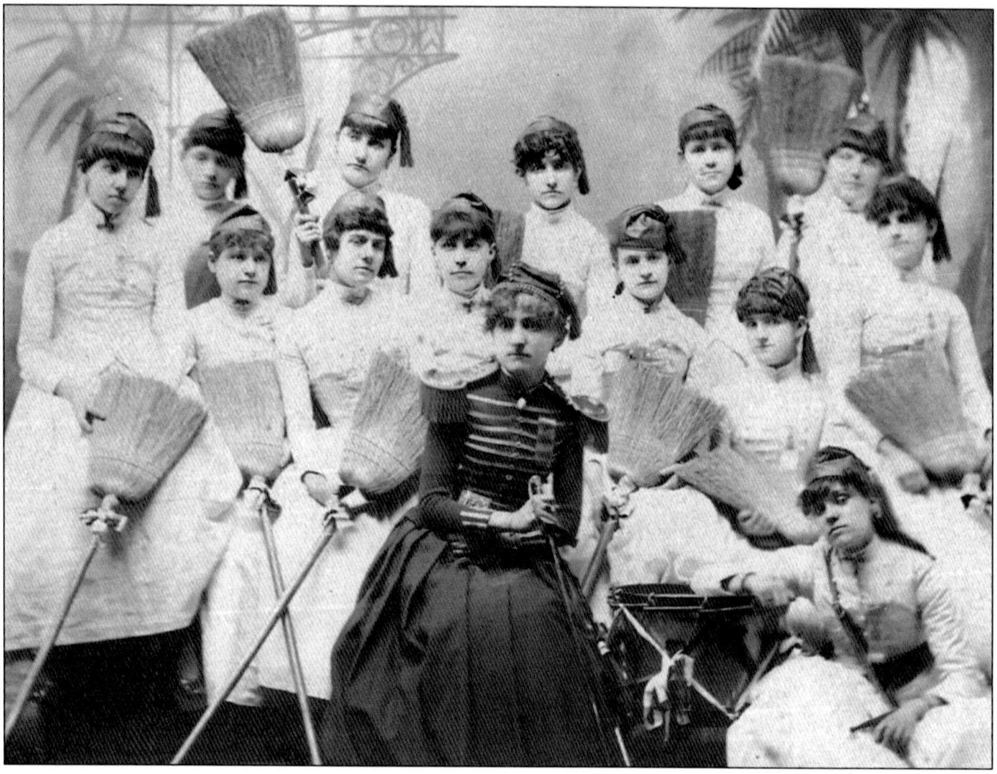

GOLDEN GONDOLA, 1899. At the beginning of the 20th century, street fairs had taken the place of many county fairs. In June 1899, the Wilmington Street Fair and Carnival Company presented an application to city council for the use of the streets to hold an exhibit from July 24 to 29. The Golden Gondola merry-go-round was built in Europe.

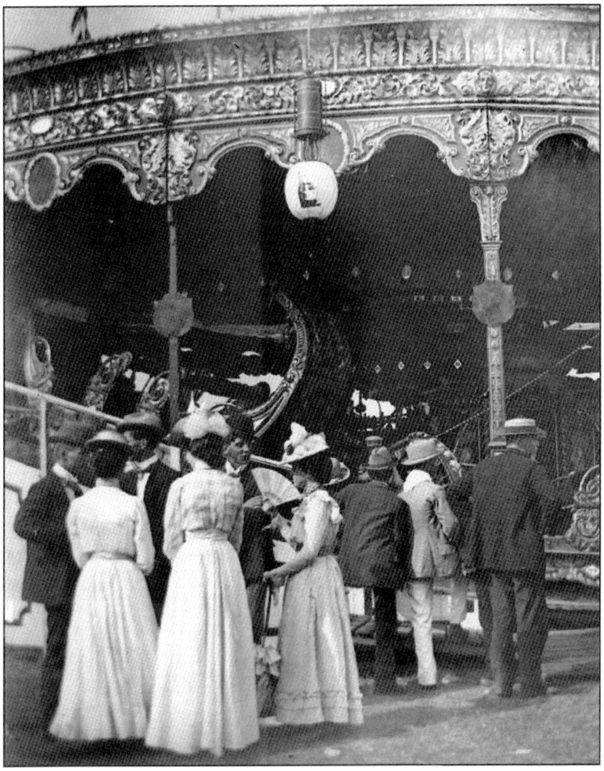

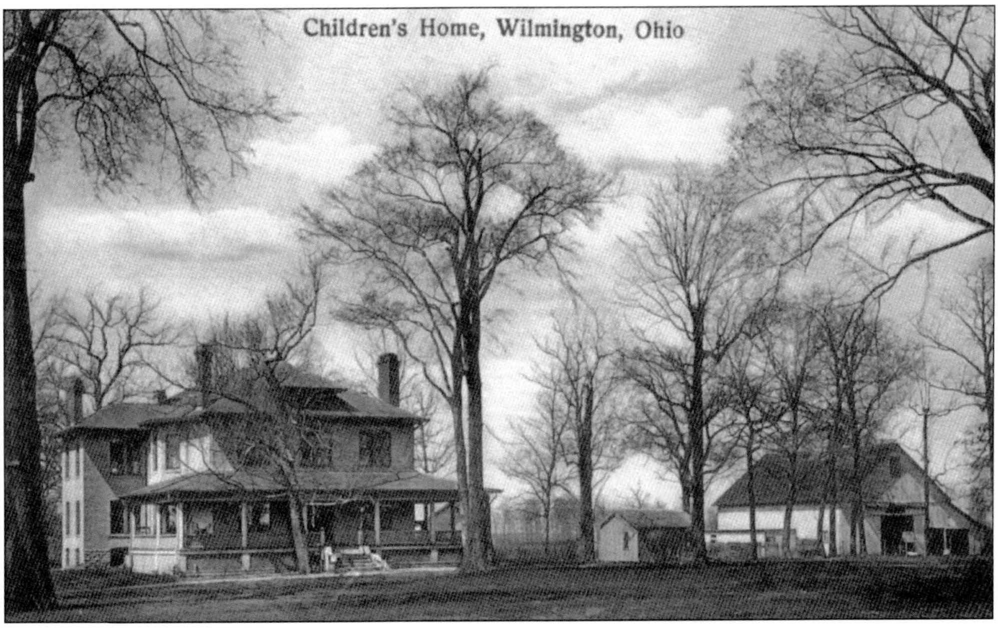

CHILDREN'S HOME. Housing the county's "unfortunate and dependent children" was first discussed in 1884 and passed by referendum. By October 1884, a site was purchased, and buildings were constructed at West Main Street and Nelson Avenue. On February 20, 1896, the building burned to the ground. In 1902, J. P. Vance won the contract to build a new home on 46 acres on State Route 68, purchased from Shipley McMillan. The building no longer exists.

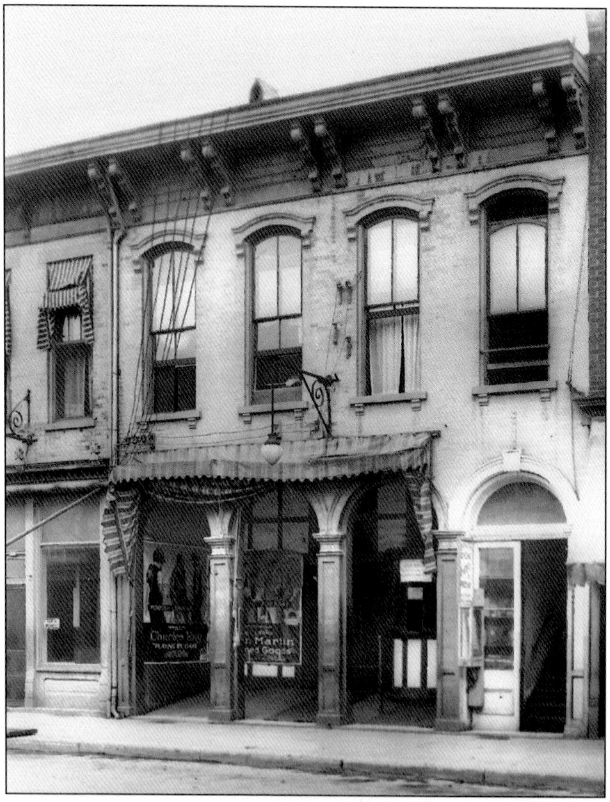

Cub Theatre, 1908. The Cub Theatre belonged to Frank Murphy, the brother of Charles Murphy (who built the Murphy Theatre). Located across the street from the Murphy, the Cub was named after the Chicago Cubs, which Charles Murphy owned, and was operated from 1908 to 1914. The West House Theatre opened in 1908 on West Main Street. The Gem Theatre, also owned by Frank Murphy, opened in 1912 at the southwest corner of Main and South Streets.

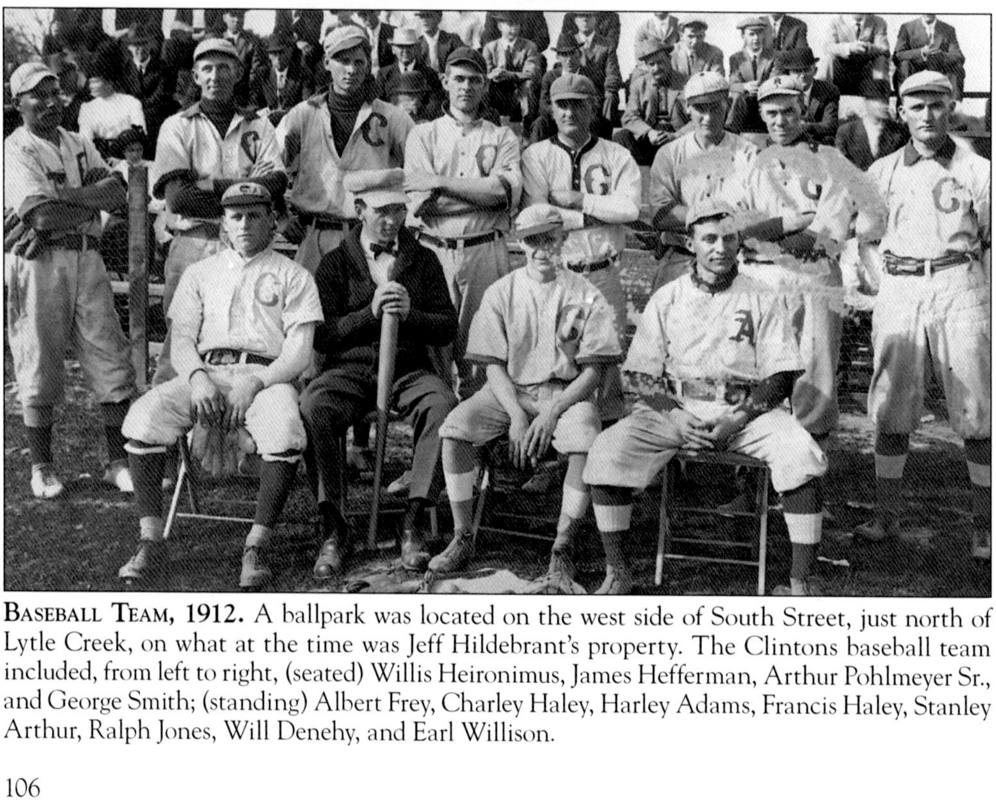

Baseball Team, 1912. A ballpark was located on the west side of South Street, just north of Lytle Creek, on what at the time was Jeff Hildebrant's property. The Clintons baseball team included, from left to right, (seated) Willis Heironimus, James Hefferman, Arthur Pohlmeyer Sr., and George Smith; (standing) Albert Frey, Charley Haley, Harley Adams, Francis Haley, Stanley Arthur, Ralph Jones, Will Denehy, and Earl Willison.

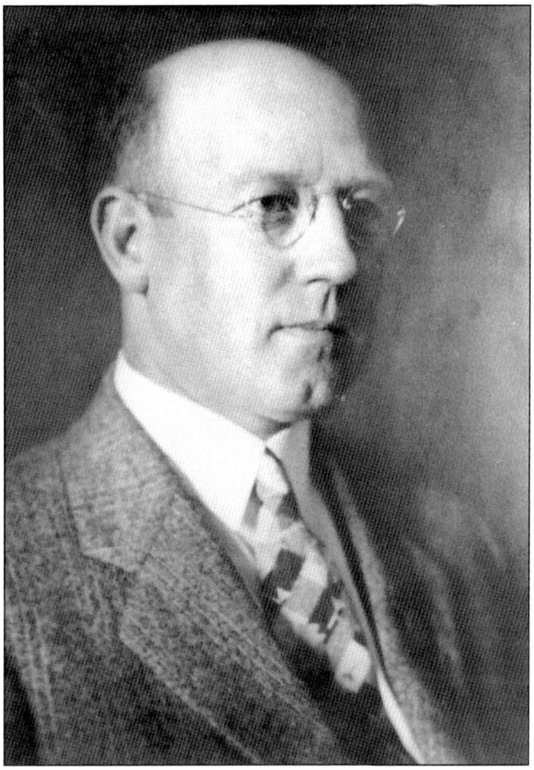

HALE HOSPITAL. Dr. Kelley Hale and his wife, Dessa, opened the first Hale Hospital at the corner of Spring and Locust Streets in 1914. The second Hale Hospital, built on West Main Street in 1923, offered care to local residents regardless of their race or their ability to pay. Dessa Hale was a registered nurse anesthetist, the service of which she introduced to Clinton County. The second Hale Hospital, shown below, featured state-of-the-art conveniences such as surgical suites, a sterilization room, and an elevator. During his time at this hospital, Dr. Hale invented many surgical tools.

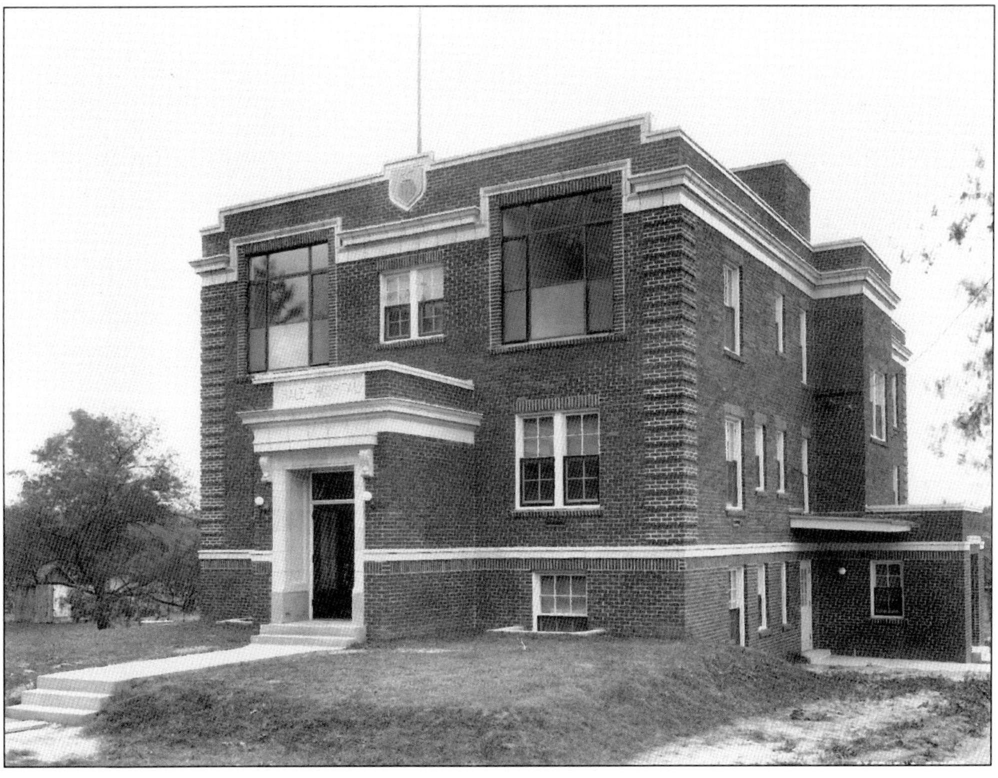

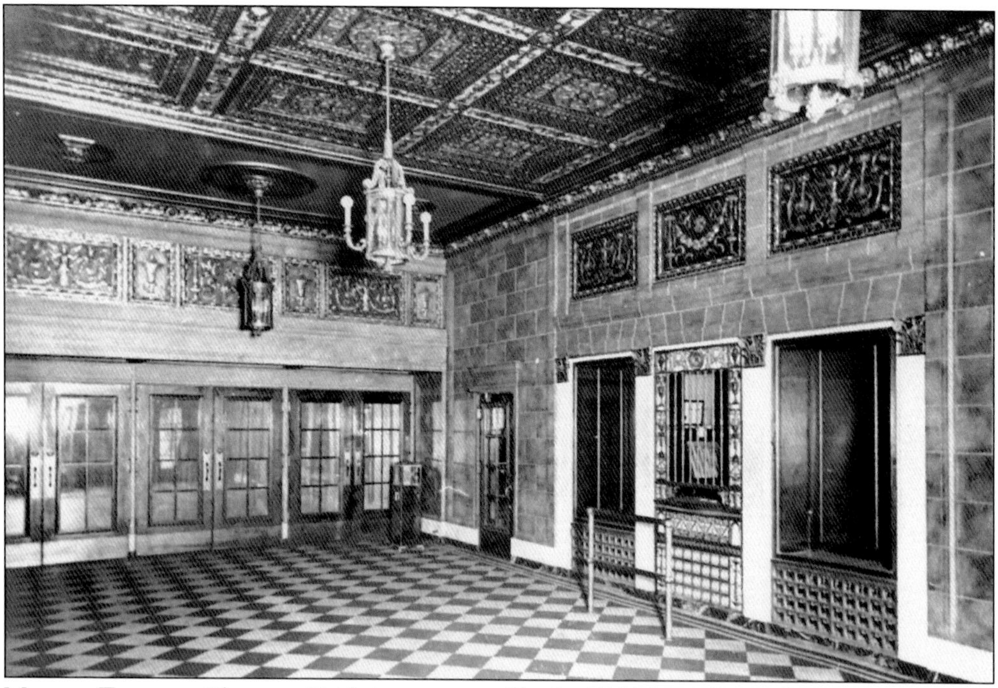

MURPHY THEATRE. The son of Irish immigrants, Charles Webb Murphy was born in Wilmington and moved to Cincinnati, eventually becoming a newspaper sports writer and then a press agent for the New York Giants. He bought the Chicago Cubs for $105,000 in 1905 with a loan from friend and former employer Charles Taft. A successful but controversial owner, Murphy sold the franchise in 1914 and returned to Wilmington, where his mother still lived, in 1916. He spent $250,000 to build the Murphy Theatre, which required European craftsmen and 200 railroad cars of material. The lobby was decorated with a sunburst chandelier, marble floors, and polished oak doors. It opened on July 24, 1918, and is still used today. Murphy died in Cincinnati in 1931 at age 63.

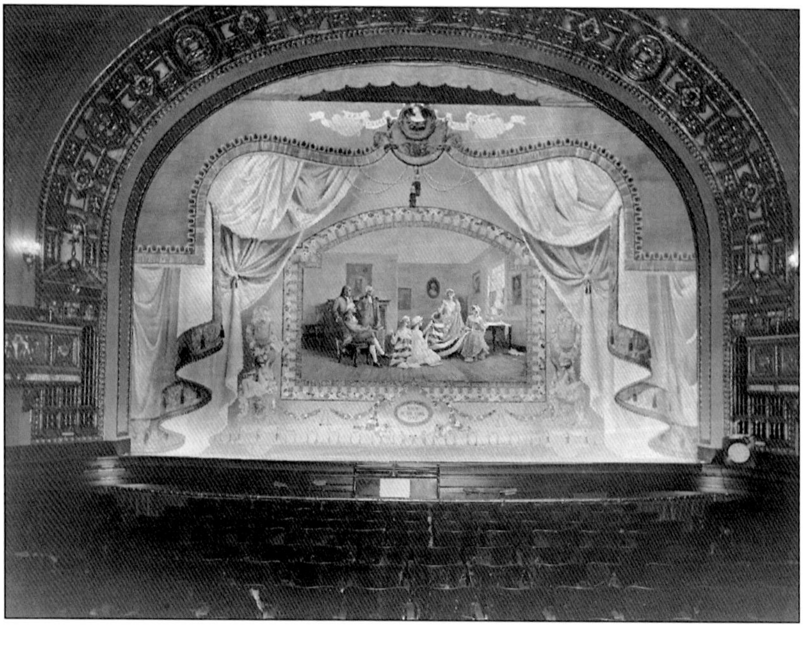

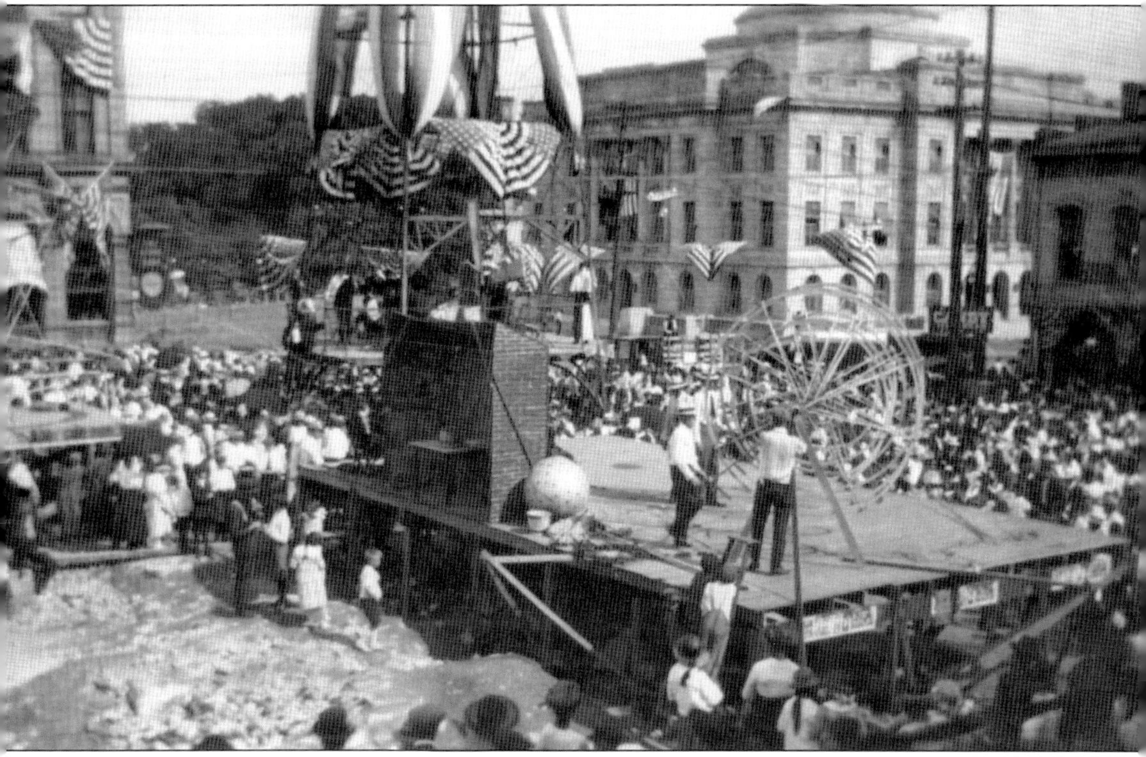

FALL FESTIVAL. On the site of the second Clinton County courthouse, which was demolished in 1918 for the third—and current—courthouse, a fall festival was held downtown in 1919. A tank cleared away the Irish bowery, "Shadagee Square," for the current courthouse. These East Main Street businesses were removed: Bing's Tobacco, Fred Dunham's Shoes, the Rodney Jones Saloon, Clark's grocery and open-air market, Pennington Auto, and Wilmington Steam and Laundry. On South Street, the probate court, the jail, Smith Brothers Dyeing, Isaac Rickman Fish Market, Hamilton Barbershop, Sam Stiff Grocery, and the Busy Bee restaurant were demolished. The 36-foot-diameter courthouse dome features murals representing agriculture, education, medicine, and industry. (Courtesy of Rita Butcher.)

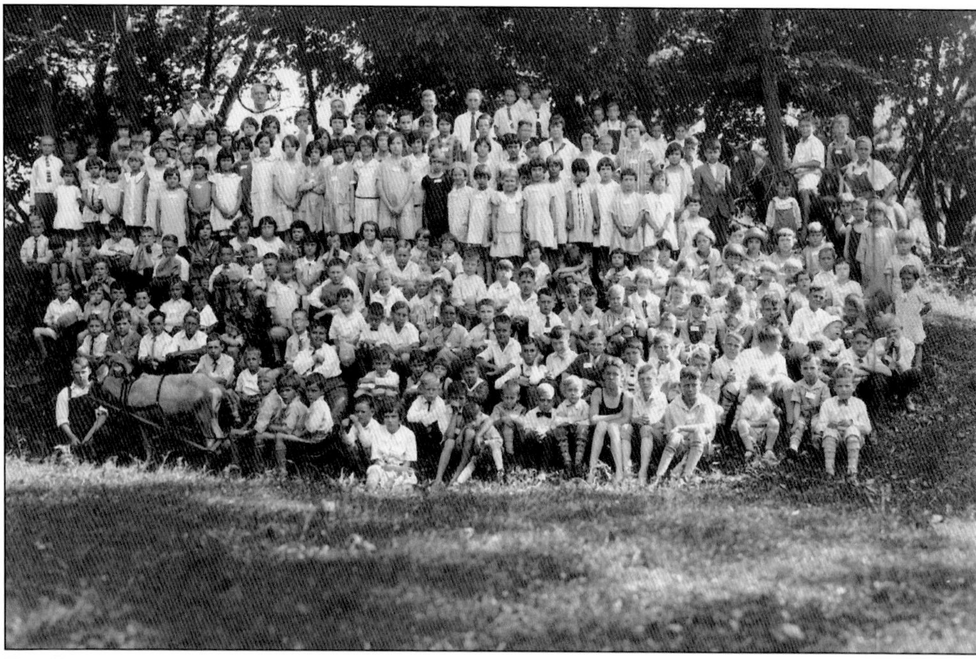

Dr. Peelle's Deliveries, 1928. This photograph, taken on Dr. Frank Peelle's 60th birthday on July 30, 1928, shows all the children delivered by Peelle, a general practitioner in Wilmington. Peelle is standing in the back row, third from left.

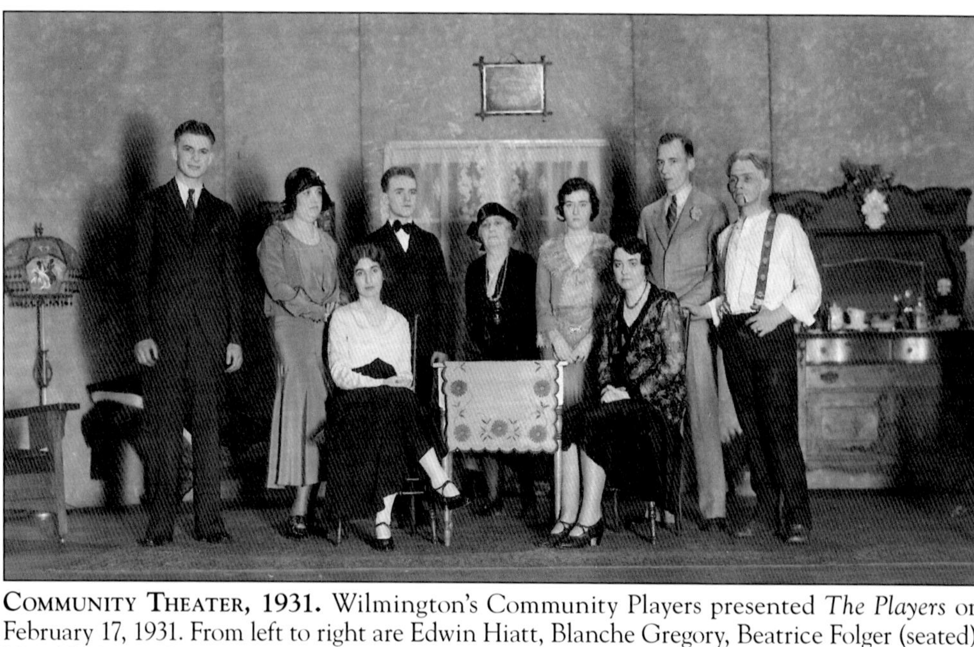

Community Theater, 1931. Wilmington's Community Players presented *The Players* on February 17, 1931. From left to right are Edwin Hiatt, Blanche Gregory, Beatrice Folger (seated), Harold Howe, director Henrietta M. Strumm, Mary Terrell, Gertrude Huls (seated), Adolph Varelmann, and Robert Hadley.

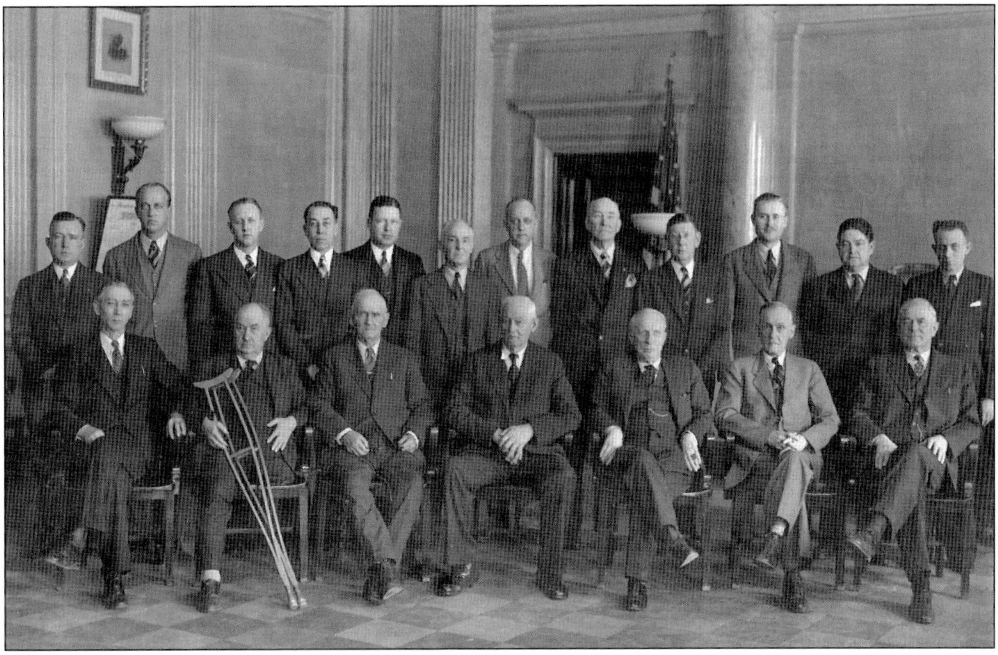

Bar Association, 1938. Members of the Clinton County Bar are pictured above. From left to right are (seated) S. W. Huls, J. M. Braut, John Harlan, Judge F. M. Clevenger, W. B. Rogers, probate judge Hugh Wright, and I. Q. Jordan; (standing) Lawrence Lyons, Howard D. Barns, Melville Hayes, C. Luther Swaim, D. K. Hempstead, Allan Smith, George Barnes, Leo Weltz, clerk Eldon Hayes, Charles Kirk, R. H. Hildebrandt, and George Schilling.

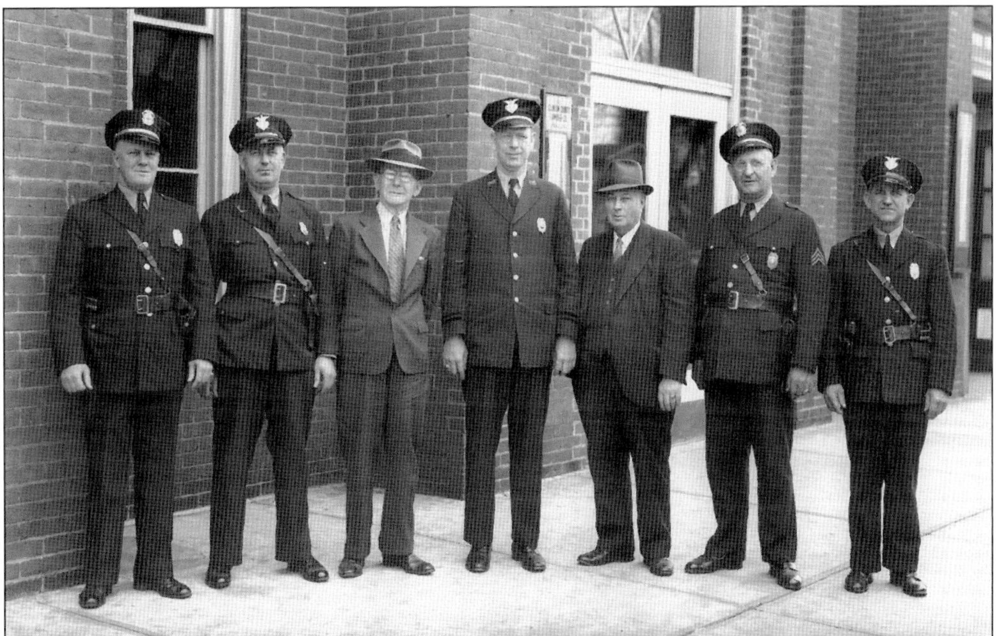

Police Force, 1941. Members of the police force include, from left to right, Sgt. Don Simmons, traffic patrolman Dwight Winkle, Mayor C. Q. Hildebrant, Chief Everett Downing, service and safety director Arthur Zimmerman, Sgt. D. A. Adams, and patrolman Arnold Conklin.

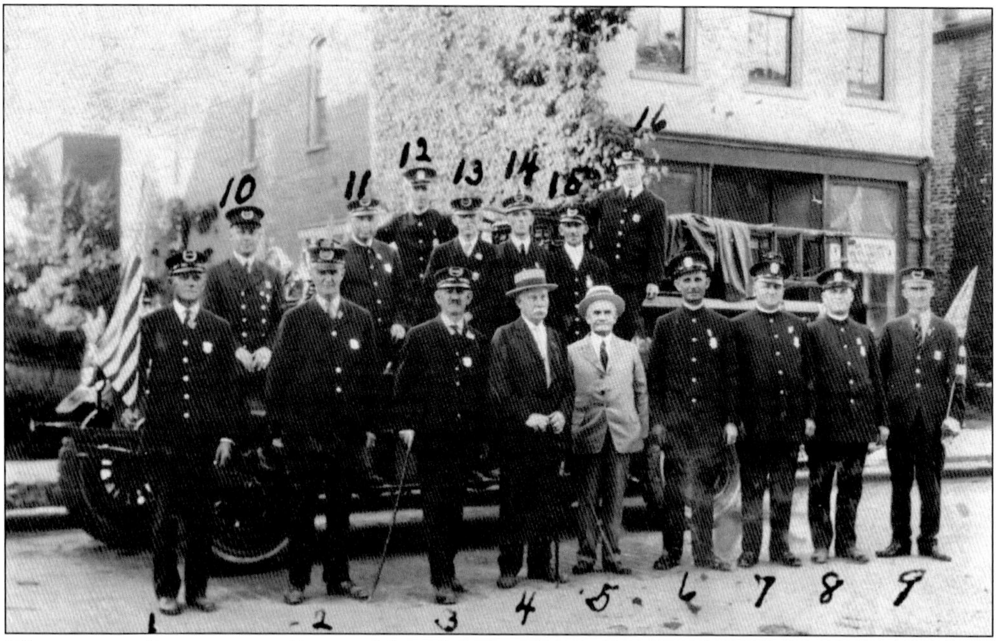

WILMINGTON FIREFIGHTERS. Pictured from left to right are (first row) firefighters Charles Hormell, Harry Ames, and Frank Pennebaker, Mayor R. C. Greene, safety director J. S. Thomas, police officer Henry Adains, chief of police Rollo Kirk, police officer William Gray, and caretaker Bert Cox; (second row) ? Carpenter and firefighters Howard Babb, Everett Downing, Clinton Olvis, Arthur Sutton, Louis Shurer, and St. Clair Fife.

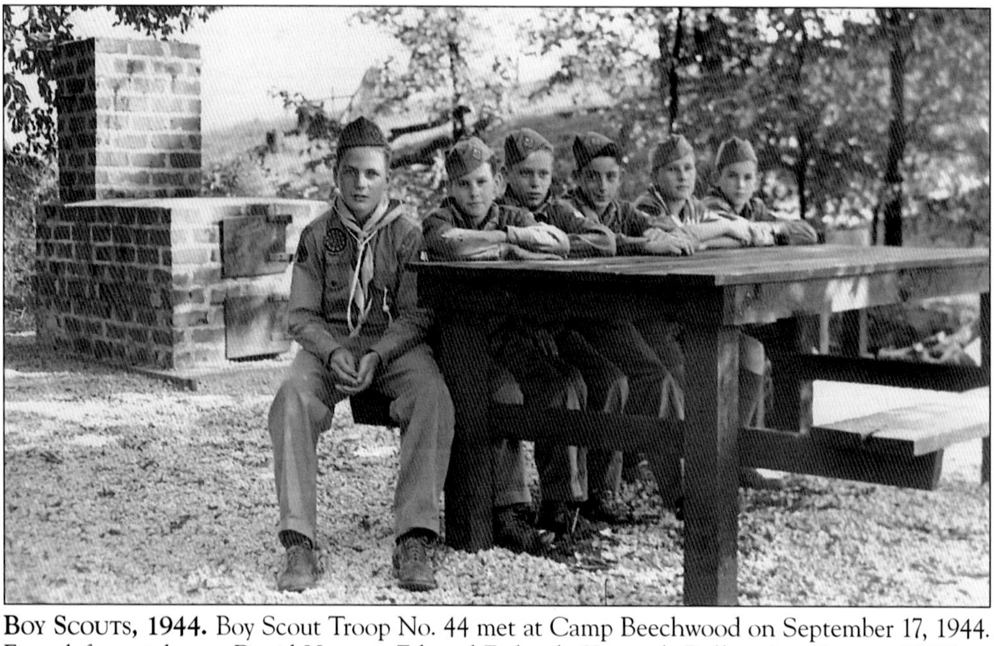

BOY SCOUTS, 1944. Boy Scout Troop No. 44 met at Camp Beechwood on September 17, 1944. From left to right are David Haynes, Edward Ewbank, Kenneth Bullen, Joe Conner, William Garinger, and Sidney Myers. In 1911, Rev. A. J. Marbet became scoutmaster and J. W. Denver Williams Sr. and O. W. Hale received registration as assistant scoutmasters. The first troop in Clinton County held early meetings in a barn behind the Williamses' house.

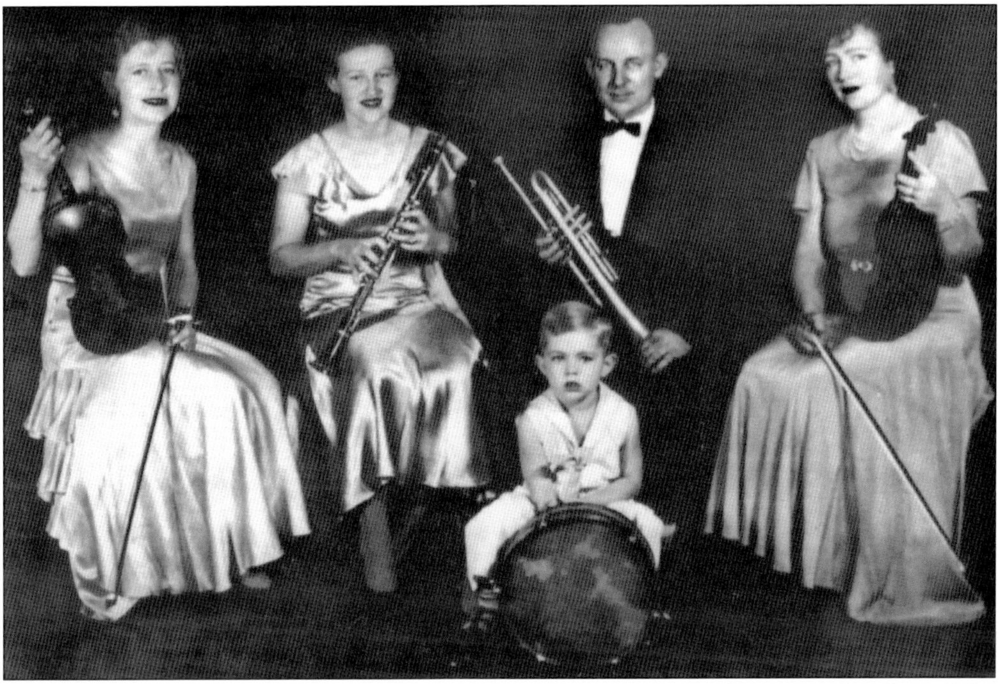

Tooker Family Musicians. In 1899, Victor Tooker, son of musician Thomas Tooker, formed the Vic Tooker Comedy Company. Victor, his wife, Nora Belle, and their children traveled together as entertainers. Son Guy met musician Alice Moore and married her in 1925, eventually creating the Tooker Traveling Troupe with Alice's sisters, Anna and Eleanor, pictured above. They played the vaudeville circuit and befriended celebrities such as W. C. Fields. Guy and Alice's son, Vic (shown below), was born in Wilmington in 1930 and by age five was playing on stage. He later spent 17 years performing on the *Delta Queen*. The Tookers always called Wilmington their home, and Vic, who died in 2000, and his parents are buried in Sugar Grove Cemetery.

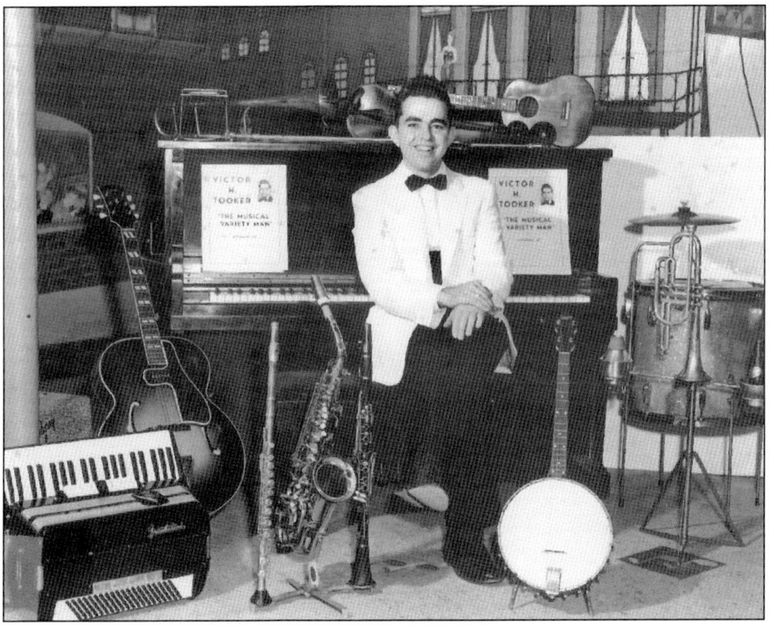

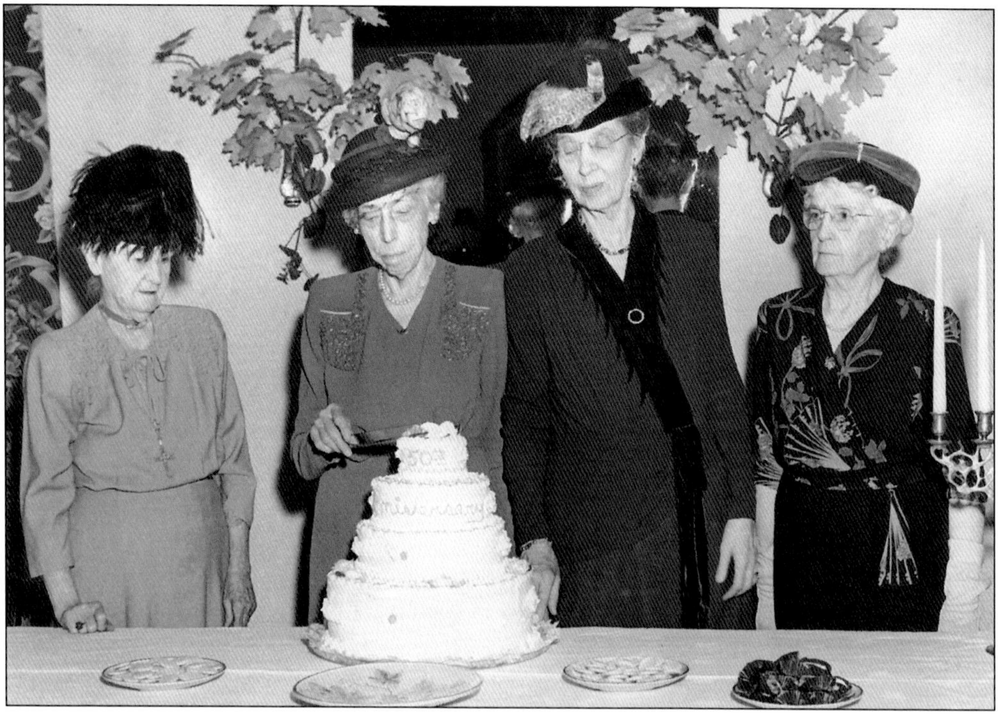

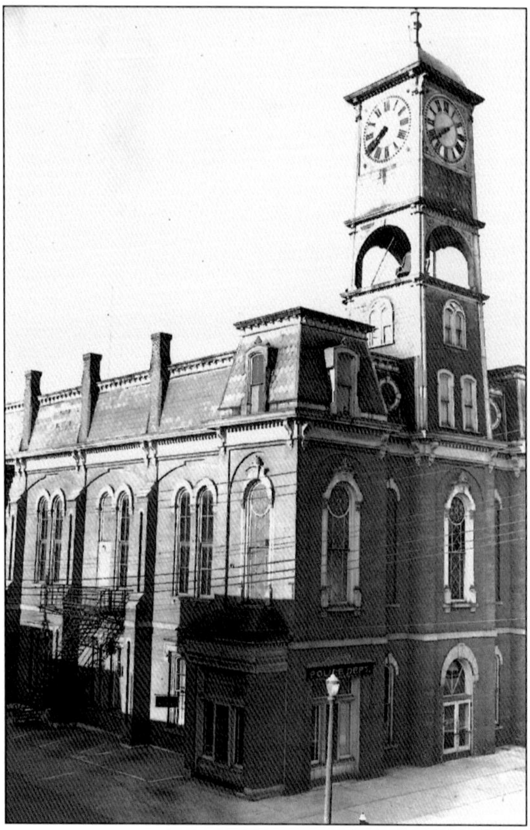

SIX AND TWENTY CLUB, 1948. Members of the Six and Twenty Club celebrated its 50th anniversary on October 29, 1948, at the General Denver Hotel. From left to right are Adda Hains Hildebrant, Marshie Austin, Tacy Walker Robinson, and Wilmina Kimbrough. The Wilmington club began in 1898 as a book discussion group. Over the years, the club has expanded its purpose to embrace many cultural activities.

CITY HALL, 1949. Wilmington's city hall, also known as the "opera house" because operas were performed on the second floor, was located on Locust Street in the current municipal building's parking lot. This photograph was taken in September 1949 before a remodeling effort. The building housed the police and fire departments. In 1941, Link's Skating Rink was located on its second floor. Basketball games were played there, too.

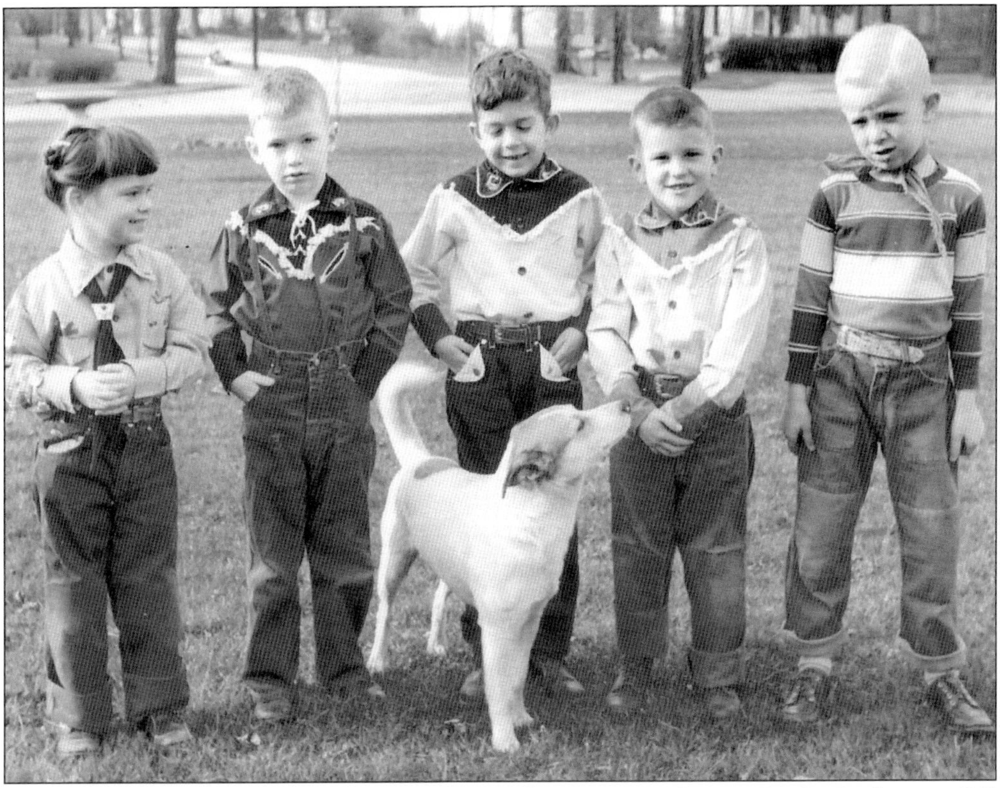

Cowgirls and Cowboys, 1951. From left to right, Janice Buchanan, Bucky Buchanan, Bill Cowgill, Chris Stephens, and Mike Walsh pose with Stephens's dog, Lucky.

Brownie Troop, 1955. A Brownie troop that held meetings at Main School is pictured at right. From left to right are Bonnie Haywood, Martha Hamilton, Doris Kistner, Ann McNemar, Carolyn Bean, Kay Schultz, Linda Grove, Jenny Bath, Susie Smith, and Nancy Lawson.

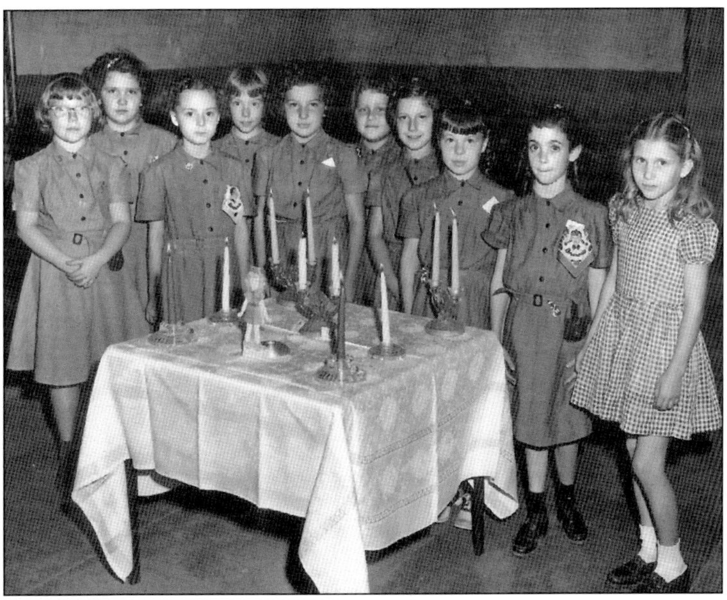

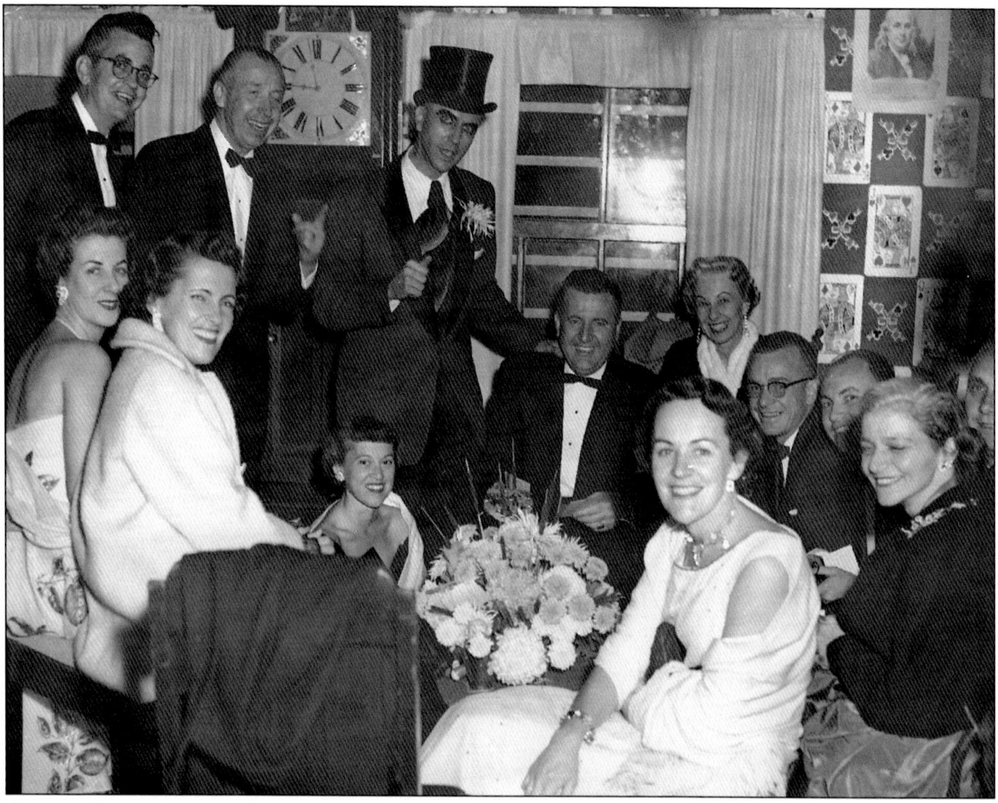

CIRCUS PARTY, 1953. George Horton, who at the time was vice president of the Wilmington Casting Company, which his father started in 1911, hosted a circus party in November 1953 at his South Street home. From left to right are (first row) Betty Yantes, Jean French, Mary Lib Creamer, Barbara Hazard, and Maude Cowgill; (second row) Don Cowgill, unidentified, Horton, Bill Creamer (seated), Gwen Bath, Dick Bath, Ed Yantes, and Frank Hazard.

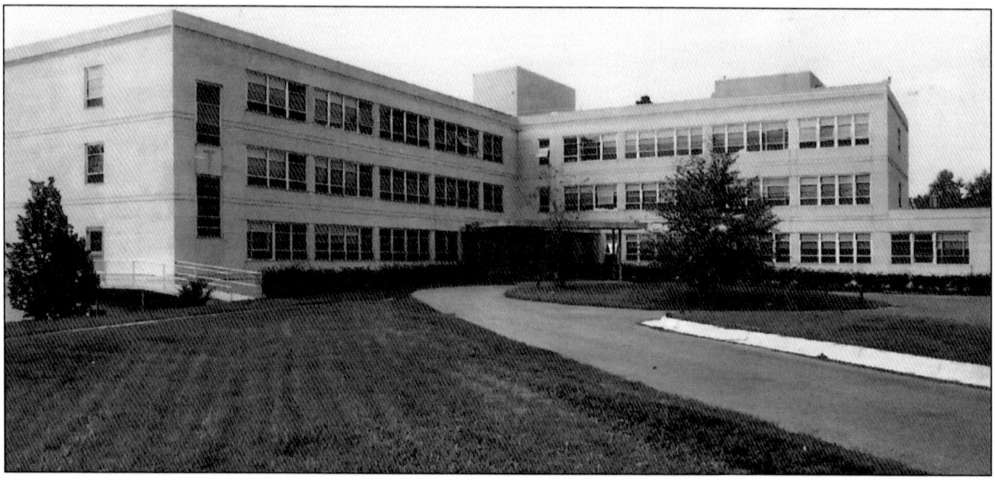

CLINTON MEMORIAL HOSPITAL. In 1947, twelve acres on West Main Street were purchased for the future Clinton Memorial Hospital. In 1951, at a cost of $950,000, a new 64-bed hospital was dedicated. Elsie Delin was named the first hospital administrator. Dr. Richard Bath was elected the first chief of staff. Vicki Priest, born October 4, 1951, was the first baby born at the hospital.

Ten

Military Service

Wilmington's connection with the armed forces can be seen in those who served in the military, in those who contributed on the home front, and in the two military installations located in Wilmington.

Wilmington has been the home to veterans from all of America's wars. Revolutionary War veterans who settled in Wilmington include Col. Thomas Gaddis, who proudly displayed his enlistment and discharge papers, both of which were signed by Gen. George Washington. Villagers also fought in the frontier wars and in the War of 1812. James W. Denver served as a captain in the Mexican-American War and as a general in the Civil War. The Civil War presented a serious moral dilemma for the local Quakers, who were unremittingly antislavery but pacific as well. Some Quakers, such as Col. A. W. Doan, chose to fight in the war.

Many Wilmington citizens have volunteered for multiple wars. Dr. Robert Conard fought in both the Spanish-American War and World War I, and he later served as an advisor during World War II.

Local residents also assisted on the home front during World War II with food and scrap metal drives, as well as by serving as German warplane spotters from atop the General Denver Hotel. Notably, Wilmington was also the location of a work camp for German prisoners of war.

Wilmington has been home to two important military installations: the Clinton County Army Airfield (later called the Clinton County Air Force Base) and the Nike missile site. The airbase has a storied history as an experimental glider base and a top-secret weather balloon base. It was also the home base of the first fully automatic flight (no pilot assistance) across the nation and the Atlantic. The base served as part of the Strategic Air Command during the 1950s and housed a special operations unit that trained gunship crews for deployment to Vietnam in the 1960s. The Nike missile site contained nuclear-capable warheads that provided the first line of defense against a Soviet missile attack at the height of the cold war. In 1971, both installations were closed.

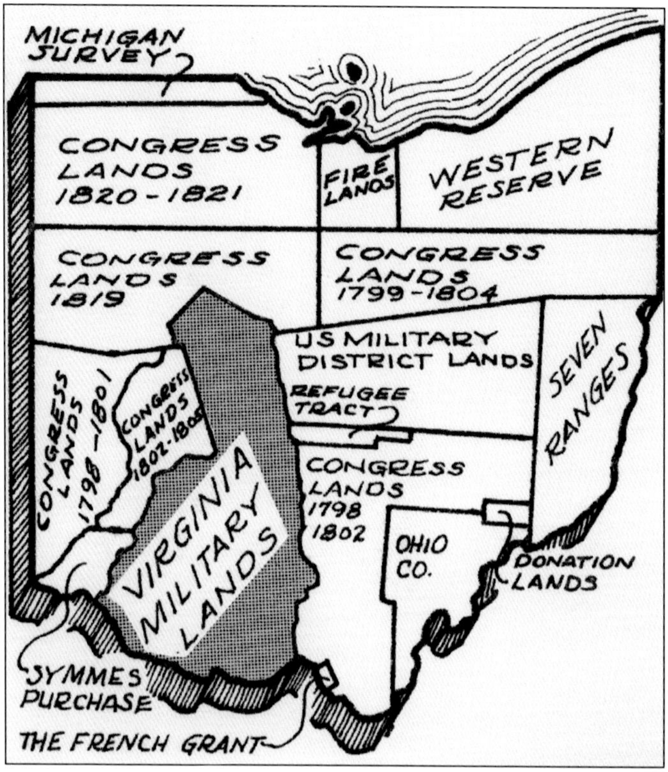

VIRGINIA MILITARY DISTRICT. This sketch depicts the Virginia Military District, which existed solely in central and southern Ohio between the Little Miami, the Scioto, and the Ohio Rivers. It is unique for its metes and bounds survey system, which caused many legal headaches for property owners. Virginia agreed to cede its claims to the lands northwest of the Ohio River in return for land for its Revolutionary War soldiers. (Courtesy of Earl Nicholson.)

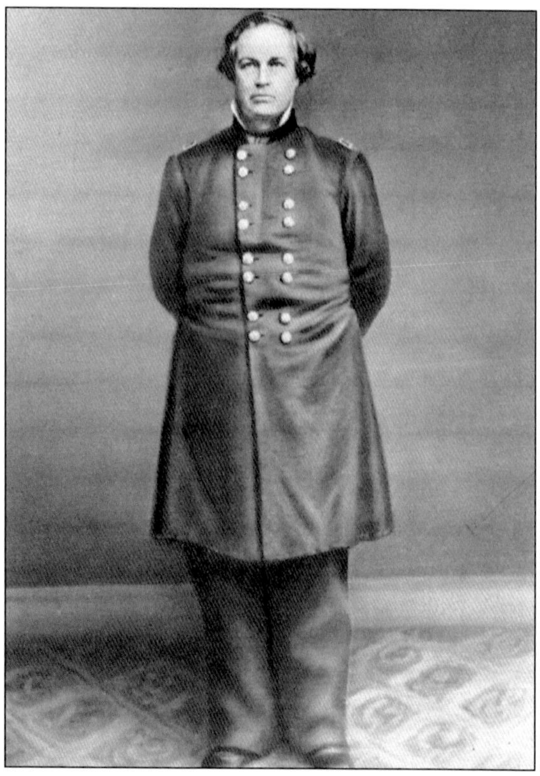

GEN. JAMES W. DENVER. Denver served in the Mexican-American War under Gen. Winfield Scott and later as the president of the National Association of Mexican War Veterans. Born in 1817 in Virginia as the son of a war veteran, Denver came to Wilmington in 1830 and graduated from Cincinnati Law School. In 1861, Pres. Abraham Lincoln appointed him a brigadier general of volunteers during the Civil War.

James W. Denver. After the Mexican-American War, Denver served as a California secretary of state and state legislator, a Kansas territorial governor during the difficult era known as "Bleeding Kansas," the Commissioner of Indian Affairs, and a U.S. congressman, and he was mentioned as a Democratic Party candidate for president. After his Civil War service, he returned to the practice of law in Wilmington and Washington, D.C. The city of Denver, Colorado, is named after him.

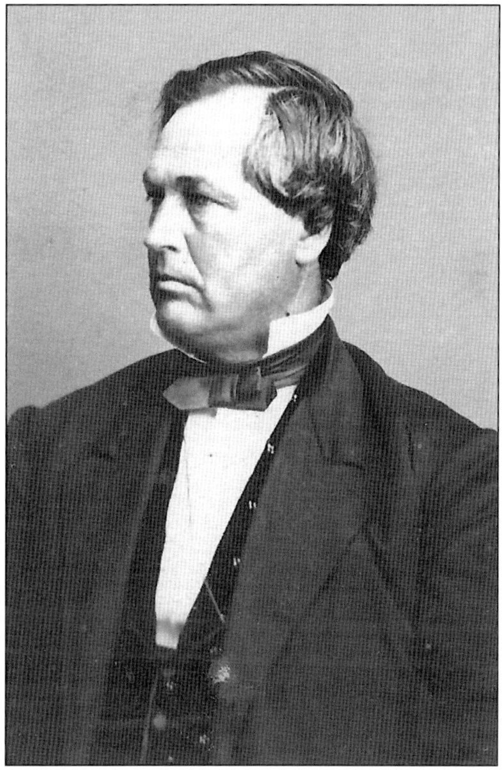

Squirrel Hunter Discharge, 1862. Squirrel Hunters were volunteers who lacked military training or equipment but responded to Gov. David Tod's call to defend Cincinnati from an imminent Confederate invasion. The invasion was deterred, and a grateful Ohio legislature printed discharge papers to thank the volunteers for their brief service.

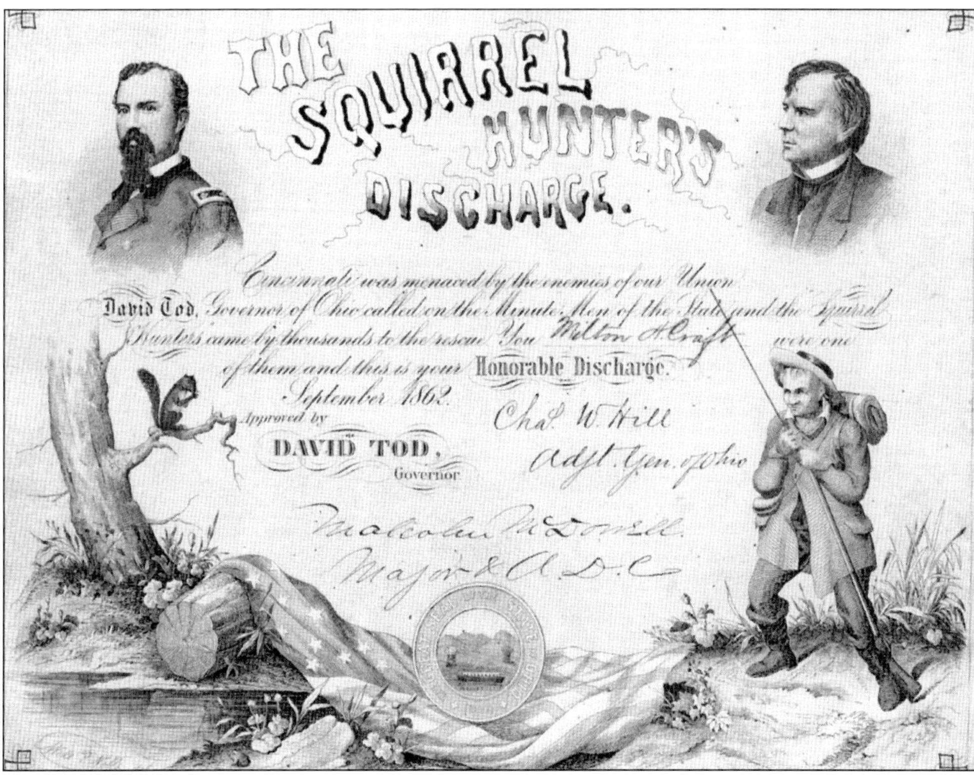

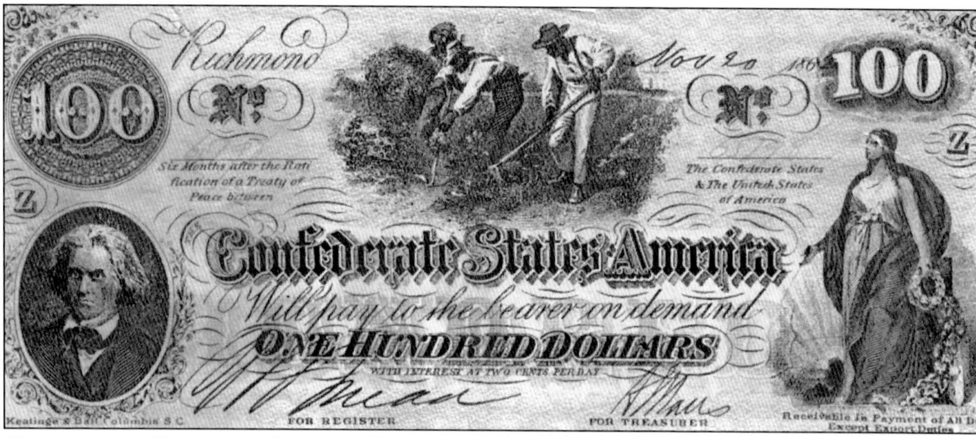

CONFEDERATE STATES OF AMERICA CURRENCY. In 1861, at the start of the Civil War, the newly formed Confederate government began issuing currency to its citizens. The North exacerbated the South's inflation woes by counterfeiting their currency to cause massive inflation. At the close of the war, Confederate notes were completely worthless, although many Northern soldiers brought them home as souvenirs of their service.

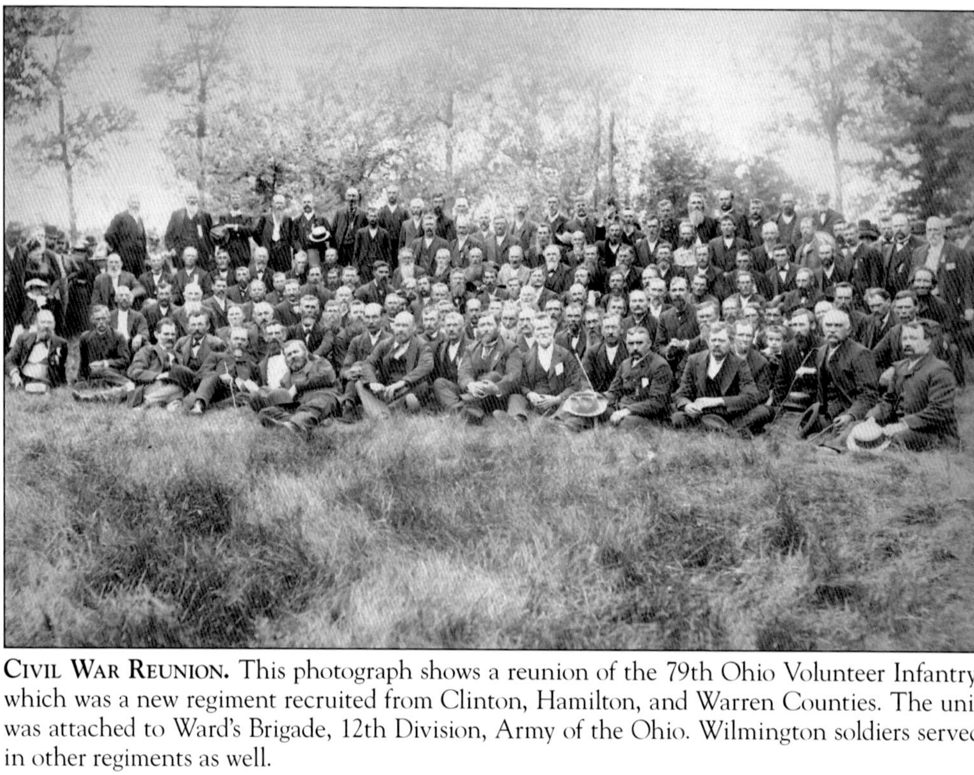

CIVIL WAR REUNION. This photograph shows a reunion of the 79th Ohio Volunteer Infantry, which was a new regiment recruited from Clinton, Hamilton, and Warren Counties. The unit was attached to Ward's Brigade, 12th Division, Army of the Ohio. Wilmington soldiers served in other regiments as well.

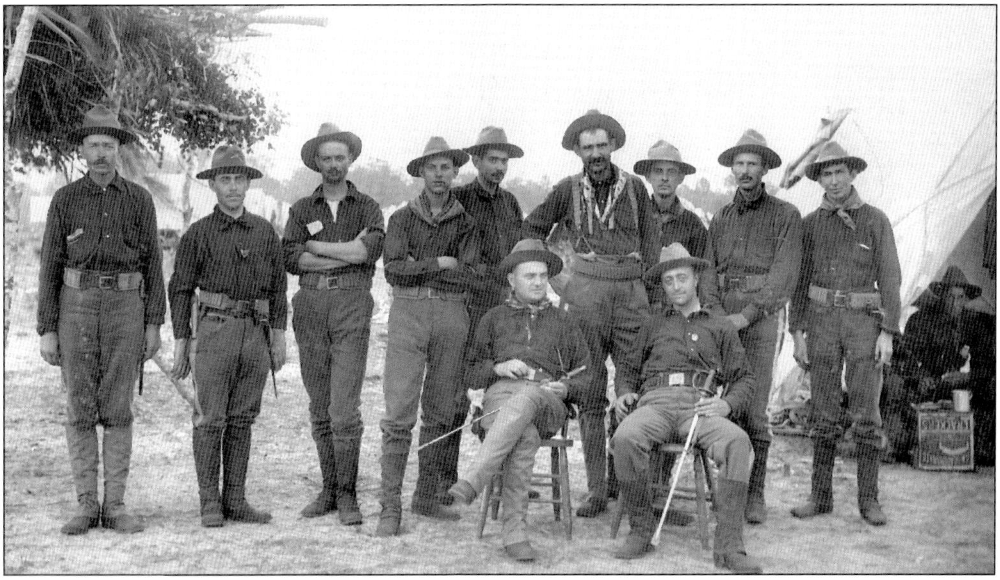

Spanish-American War, c. 1899: Pictured from left to right are (seated) Boyer and Hamilton; (standing) Schlagle, Griffin, Anderson, Mills, Weichert, Rausch, Smith, Kemp, and Owens; the soldier in the tent was known as "The Kid." The Flying Squadron (an armored cruiser unit) was known as "The Old Crow," presumably after the Kentucky bourbon popular at that time.

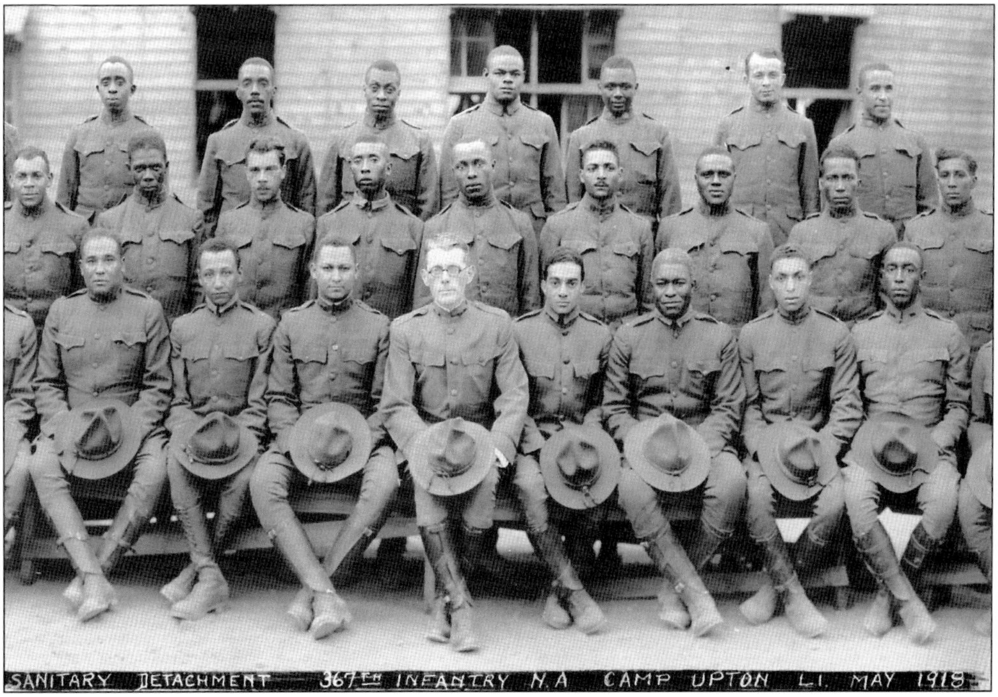

Dr. Robert Conard. Conard served in the Spanish-American War as a hospital steward and later commanded the ambulance trains. He continued his military service with the Ohio National Guard from 1910 to 1917 and was called to active service as a major during World War I. During World War II, he was state coordinator of medical officers. In 1948, he retired from the army reserve as a colonel.

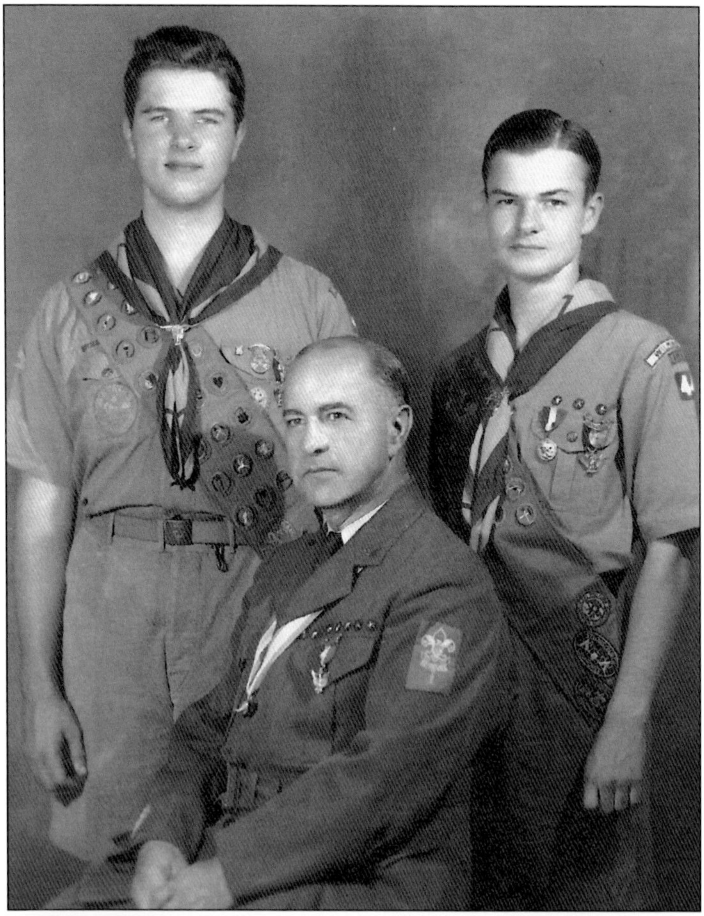

James William Denver Williams Jr., c. 1941. Pictured as Eagle Scouts, from left to right, are James William (J. W.) Denver Williams Jr., James William Denver Williams, and David Rombach Williams. Denver Williams Jr. enlisted in the U.S. Marine Corps and was killed while leading a charge in Okinawa in 1945. His parents donated the land for the J. W. Denver Williams Jr. Memorial Park in his honor.

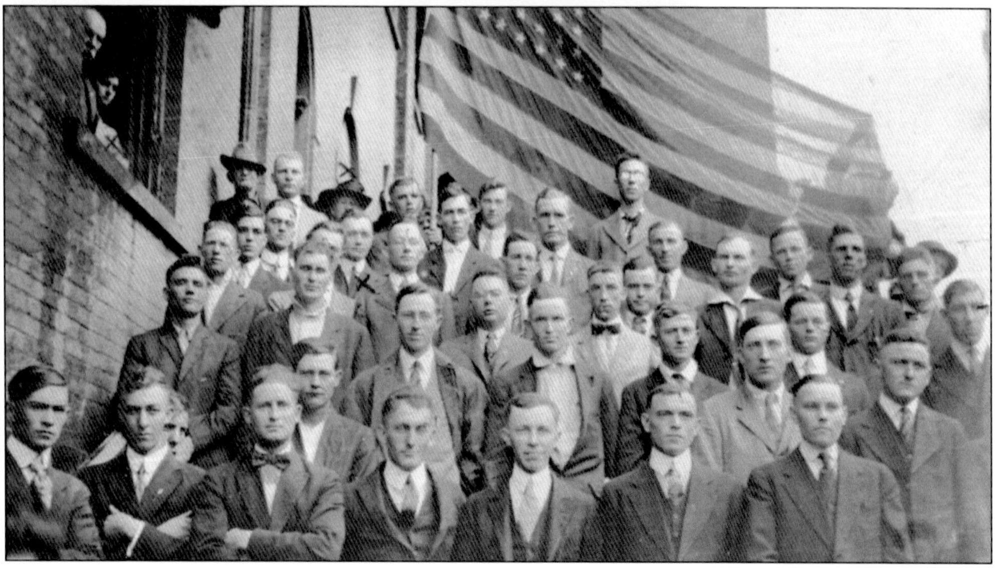

World War I Soldiers, c. 1918. This photograph shows the first group of soldiers from Clinton County to leave for World War I. (Courtesy of Rita Butcher).

CLAUDE CASHMAN, C. 1918. During World War I, Cashman served with the Motor Transport Corps. After the war, he operated an automotive electrical repair shop on North Spring Street and designed a radio broadcast system using telephone lines to broadcast away football games.

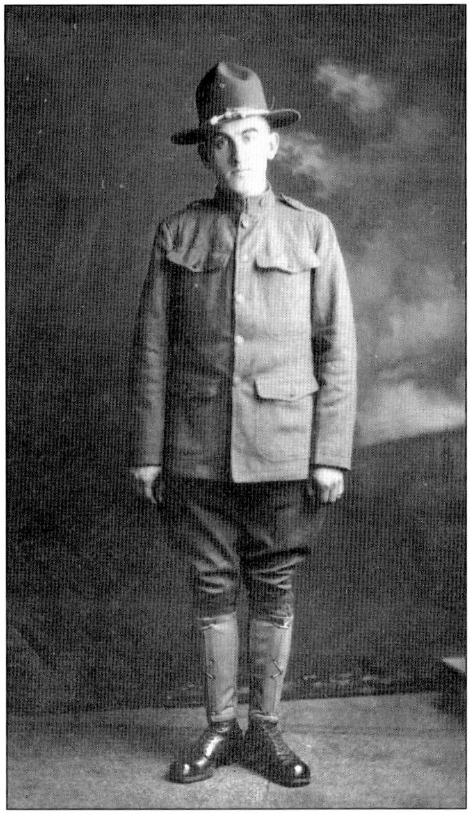

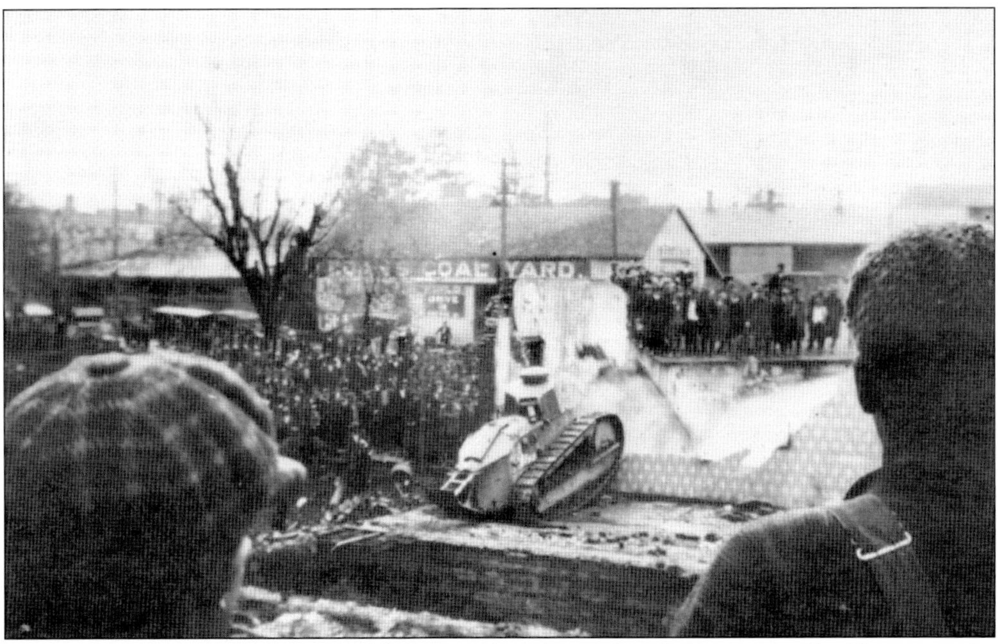

WORLD WAR I TANK, 1918. A World War I tank is shown demolishing several buildings to make room for the new courthouse. In 1942, the U.S. War Department allowed the tank to be sold as part of a nationwide campaign to recycle metal for the war effort.

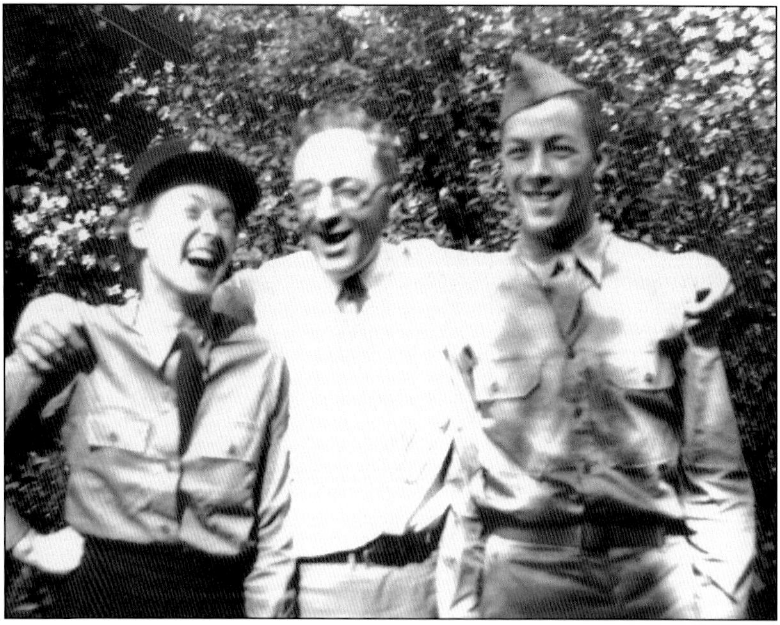

Metzger Family, 1942. Pictured from left to right are Louisa Metzger Swaim, Harry Metzger, and J. Hayes Metzger. Siblings Louisa and Hayes joined the army at the same time. Their father was a World War I veteran who helped start the American Legion Post No. 49 in Wilmington.

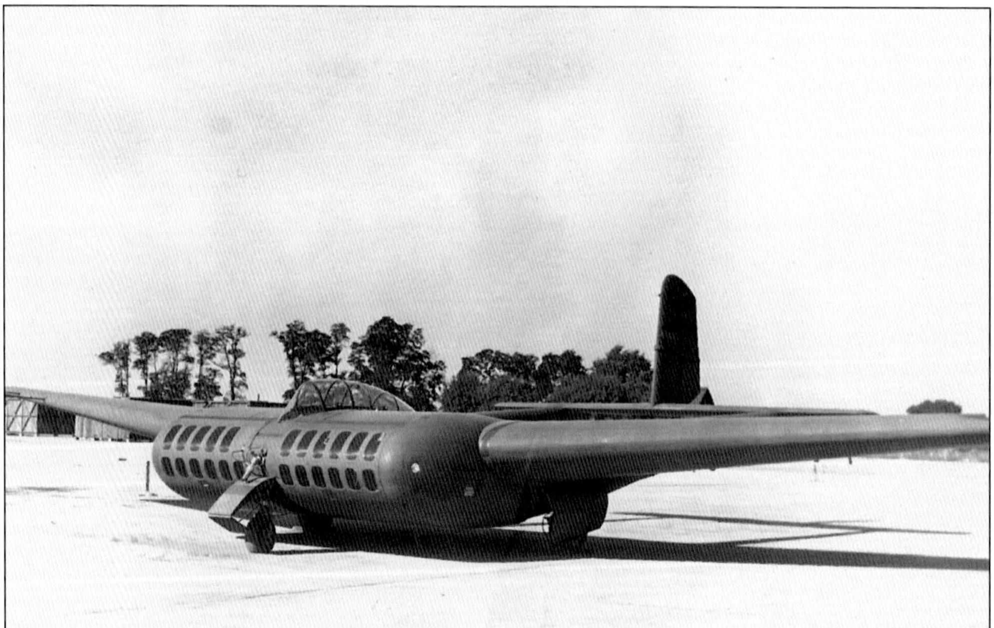

Experimental Gliders, 1944. In 1942, the army took control of the local airfield for its experimental glider testing program, which was affiliated with the glider training program at Wright Field. This picture was taken during an open house.

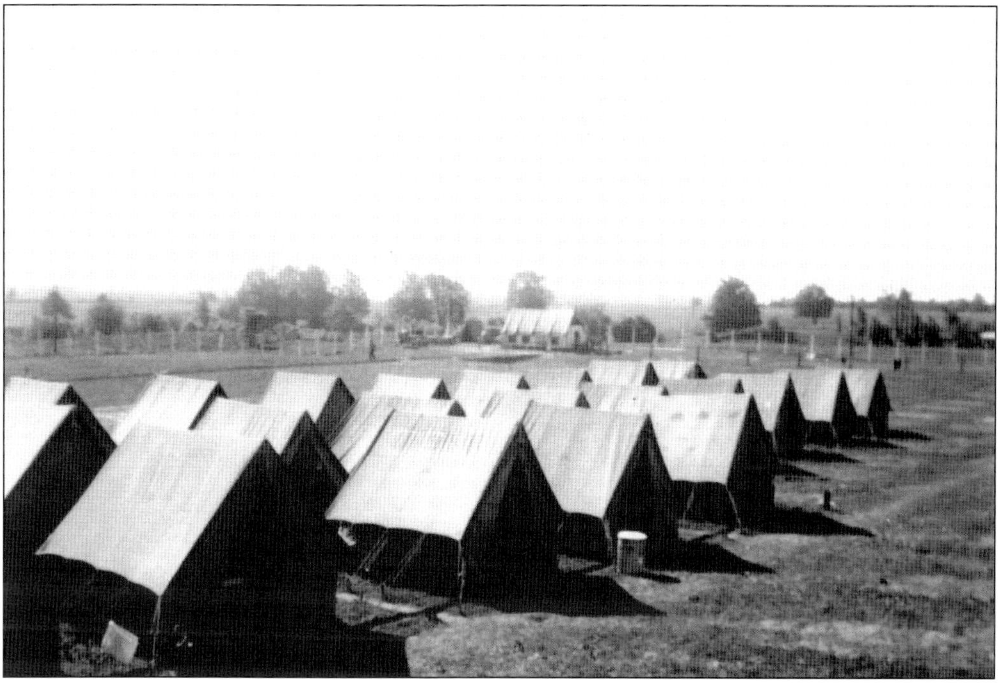

POW CAMP. During the summer of 1945, a work camp for German prisoners of war was located near Wilmington College to help with the local labor shortage. Some prisoners detasseled corn, while others worked in canneries in Jamestown and Blanchester. While at the camp, the prisoners were treated well, and one prisoner wrote in a letter after his return to Europe that he sorely missed the good food and other luxuries he had been given in Wilmington.

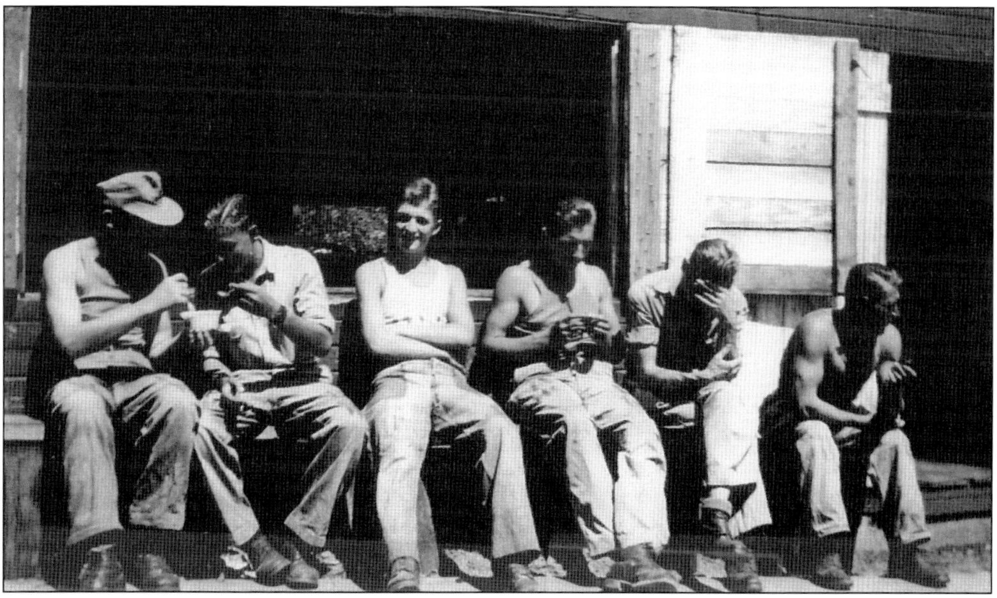

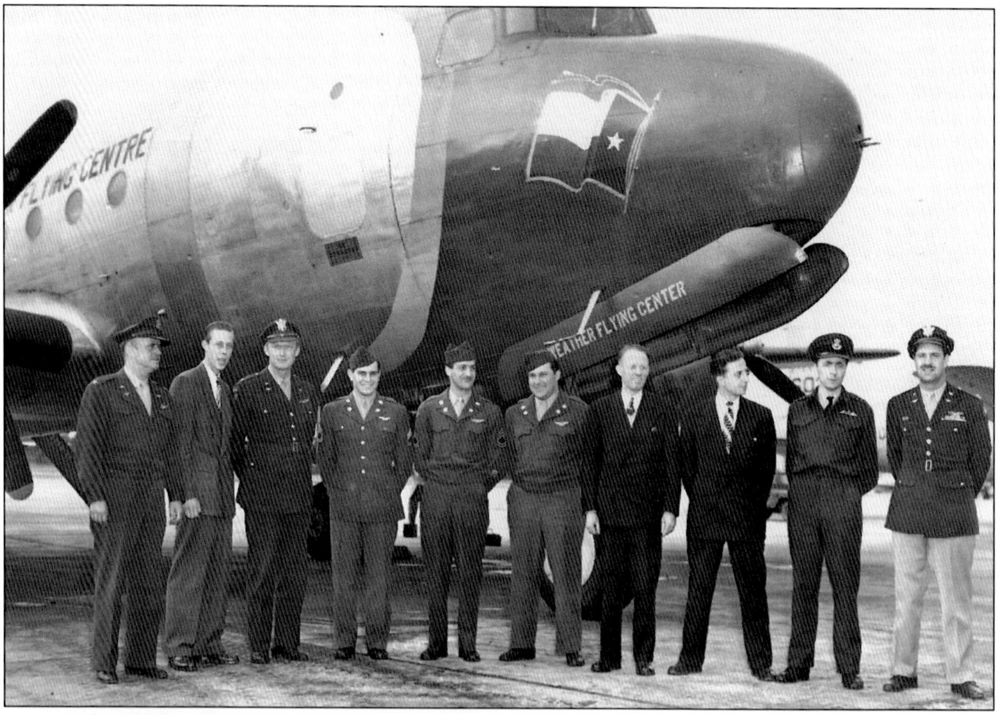

All Weather Flying Division, 1947. Pictured is the C-54 airplane *Robert E. Lee* after its return from England. Pictured from left to right are Col. James Gillespie, George Johnson, Capt. Thomas Wells, Tech. Sgt. Welker McKee, Tech. Sgt. Raymond Centolella, Staff Sgt. John Nimon, Charles Franklin, James Anast, T. R. Jeff, and Capt. Ramon Witting.

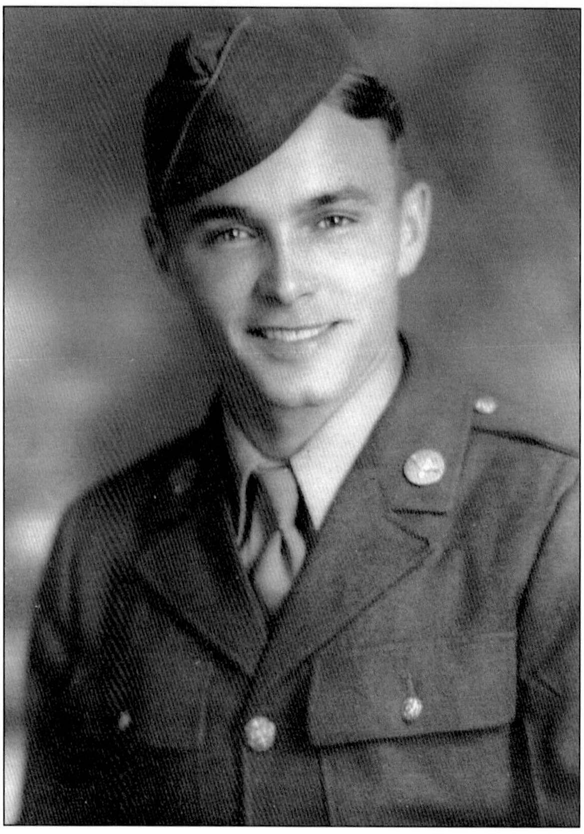

Tom Browning, 1940s. During World War II, Rowena and James Browning had three sons and two sons-in-law in the war at the same time. All five—Charles Browning, Tom Browning, James Browning, Dwight Hyde (married to Hazel Browning), and Bill Shearer (married to Betty Browning)—were from Wilmington. Tom Browning, a B-24 gunner, was awarded the Distinguished Flying Cross twice, the Presidential Unit Citation twice, and the Air Medal four times. (Courtesy of Beverly Browning.)

Joseph Roberts, 1952. Joseph "Joe" Roberts served in the U.S. Marine Corps during the Korean War. From 1979 to 1980, he served as the commander of the American Legion Post No. 49 in Wilmington.

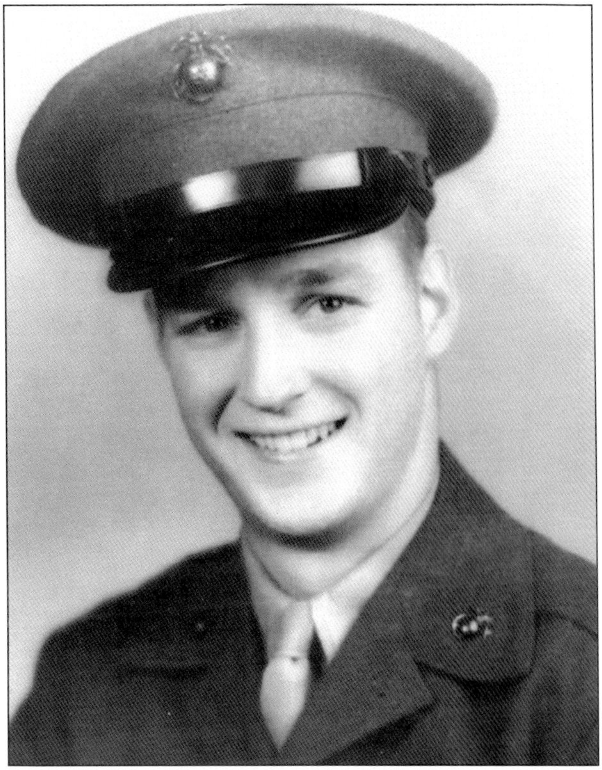

Nike Missile Silos, 1960–1971. These two army soldiers explain to civilians the function of the Ajax missile on Armed Forces Day in 1960. At the height of the cold war, the United States built approximately 250 Nike missile sites for selected cities and strategic military locations. Located off State Route 730, the Wilmington site had two distinct areas: the administration area and the launch area. (Courtesy of Paul Presta.)

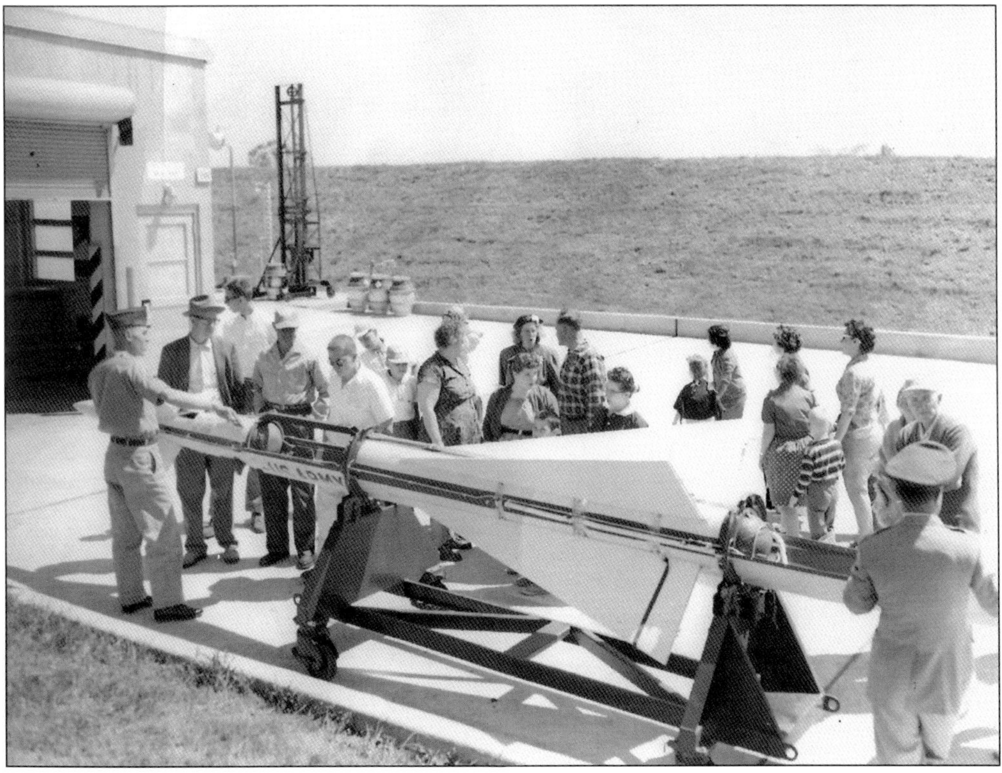